NEW TESTAMENT GREEK

NEW TESTAMENT GREEK

An Introductory Grammar

WATSON E. MILLS
B.A., B.D., M.A.,
Th.M., Th.D., Ph.D.

The Edwin Mellen Press
New York/Toronto

Also by the author:

Understanding Speaking in Tongues
Speaking in Tongues: Let's Talk about It
The Lure of the Occult
Review of New Testament Books Between 1900-1950
Charismatic Religion in Modern Research: A Bibliography
A Theological/Exegetical Approach to Glossolalia
Glossolalia: A Bibliography

Library of Congress Cataloging in Publication Data

Mills, Watson E.
   New Testament Greek
   Bibliograpgy: p. 188
   Includes indexes.
   1. Greek language, Biblical--Grammar--1950-
I. Title.
PA817.M53   1985   487'.4   85-11540
ISBN 0-88946-200-3
ISBN 0-88946-201-1 (pbk.)

For information contact:

The Edwin Mellen Press

P. O. Box 450   Box 67
Lewiston, New York   Queenston, Ontario
USA 14092   Canada L0S 1L0

Printed in the United States of America

Dedication

αὐτῇ ἣν ἀγαπῶ μετὰ πάσης τῆς καρδίας μου

Contents

Introduction

Studying, teaching and now writing about New Testament Greek has been one of the more exhilarating experiences of my life. After working with New Testament Greek for more than twenty-five years, I still marvel at its intracacies and precision in sharp contrast to the Romance languages spoken today. Indeed, the glory of the language of the New Testament resides not in its seemingly endless paradigms, but in the precision of expression it afforded the writers of the New Testament and consequently the almost inexhaustible possibilities for interpretation it offers those who learn it today. It is safe to say that once you begin a study of Greek, the New Testament will be transformed into an infinitely greater literary treasure whose depths are barely touched by English.

The purpose of this volume is to introduce you to the *Koine* Greek of the New Testament. As with any "introductory" textbook, sticky questions arise: What to include? What to exclude? What order? How much detail? There is the ever-present tendency toward over-simplification.

In facing these, and other difficulties, I set out from the beginning to attempt to blend an emphasis upon syntax with vocabulary and paradigms in such a way that upon completion you will be able (with the aid of a lexicon) to handle the text of 1 John. But more importantly, I set as a goal something much less quantifiable, but nonetheless real: to whet your appetite for the study of Greek in such a way as to motivate you to delve deeper in your studies—far beyond the scope of this book. In the degree that this worthy goal is achieved, I can say this grammar has succeeded.

There is in these pages enough syntax, vocabulary, and paradigms to "teach" you that there is truly no limit to the treasures of New Testament interpretation open to those who know Greek.

I wish to thank my assistant, Ms. Irene Pace, who typed the text of this grammar (through many drafts). Her skill and patience is gratefully acknowledged. I also wish to thank Robert G. Bratcher, who read the manuscript and made many helpful suggestions for its improvement. He gently marked my errors; however, those that remain are mine, not his.

Lastly, I am grateful to be affiliated with a great University like Mercer where the administration values and supports the research and writing as a logical extension of the goals of the institution.

WATSON E. MILLS

Mercer University
Macon, Georgia
June 1985

Lesson 1

Writing Greek

§1. *Introduction*. The Greek alphabet consists of 24 letters, some of which are virtually identical to the Latin alphabet still used today. Both the Latin and the Greek alphabets took their origin from the Phoenician alphabet as did the Hebrew.

Some of the Greek characters will be recognizable immediately: the term *alphabet* for example is but the name of the first two letters of the Greek alphabet; Revelation 1:8 speaks of the *alpha* and *omega*, the first and the last letters; those who have studied math will recognize the Greek π.

There are look alikes too! The Greek *delta* (δ) resembles a *d*; epsilon (ε) an *e*; kappa (κ) a *k*; omicron (o) an *o*; sigma (ς) an *s*; tau (τ) a *t*; upsilon (υ) a *u*.

Capital letters are listed in the accompanying chart but they are not nearly so important as the lower case letters.

Capital letters are used in the first letter of proper names, but not at the beginning of a sentence. In fact, most of the capital letters are very much like their lower case equivalents, or the equivalent English capital. Once you have mastered the lower case letters, there are only 10 capital letters that require any special consideration.

(1) Δ can be easily remembered since the Nile River delta resembles the shape of this letter (upside down).

(2) P and X are much like the lower case letters ρ and χ, but must be distinguished from the upper case English *P* and *X*.

(3) H and Y are η and υ not English *H* and *Y*.

(4) Γ Λ Ξ Σ Ω have Greek forms different from all English letters and different from their lower case equivalents.

§2. *The Greek Letters*.

LETTER		NAME		PRONOUNCIATION
UPPER	LOWER	GREEK	ENGLISH	
Α	α	ἄλφα	alpha	*a* as in *father*
Β	β	βῆτα	beta	*b* as in *barber*
Γ	γ	γάμμα	gamma	*g* as in *girl*[1]
Δ	δ	δέλτα	delta	*d* as in *doubt*
Ε	ε	ἒ ψιλόν	epsilon	*e* as in *get*
Ζ	ζ	ζῆτα	zeta	*z* as in *zoo*
Η	η	ἦτα	ēta	*a* as in *gate*
Θ	θ	θῆτα	thēta	*th* as in *thug*
Ι	ι	ἰῶτα	iōta	*i* as in *picnic*
Κ	κ	κάππα	kappa	*k* as in *kumquat*
Λ	λ	λάμβδα	lambda	*l* as in *lump*
Μ	μ	μῦ	mu	*m* as in *mud*
Ν	ν	νῦ	nu	*n* as in *nonsense*
Ξ	ξ	ξῖ	xi	*x* as in *relax*
Ο	ο	ὂ μικρόν	omicron	*o* as in *omelet*
Π	π	πῖ	pi	*p* as in *price*
Ρ	ϱ[2]	ῥῶ	rhō	*r* as in *rang*
Σ	σ, ς[3]	σίγμα	sigma	*s* as in *successful*
Τ	τ	ταῦ	tau	*t* as in *tight*
Υ	υ	ὖ ψιλόν	upsilon	*u* as in *upper*
Φ	φ	φῖ	phi	*ph* as in *phosphorus*
Χ	χ	χῖ	chi	*ch* as in German *ich*
Ψ	ψ	ψῖ	psi	*ps* as in *lips*
Ω	ω	ὦ μέγα	omega	*o* as in *note*

§3. *Orthography.* You must practice writing the letters and repeating the names of each out loud until you can do so without hesitation. This section suggests a pattern for writing each letter. The small *b* suggests where to *begin* movement for those letters that require only one stroke. Letters requiring more than one stroke are marked b_1 and b_2, etc.

§3.1. *Greek letters that do not extend above or below the line.*

---

[1] Double γ, γκ, γχ are pronounced like *ny* in "canyon," i.e., ἄγγελος (angel).

[2] At the beginning of a word ϱ is written with a rough breathing ῥ.

[3] ς is used instead of σ when sigma occurs at the end of a word, i.e., σώζω but λόγος. The sigma final (ς) *may* also occur *within* compound words like προςφερω when the prefix ends with a sigma.

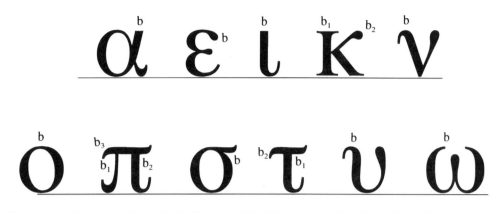

Note: ν and υ are virtually indistinguishable except for the pointed bottom on the ν and the rounded bottom on the υ.

§3.2. *Greek letters that extend above the line.*

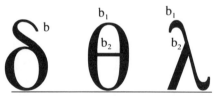

§3.3. *Greek letters that extend below the line.*

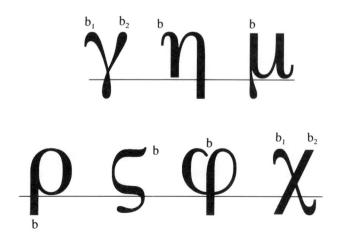

§3.4. *Greek letters that extend above and below the line.*

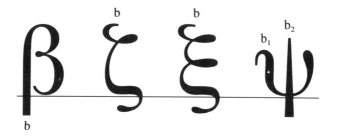

§3.5. *Letters to distinguish carefully.* In writing these letters, be careful to note that there is only one slight variation in the structure of each member in the following pairs:

φ and ψ

ν and υ

ν and γ

§4. *Transliteration.* At times it is necessary to transliterate Greek words into English letters: for example, when no Greek typewriter or type font is available. This method of representing Greek letters with English ones is called *transliteration.* It is usually employed only for single words or short phrases; *never for longer passages.* This sys- tem for transliteration is offered only for use in certain cases and is intended to be an aid to learning. It must never be used as a substitute for mastering the Greek letters.

§4.1. *Transliteration equivalents.*

α = a	η = ē	ν = n	τ = t
β = b	θ = th[5]	ξ = x	υ = u, y[6]
γ = g[4]	ι = i	o = o	φ = ph[5]
δ = d	κ = k	π = p	χ = ch[5]
ε = e	λ = l	ϱ = r	ψ = ps[5]
ζ = z	μ = m	σ, ς = s	ω = ō

§4.2. *Examples of transliteration.*

GREEK	TRANSLITERATION	MEANING

---

[4]In combination with another γ or a κ, ξ or χ, transliterate γγ as ng; γκ as nk; γξ as nx; and γχ as nch.

[5]The Greek letters θ, φ, χ, and ψ are transliterated with *two* English letters.

[6]The Greek υ is transliterated as *u* in the combinations αυ, ευ, ου, υι, ηυ. In all other cases it is rendered *y*. Example: κύϱιος = *kyrios* but οὐκ = *ouk.*

ἄγγελος	angelos	messenger
δόγμα	dogma	decree
ἐγώ	egō	I
θεός	theos	God

§5. *Punctuation*. There are four punctuation marks in Greek. Both the comma and the period correspond exactly to the English comma and period. The Greek colon (·) corresponds to the English colon and the English semi-colon. Note that it is written above the line. The Greek question mark (;) corresponds in appearance to the English semi-colon.

§6. *Breathing Marks*. When a vowel (§8) begins a word in Greek, it is marked by a symbol called a breathing mark. This symbol appears *above* the vowel: ἀπόστολος. The breathing mark may occur *together with* an accent mark: ἄγγελος. If the word begins with a diphthong (§9) the breathing mark occurs over the close (second) vowel: εὐλογέω. When the initial vowel is a *capital letter* the breathing is set to the left of the word: Ἰησοῦς. Notice that an initial υ or an initial ρ always receive the rough breathing (in the case of a υι diphthong the rough breathing is placed over the ι).

There are two such breathing marks in Greek: the smooth breathing (᾿) and the rough breathing (῾). In reality, these marks resemble an apostrophe that may be turned outward (᾿) (soft breathing) or turned inward (῾) (rough or aspirate breathing). The smooth breathing makes no difference in pronunciation. The rough breathing is sounded like the English *h* when it occurs over the initial letter of a word.

Lesson 2

Pronouncing Greek

§7. *System of Pronunciation*. The system of pronunciation offered here is essentially the traditional one that is used throughout most of the English-speaking world. It is *not* the one used by the Apostle Paul, or Plato or persons who speak modern Greek. In fact each of these systems, and many others, were themselves widely divergent. The purpose of any system of pronunciation is simply to facilitate oral reference to the various forms by teachers and students alike.

§8. *Vowels*. A vowel is a speech sound that results when the breath channel is not blocked. There are seven vowels in Greek (α, ε, ι, ο, υ, η, ω). Of these ε and ο are always short; η and ω are always long; α, ι, and υ are sometimes short and sometimes long. The long and short forms, however, are not distinguished by different characters. Thus, only by observation is it possible to learn the tone value of α, ι, and υ in specific *Greek* words.

   α, ε, ο, η, and ω are pronounced with the mouth more or less open when the sound is made. These vowels are thus called *open vowels*. ι and υ are pronounced with the mouth more or less in a closed position. These vowels are thus referred to as *close vowels*.

§9. *Diphthongs*. The term diphthong (from δίφθογγος, "having two sounds") is the resulting combination of an open and a close vowel (in that order except for υι). The common or "proper" diphthongs are:

αι	=	*ay* in aye
αυ	=	*au* in naught
ει	=	*ei* in height
οι	=	*oi* in oil
ου	=	*ou* in out
ευ	=	*eu* in neuter
υι	=	*wi* in wine

Sometimes the two adjoining vowels (open and close) are *not* to be treated as a diphthong, but are to be pronounced as separate syllables. In these cases, a diaeresis (¨) is employed over the second of the two vowels. Example: Ἠσαΐας (John 1:23). Notice that in the example the diaeresis is *combined* with the accute accent.

When a small ι is written beneath a vowel (ᾳ), it is called an *iota subscript*. Its presence does not change the pronunciation of the vowel (α), but when it combines with another vowel it is referred to as an "improper diphthong." The improper diphthongs are:

ᾳ	=	*a* in father
ῃ	=	*a* in gate
ῳ	=	*o* in note

In transliteration the improper diphthongs are written āi, ēi, ōi (the long accent mark serves to distinguish them from the proper diphthongs which would be transliterated ai, ei, oi).

§10. *Consonants.*

§10.1. The following consonants are pronounced like their English equivalents:

β	=	b
δ	=	d
κ	=	k
λ	=	l
μ	=	m
ν	=	n
π	=	p
τ	=	t
φ	=	ph
ψ	=	ps

§10.2. The remaining seven consonants require special attention: γ is pronounced like the *g* in *gun*, never as the *g* in *gin*. When it occurs in combination with another γ or κ, ξ, or χ, it is pronounced as follows:

γγ	=	*ng* in angel
γκ	=	*nk* in tinker
γξ	=	*nx* in lynx
γχ	=	*ng* in sing plus a hard *ch* as in the German *ich*.

ζ is pronounced like the *z* in daze. Example: σώζω, *I save*.

θ is pronounced like *th* in *th*in, never as *th* in *th*en. Example: θεός, *God*.

ξ is pronounced like *x* in e*x*act. Example: ξύλον, *wood, tree*.

ϱ is pronounced like *r* in *r*un. Example: παρά, *beside*.

σ is pronounced like the *s* in *s*ing never like the *s* in ro*s*e. Example: συνάγω, *I gather together*.

χ is pronounced like *ch* in *ch*emical. Example: χαρά, *joy*.

The Greek consonants may be divided into three general classes: liquids, mutes, and sibilants.

§10.3. *Liquid Consonants*. The liquid consonants are λ, μ, ν, ϱ. These are pronounced with a smooth even flow of air. An initial ϱ takes rough breathing and is usually transliterated as *rh*. Example: ῥῆμα, *word*.

§10.4. *Mute Consonants*. There are nine consonants in this category. Each is pronounced with a momentary closing of the air passage. The mutes may be arranged according to the part of the body involved in their formation. π, β, φ are labials (involving the lips); κ, γ, χ are gutturals (involving the throat); τ, δ, θ are dentals (involving the tongue pressed against the teeth).

	sharp	flat	aspirate	
labials	π	β	φ	(*p*-sounds)
gutturals	κ	γ	χ	(*k*-sounds)
dentals	τ	δ	θ	(*t*-sounds)

§10.5. *Sibilants*. The sibilant consonants all have a ''s'' sound. They are σ, ξ, ζ, ψ. Three of these (ζ, ξ, ψ) are double consonants resulting as follows:

π, β, φ	+	σ	=	ψ	(*p*-sound)
κ, γ, χ	+	σ	=	ξ	(*k*-sound)
δ	+	σ	=	ζ	(*d*-sound)

σ is a simple sibilant; in combination with a *p* sound mute it gives a ψ; with a *k* sound mute it gives a ξ; with a δ it gives a ζ.

§11. *Accents*. There are three accent marks in Greek: the acute accent (´); the grave (`) the circumflex (˜). Except in a few cases these accents will occur *only* on the last three syllables of a word. Generally, the accents may be ignored in *writing* Greek except in a few cases where the accent actually serves to distinguish one word from another. The general rules for accenting are discussed with examples in *Appendix 1*. Note that breathing marks are *not* accent marks and that these must be treated as an essential part of the vocabulary. When a word has *both* a breathing mark and an accent mark, the breathing mark always precedes, except in the case of the circumflex, which stands over the top of the breathing mark. Examples: ἄνθρωπος; αἷμα; ἅγιος.

§12. *Elision and Crasis*. Some words lose a final vowel before an initial vowel in the succeeding word. Example: διὰ ἀδελφοῦ becomes δι' ἀδελφοῦ. When this occurs the vowel is said to elide, thus the term *elision*. In some cases the final and initial vow-

vowels are *blended* or *mixed* so that the two words become one. This process is referred to as *crasis*. Example: τὰ αὐτά becomes ταῦτα.

§13. *Practice*. Repetition is the key to the mastery of the Greek alphabet. After learning to recognize each letter and recite the name of each *in order and from memory* you must practice again and again. Any new language, especially one that involves an alphabet different from your native one, must be learned *visually* and *auditorially*. But equally important is the *motor* path to learning. This simply means that you pronounce the letter, write the letter, and see the letter simultaneously.

§14. *Exercises*. There follows a transliterated section from the Greek text of John 1:1-8. Your task is to write it out in *Greek* letters, inserting breathing marks where necessary. All vowels are short unless marked with a long stroke over the "e" (η) or the "o" (ω). The inferior "i" (ᵢ) indicates that an iota subscript should be written under the preceding vowel. The apostrophe (denoting elision) should be reproduced by an apostrophe in Greek.

en archē᷂ ēn ho logos, kai ho logos ēn pros ton theon, kai theos ēn ho logos. houtos ēn en archē᷂ pros ton theon. panta di' autou egeneto kai chōris autou egeneto oude hen. ho gegonen en autō᷂ zōē ēn, kai hē zōē ēn to phōs tōn anthrōpōn. kai to phōs en tē᷂ skotia᷂ phainei, kai hē skotia auto ou katelaben. egeneto anthrōpos, apestalmenos para theou, onoma autō᷂ iōannēs. houtos ēlthen eis marturian, hina marturēsē᷂ peri tou phōtos, hina pantes pisteusōsin di' autou. ouk ēn ekeinos to phōs, all' hina marturēsē᷂ peri tou phōtos.

Lesson 3
Present Active Indicative

§15. *Vocabulary.*
ἀκούω, *I hear*
βλέπω, *I see*
γινώσκω, *I know*
γράφω, *I write*
διδάσκω, *I teach*
ἔχω, *I have*
λαμβάνω, *I take, I receive*
λέγω, *I say*
λύω, *I loose, I destroy*
πέμπω, *I send*

§16. *Forms.* The present tense, active voice, indicative mood, of λύω:

	SINGULAR	PLURAL
1st per	λύω, *I am loosing*	λύομεν, *we are loosing*
2nd per	λύεις, *you are loosing*	λύετε, *you are loosing*
3rd per	λύει, *he, she, it is loosing*	λύουσι(ν), *they are loosing*

Notice that the third personal plural form may be written λύουσι or λύουσιν. This final ν is called movable ν, and is found at the end of several Greek forms. There are no hard and fast rules for its use.

§17. *Formation of the ω Verbs.* All of the verbs in the vocabulary (§15) end with an ω. Each Greek verb may be divided into two parts: the stem (λυ) and the personal ending (ω). The stem is that part of the verb that remains constant throughout the conjugation and which denotes the fundamental meaning of the verb itself (λυ = loose).

λύ-ω	λύ-ομεν
λύ-εις	λύ-ετε
λύ-ει	λύ-ουσι(ν)

The stem identifies the action of the verb (to loose); the ending specifies which person(s) is performing that action.

§18. *Syntactical Study*. Like the verbs of many other languages Greek verbs have mood, tense, voice, person and number.

§18.1. *Mood*. Mood is that quality of the verbal idea that lets the hearer (reader) know what relationship the statement being made bears to reality. Is the statement descriptive of a real set of events (example: *it is raining today*) or is it only a wish in the speaker's mind (example: *I wish I knew all there is to know about Greek*)? The indicative mood communicates that *from the vantage point of the speaker's mind the action described is actually taking place in the real world.*

§18.2. *Tense*. In the Greek verb system tense (in the indicative mood) serves to indicate two things about the action being described: (1) *when* the action is occurring; (2) what *kind* is occurring.

Obviously, in the first instance, the present tense tells you that the action is occurring in the *present* time. Secondly, the present tense describes action that is *durative*, i.e., *continuous* in nature. That is, the present tense is used to describe action that is occurring in the *present* time and that is *continuous* in nature. Example: λύω, *I am loosing* (present time, the action is continuous).

§18.3. *Voice*. Voice functions to indicate the relationship of the subject of the sentence to the action being described by the verb. In Greek, there are three voices: active, middle (sometimes called *reflexive*), and passive.

The active voice is the most common because it indicates that the subject is doing the acting. Example: *I am loosing the men*. In this sentence the subject of the verb (''I'') is performing the action indicated by the verb.

The passive voice indicates the subject of the sentence is *receiving* the action indicated by the verb. Example: *The men are being loosed by the disciple*. In this example the subject of the sentence (''the men'') is the recipient of the action specified by the verb.

The middle (reflexive) voice indicates that the subject is doing the action, but doing it in such a way as to participate in the results of that action. Example: *I am washing myself*. Here the subject (''I'') is doing the washing, but note that the washing is also being done to the subject. This middle voice is also known as the reflexive voice.

§18.4. *Person*. Person functions to indicate whether the subject of the sentence is doing the speaking (1st person), being spoken to (2nd person), or being spoken of or about (3rd person). Example: I am loosing (1st person), you are loosing (2nd person), they are loosing (3rd person).

§18.5. *Number*. Number is that quality of the verb that indicates whether the subject is one (singular) or two or more (plural). Example: I am loosing (singular), we are loosing (plural).

Take special note that the second person forms in modern English are the same in both the singular and the plural, i.e., "you." *These forms are not the same in Greek*, and the student must use great care at this point.

§18.6. *Locating a verb*. To analyze or locate a verb, you should supply the following information: tense, voice, mood, person, number and the lexical form of the verb. Example: locate λύω = present tense, active voice, indicative mood, first person, singular number from the verb λύω. In most cases the information is shortened to: present, active, indicative, first, singular, from λύω.

§19. *Exercises.*

§19.1. *Translate into English*:
1. ἀκούομεν, λέγει, ἔχετε
2. γράφετε, βλέπεις, ἔχουσι
3. γινώσκω, λαμβάνει, λέγω

§19.2. *Translate into Greek*:
1. They are having, you (pl) are seeing
2. You (sing) are knowing, she is hearing
3. We are receiving, I am hearing

§19.3. *Locate these verbs*:
1. λαμβάνω, ἔχει, γινώσκομεν
2. ἔχομεν, ἀκούετε, λαμβάνουσι
3. βλέπεις, λύουσι, γράφομεν

Lesson 4

εω **Contract Verbs**

§20. *Vocabulary.*
εὐλογέω, *I bless*
ζητέω, *I seek*
θεωρέω, *I behold*
ὁμολογέω, *I confess*
παρακαλέω, *I comfort, I exhort*
περιπατέω, *I walk about*
καλέω, *I call*
ποιέω, *I do, I make*
λαλέω, *I speak*

§21. *Inflection.* There are two major classes of verbs in Greek. The ω class (§16) and the μι class (§180). The contract verbs form a special class of the ω conjugation. A contract verb is any verb whose stem ends in a vowel. In this lesson we will study those verbs whose stems end in εω. When this occurs the following contractions take place *in the present and imperfect tenses only*:

	SINGULAR	PLURAL
1st per	ποιέω = ποιῶ	ποιέομεν = ποιοῦμεν
2nd per	ποιέεις = ποιεῖς	ποιέετε = ποιεῖτε
3rd per	ποιέει = ποιεῖ	ποιέουσι = ποιοῦσι

§22. *Rules for Contraction.* Rules for contraction for verbs ending in εω:

ε	+	ω	=	ω	(1st person sing)
ε	+	ει	=	ει	(2nd person sing)
ε	+	ει	=	ει	(3rd person sing)

ε	+	o	=	ου	(1st person pl)
ε	+	ε	=	ει	(2nd person pl)
ε	+	o	=	ου	(3rd person pl)

§23. The εω verbs are listed in their lexical vocabulary form (§20) in the *un*contracted form so the student may recognize its type of configuration readily.

§24. *Exercises*.

§24.1. *Translate into English*:

1. ἀκούουσι, γράφουσι, διδάσκουσι.
2. καλεῖ, ζητεῖ, ποιεῖ.
3. θεωροῦσι, λαλοῦσι, βλέπουσι.
4. λύετε, εὐλογεῖτε, θεωρεῖτε.
5. ἔχομεν, περιπατοῦμεν, ζητοῦμεν.

§24.2. *Translate into Greek*:

1. I am destroying, I am calling, I am comforting.
2. You (sing) are speaking, you (sing) are writing, you (sing) are hearing.
3. We are giving thanks, we are calling, we are seeking.
4. They are exhorting, they are walking about, they are calling.
5. He is making, she is calling, he is seeking.

Lesson 5
Second Declension Nouns

§25. *Vocabulary.*
ἄγγελος, ὁ *messenger, angel*
ἀδελφός, ὁ, *brother*
ἄνθρωπος, ὁ, *man*
ἀπόστολος, ὁ, *apostle*
ἄρτος, ὁ, *bread*
γάμος, ὁ, *marriage*
δοῦλος, ὁ, *slave, servant*
δῶρον, τό, *gift*
θάνατος, ὁ, *death*
θεός, ὁ, *God*
ἱερόν, τό, *temple*
καί, *and*
λόγος, ὁ, *word*
νόμος, ὁ, *law*

§26. *Inflection.* Inflection is indicated in verbs by *conjugation*; in nouns by *declension*. Greek has three declension systems for its substantives (nouns, adjectives, pronouns and participles). A declension ''system'' refers to the ending applied to the noun stem to indicate case function. In the second declension the ος sound predominates.

§27. *The Article.*

§27.1. *Indefinite article.* Greek has no indefinite article analogous to the English *a* or *an*. Thus ἀπόστολος means *apostle* or *an apostle* and ἀπόστολοι means *apostles,* not *the apostles.* There are other ways to indicate indefiniteness in Greek; these will be studied later (§197).

§27.2. *Definite article.* Notice that each of the nouns in the vocabulary (§25) is followed either by ὁ or by τό. These are the masculine and neuter definite articles respectively. Thus οἱ ἀπόστολοι is translated *the apostles* and τὰ δῶρα is translated *the gifts*.

The definite article functions to point out *specific identity*. It is a *certain* indicator of the case of the noun that appears with it.

Notice that the masculine singular and plural forms of the definite article are not accented. They are pronounced together with the substantive and are called *proclitic* (§71.2).

§28. *Forms of the Second Declension.* Declension of o stem nouns together with the definite article:

§28.1. *Masculine.*

CASE	SINGULAR		PLURAL	
Nom	ὁ	λόγος	οἱ	λόγοι
Gen	τοῦ	λόγου	τῶν	λόγων
Abl	τοῦ	λόγου	τῶν	λόγων
Dat	τῷ	λόγῳ	τοῖς	λόγοις
Loc	τῷ	λόγῳ	τοῖς	λόγοις
Inst	τῷ	λόγῳ	τοῖς	λόγοις
Acc	τὸν	λόγον	τοὺς	λόγους

§28.2. *Neuter.*

CASE	SINGULAR		PLURAL	
Nom	τὸ	δῶρον	τὰ	δῶρα
Gen	τοῦ	δώρου	τῶν	δώρων
Abl	τοῦ	δώρου	τῶν	δώρων
Dat	τῷ	δώρῳ	τοῖς	δώροις
Loc	τῷ	δώρῳ	τοῖς	δώροις
Inst	τῷ	δώρῳ	τοῖς	δώροις
Acc	τὸ	δῶρον	τὰ	δῶρα

Notice that neuter plural nouns take a *singular* verb. Also, note that the definite article and the case ending are identical in the neuter singular nominative and accustaive and in the neuter plural nominative and accusative. The *function* in a given sentence will enable you to locate these properly.

§29. *Location.* To locate (parse) a Greek noun four bits of information are required: declension, case, gender, number. ὁ ἀπόστολος is located: 2nd declension, nominative, masculine, singular. τοὺς λόγους is 2nd declension, accusative, masculine, plural. τῶν δώρων is 2nd declension, genitive/ablative, neuter, plural.

§30. *Case*. There are seven case functions in Greek[1] *Case function* lets the reader know how the noun relates to the verb or other segments of the sentence. These functions are indicated by different (inflected) forms. Since there are seven distinct case functions and only four forms you can see that some forms represent more than one case function, i.e., the form τῷ ἀποστόλῳ represents three functions: dative, locative, and instrumental.

Only the nominative case is thought of as falling into a direct or perpendicular relationship to the sentence; the other cases are thus said to be *oblique* cases.

Study the following table:

SINGULAR	PLURAL	CASE	IDEA
λόγος	λόγοι	Nominative	Designation
λόγου	λόγων	Genitive	Description
λόγου	λόγων	Ablative	Separation
λόγῳ	λόγοις	Dative	Interest
λόγῳ	λόγοις	Locative	Location
λόγῳ	λόγοις	Instrumental	Means
λόγον	λόγους	Accusative	Limitation

With the definite article the declension is:

CASE	SINGULAR		PLURAL	
Nom	ὁ λόγος	*the word*	οἱ λόγοι	*the words*
Gen	τοῦ λόγου	*of the word*	τῶν λόγων	*of the words*
Abl	τοῦ λόγου	*from the word*	τῶν λόγων	*from the words*
Dat	τῷ λόγῳ	*to the word*	τοῖς λόγοις	*to the words*
Loc	τῷ λόγῳ	*in the word*	τοῖς λόγοις	*in the words*
Inst	τῷ λόγῳ	*by the word*	τοῖς λόγοις	*by the words*
Acc	τὸν λόγον	*the word*	τοὺς λόγους	*the words*

Study these sentences:
I am hearing the word = ἀκούω τὸν λόγον.
We are seeing the apostles = βλέπομεν τοὺς ἀπόστολους.
The men are blessing God = οἱ ἄνθρωποι εὐλόγουσι τὸν θεόν.

---

[1]There are actually *eight* cases if the *vocative* is included. The vocative is *not* included in the paradigms in this text because the vocative bears no syntactical relation to the other parts of the sentence, because it is relatively infrequent in its occurrence in the New Testament, and because the vocative generally assumes the same form as the nominative (note that the vocative form of nouns of the second declension [ος type] is obtained by adding an ε to the noun stem. Thus the vocative form of κύριος is κύριε).

§31. *Case Functions*. The seven case functions are as follows:

§31.1. *Nominative case*. The nominative case *names* the subject of the action. ὁ ἄγγελος βλέπει τὸν ἄνθρωπον = *the messenger is seeing the man*. The nominative ending ος is attached to the stem ἄγγελ- because ἄγγελος *functions* as the subject of the sentence.

§31.2. *Genitive case*. The genitive case *decribes* or *specifies*. Among other things, the genitive case indicates *possession*. ὁ λόγος *τοῦ νόμου* is a phrase in which τοῦ νόμου describes ὁ λόγος by indicating which λόγος.

§31.3. *Ablative case*. The ablative case is the case of *separation* indicating source, separation, or departure. Notice that the ablative case has the same form as the genitive. In the sentence ὁ ἀδελφός βλέπει τὸν ἄγγελον *τοῦ θεοῦ* the τοῦ θεοῦ functions in the ablative. Of course, as far as *form* is concerned, this sentence could be translated either: (1) *The brother is seeing the angel of God* (genitive); or (2) *the brother is seeing the angel from God* (ablative). In a later lesson you will study prepositions. These assist in clarifying case function in those instances where *form* alone is not sufficient.

§31.4. *Dative case*. The dative case indicates *personal interest*. It is the case of the indirect object (i.e., the noun that indicates "to whom" or "for whom" something is done). οἱ ἄγγελοι λέγουσι τοὺς λόγους *τοῖς ἀποστόλοις*, *the angels are speaking the words to the apostles*. Thus the dative case is employed to indicate to whom the action is occurring.

§31.5. *Locative case*. The locative case indicates *location* or *position*. Note that the form of the locative is the same as that of the dative. Example: οἱ ἄγγελοι λέγουσι τοὺς λόγους *τῷ ἱερῷ* = *the angels are speaking the words in the temple*.

§31.6. *Instrumental case*. The instrumental case indicates *means* by which something is accomplished. Example: ὁ ἄνθρωπος διδάσκει λόγοις = *the man is teaching by means of words*. Note again that the form is the same as that of the dative and locative.

§31.7. *Accusative case*. The accusative case *limits* the action of the verb. Its main function is that of the direct object. Example: ὁ ἀδελφὸς βλέπει τὸν ἄνθρωπον = *the brother is seeing the man*.

§32. *Word Order and Case*. In English the relationship among the various words that make up the sentences is indicated by word order. The usual pattern is subject-predicate-object. In Greek word order is secondary as a way of indicating the function of words within a sentence. *Case endings* regularly indicate the function of most parts of speech in a Greek sentence.

The relationships among words are indicated in Greek by *case endings* (and by prepositions which evolved later to make even clearer the basic case ideas). Originally, there were seven case *forms* and *functions*. Gradually the dative, locative, and instrumental case *forms* evolved into the same *form* though their separate case *functions* have persisted. The same is true of the genitive and ablative cases; the *forms* are the same but each case retains a separate *function*.

§33. *Gender*. There are three genders in Greek: masculine, feminine, and neuter. In Greek, however, the gender does not necessarily refer to the actual sex identification associated with the word as is often the case in English. In Greek, gender is a *grammatical* function. As such, gender is indicated by the article:

ὁ λόγος   *the word*
ἡ ἀλήθεια   *the truth*
τὸ δῶρον   *the gift*

The gender of individual nouns *must be learned as part of the vocabulary*. Most of the nouns of the second declension ending in ος are masculine (but not all!); all nouns of the second declension ending in ον are neuter.

§34. *Number*. There are two numbers in Greek: singular and plural. The singular represents *one*; the plural represents *two or more*.

§35. *Exercises*.

§35.1. *Translate into English*:
(1) ἀδελφὸς τοῦ ἀποστόλου γράφει τὸν νόμον. (2) οἱ ἀπόστολοι γινώσκουσι τὸν νόμον. (3) δοῦλοι λύουσιν ἱερά. (4) ἔχομεν δῶρα καὶ γράφομεν τοῖς ἀνθρώποις. (5) γράφετε τοῖς δούλοις τοὺς λόγους τῶν ἀδελφῶν. (6) πέμπει ἀδελφὸς τὸ δῶρον. (7) ἄγγελοι παρακαλοῦσι τοὺς ἀδελφούς. (8) οἱ ἀδελφοὶ γινώσκουσι θάνατον καὶ διδάσκουσιν ἀνθρώπους. (9) ὁ δοῦλος ζητεῖ τὸ ἱερόν. (10) ὁ ἄνθρωπος ἔχει τὸν νόμον καὶ ἄνθρωποι διδάσκουσι τοὺς ἀδελφούς.

§35.2. *Translate into Greek*:
(1) The men are destroying the temple of God. (2) An apsotle is knowing a slave. (3) The slave is receiving a gift in the temple. (4) The men are calling the messengers. (5) He is receiving gifts from the men. (6) Slaves from the apostle are hearing the words of death. (7) She is speaking the words of the law to a slave. (8) An apostle is receiving the word from God. (9) Messengers and apostles are seeing temples. (10) The man of God is receiving a gift.

Lesson 6
Present Passive Indicative

§36. *Vocabulary.*
βάλλω, *I throw*
βαπτίζω, *I baptize*
ἐγείρω, I raise up
ἐν, *in* (location, with the locative case)
    by (impersonal agency, with the instrumental case)
κηρύσσω, *I preach, I proclaim*
κόσμος, ὁ, *world*
μένω, *I abide*
σῴζω, *I save*
τέκνον, τό, *child*
τόπος, ὁ, *place*
ὑπό, *by* (direct agency, with the ablative case)
φέρω, *I bear, I bring*

§37. *Passive Voice.* As in English the passive voice functions in Greek to indicate that the *subject is being acted upon*, i.e., the subject is the recipient of the action. "I am being raised up!" Because we are still studying the *present tense*, this action is *continuous* action in present time.

§38. *Passive Voice Forms.* The present passive indicative forms for the ω conjugation are:

	SINGULAR	PLURAL
1st per	λύομαι, *I am being loosed*	λυόμεθα, *we are being loosed*
2nd per	λύῃ, *you are being loosed*	λύεσθε, *you are being loosed*
3rd per	λύεται, *he, she, it is being loosed*	λύονται, *they are being loosed*

For the εω verbs the present passive endings are:

	SINGULAR	PLURAL

1st per φιλοῦμαι, *I am being loved*   φιλούμεθα, *we are being loved*
2nd per φιλῇ, *you are being loved*   φιλεῖσθε, *you are being loved*
3rd per φιλεῖται, *he, she, it is being loved*   φιλοῦνται, *they are being loved*

§39. *Uses of the Passive Voice.* There are three distinct uses of the passive voice in the New Testament.

§39.1. To identify the original (direct) agency that is producing the action on the subject. This construction usually involves the preposition ὑπό with the noun following in the ablative case. Example: οἱ νόμοι γράφονται ὑπὸ τοῦ θεοῦ = *the laws are being written by God.*

§39.2. To identify impersonal agency. Here the instrumental case is used with or without the preposition ἐν. Example: ὁ ἀδελφὸς σῴζεται ἐν τῷ λόγῳ or ὁ ἀδελφὸς σῴζεται τῷ λόγῳ (without the preposition ἐν) = *the brother is being saved by the word.*

§39.3. Sometimes the passive voice occurs when no agency, direct or impersonal, is used. Example: καλεῖται = *he is being called.*

§40. *Translating the Passive Voice.* The passive voice should be rendered in English to indicate activity that is occuring in the present time and that is *durative* in nature. διδάσκομαι, *I am being taught.*

You learned in lesson 3 that *present, active, indicative verbs* could be rendered in English in at least two ways: λύω, *I am loosing* = or *I loose.* In order to indicate the *durative* nature of the present tense the former translation is preferred. The same is true in the *present passive,* i.e., *I am being loosed* is to be preferred over *I am loosed.*

§41. *Exercises.*

§41.1. *Translate into English*:
(1) οἱ ἄνθρωποι βαπτίζονται ὑπὸ τῶν ἀποστόλων. (2) οἱ ἀδελφοὶ λύονται ὑπὸ τοῦ ἀγγέλου τοῦ θανάτου. (3) ὁ θεὸς γινώσκει τὸν νόμον. (4) οἱ δοῦλοι σῴζονται ὑπὸ τοῦ ἀγγέλου τοῦ θεοῦ. (5) γράφομεν λόγους τοῖς ἀδελφοῖς. (6) οἱ νόμοι τοῦ θεοῦ κηρύσσονται ὑπὸ τὸν ἄνθρωπον. (7) οἱ ἄνθρωποι διδάσκονται ὑπὸ τὸν δοῦλον. (8) ὁ δοῦλος θεωρεῖ τὸν θεόν. (9) γάμος μένει τὸν νόμον τοῦ κόσμου. (10) ὁ θεὸς ἐγείρει τοὺς ἀνθρώπους.

§41.2. *Translate into Greek*:
(1) The man is being raised up by God. (2) The apostle is being comforted by words. (3) We are being called. (4) The law is being heard by the apostles. (5) The angels are being seen by the slaves. (6) God is calling the brothers and the apostles. (7) You (pl) are being saved from death by God. (8) The children are hearing the words of the law. (9) Death is having a place in the world. (10) I am being baptized by the brother.

Present Middle Indicative

§42. *Vocabulary*.
ἄγω, *I lead*
αἴρω, *I take up*
δοξάζω, *I glorify*
ἐσθίω, *I eat*
καρπός, ὁ, *fruit*
κρίνω, *I judge*
λίθος, ὁ, *stone*
οἶκος, ὁ, *house*
οὐρανός, ὁ, *heaven*
ὄχλος, ὁ, *crowd*
υἱός, ὁ, *son*

§43. *Middle Voice*. The middle voice indicates that the subject is acting in such a way as to participate in the results of the action. There is no exact English equivalent with which to translate this construction: ὁ δοῦλος εὐλογεῖται = *the slave is blessing himself.*

§44. *Middle Forms*. The forms for the middle voice in the present, imperfect and perfect tenses are the same as those for the passive. The difference is a grammatical one; *not one of form.*

ὁ δοῦλος εὐλογεῖται (as middle) = *the slave is blessing himself.*
ὁ δοῦλος εὐλογεῖται (as passive) = *the slave is being blessed.*

The *context* of any given sentence will usually indicate which function is meant.

Since the middle forms are the same as those of the passive (in the present tense) you need only review those forms already learned in §38.

§45. *Uses of the Middle Voice*. There are at least three uses for the middle voice:

§45.1. *Reflexive middle*. The reflexive middle is employed when the result of the action "reflects" upon the subject of the sentence. ὁ δοῦλος ἐγείρεται = *the servant is raising himself up*.

§45.2. *Intensive middle*. The intensive middle stresses the agent that is producing the action. ὁ δοῦλος γράφεται τὸν νόμον = *the servant* (and nobody else) *is writing the law*.

§45.3. *Reciprocal middle*. Here the plural is employed and there is an interchange of action. οἱ ἄνθρωποι παρακαλοῦνται = *the men are comforting each other*.

§46. There follows a complete paradigm for all voices, persons, and for each number of the present tense. *These forms must be mastered*.

ACTIVE VOICE

	SINGULAR	PLURAL
1st per	λύω, *I am loosing*	λύομεν, *we are loosing*
2nd per	λύεις, *you are loosing*	λύετε, *you are loosing*
3rd per	λύει, *he, she, it is loosing*	λύουσι, *they are loosing*

MIDDLE VOICE

	SINGULAR	PLURAL
1st per	λύομαι, *I am loosing myself*	λυόμεθα, *we are loosing ourselves*
2nd per	λύῃ, *you are loosing yourself*	λύεσθε, *you are loosing yourselves*
3rd per	λύεται, *he is loosing himself* *she is loosing herself* *it is loosing itself*[1]	λύονται, *they are loosing themselves*

PASSIVE VOICE

	SINGULAR	PLURAL
1st per	λύομαι, *I am being loosed*	λυόμεθα, *we are being loosed*
2nd per	λύῃ, *you are being loosed*	λύεσθε, *you are being loosed*
3rd per	λύεται, *he is being loosed*	λύονται, *they are being loosed*

§47. *Exercises*.

§47.1. *Translate into English*:

(1) οἱ ἄγγελοι πέμπονται ἄρτον καὶ καρπόν. (2) οἱ ἄνθρωποι βαπτίζονται. (3) οἱ ὄχλοι σῴζονται ἐν τῷ λόγῳ τοῦ ἀποστόλου. (4) τὰ τέκνα τοῦ κόσμου γινώσκεται ὑπὸ τοῦ θεοῦ. (5) λίθοι βάλλονται ὑπὸ τῶν τέκνων εἰς τὸν οἶκον τοῦ ἀποστόλου. (6) κρίνεται ἐν τῷ λόγῳ καὶ τῷ νόμῳ.

---

[1]From this point in the text, the middle voice will be translated into English only in the third person masculine so as to conserve space.

(7) οἱ υἱοὶ τοῦ θεοῦ κηρύσσουσι πρὸς τοὺς ὄχλους ἀνθρώπων καὶ τέκνων. (8) ἄνθρωποι τοῦ κόσμου δοξάζονται ἐν τῷ δώρῳ τοῦ θεοῦ. (9) αἴρομεν λίθους καὶ βάλλομεν τοὺς δούλους ἐκ τοῦ ἱεροῦ. (10) οἱ ὄχλοι ἐσθίουσιν ἄρτον καὶ εὐλογοῦσι τὸν θεόν.

§47.2. *Translate into Greek*:

(1) The Son of God is teaching the crowd. (2) The children are being baptized by the apostles from God. (3) The bread of heaven is being eaten. (4) The word of God is being preached to the slaves by the brothers. (5) The son is leading the crowd to the temple. (6) The child is being sought by the apostles. (7) The apostle and no other is calling the servant. (8) The apostle is baptizing the children. (9) The brothers are being baptized by the apostles. (10) The apostles are teaching each other the word of God.

Lesson 8
Prepositions

§48. *Vocabulary.*

§48.1. *Prepositions used with one case*:

§48.1.1. With the *genitive* case:
ἀντί, *over, against*

§48.1.2. With the *ablative* case:
ἀπό, *from, away from*
ἐκ (ἐξ before a vowel), *out of*
πρό, *in front of, before*

§48.1.3. With the *instrumental* case:
σύν, *with*

§48.1.4. With the *accustaive* case:
ἀνά, *through, by*
εἰς, *into*

§48.2. *Prepositions used with two different cases*:

§48.2.1. With the *genitive/ablative* cases:
διά, *through, by*
κατά, *down, down from*
μετά, *with*
περί, *about, concerning*
πρός, *at*
ὑπέρ, *in behalf of, instead of*
ὑπό, *by*

48.2.2. With the *locative* case:
ἐν, *in, on*

48.2.3. With the *instrumental* case:
ἐν, *by*

§48.2.4. With the *accusative* case:
διά, *because of*
κατά, *along, according to*
μετά, *after*
περί, *beside, beyond*
πρός, *to, toward, at*
ὑπέρ, *over, above, beyond*
ὑπό, *under*

§48.3. *Prepositions used with three different cases*:

§48.3.1. With the *genitive/ablative* cases:
ἐπί, *upon, on* (contact)
παρά, *from*

§48.3.2. With the *dative/locative* cases:
ἐπί, *upon, on* (position)
παρά, *before, by the side of*

§48.3.3. With the *accusative* case:
ἐπί, *upon, on, to* (motion)
παρά, *beside, beyond, along*

§49. *Prepositions*. A preposition is *positioned* in front (''pre'') of a noun and functions to assist that noun in expressing its case idea. Since τοῦ λόγου could be translated either *of the word* or *out of the word* you can readily see the assistance prepositions provide:

Genitive	τοῦ λόγου	*of the word*
Ablative	ἐκ τοῦ λόγου	*out of the word*

§50. *Compounded Prepositions*. Frequently a preposition will be compounded with a verb so as to heighten (or sometimes, change) the meaning of the verb:
γινώσκω, *I know*
ἐπιγινώσκω, *I know fully*
ἀναγινώσκω, *I read*
Compound prepositions are normally, though not always, repeated after the noun: ὁ δοῦλος ἐκβάλλει τοὺς λίθους ἐκ τοῦ οἴκου = *the slave is casting the stones out of the house*. The following prepositions are the ones most frequently repeated after verbs: ἀπό, ἐκ, εἰς, ἐν, ἐπί (review §20 and identify all compounds verbs in that vocabulary).

§51. *Visualizing Prepositions*. The following diagram will assist you in forming a mental picture of the prepositions that indicate direction or motion.

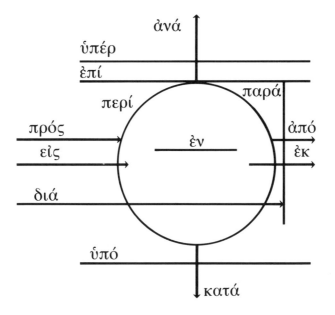

§52. *Elision*. Prepositions that end in a vowel (except περί and πρό) drop the final vowel when the next word begins with a vowel. δοῦλος παρακαλεῖται ὑπ' ἀδελφοῦ = *a slave is being comforted by a brother*. This practice is referred to as *elision*. Notice that the final vowel of the preposition is replaced by an apostrophe *except* when the preposition is combined with a verb ἀπό + ἄγω (*I lead*) = ἀπάγω (*I lead away*)

§53. *Exercises*.

§53.1. *Translate into English*:

(1) οἱ υἱοὶ ἀνθρώπων μένουσιν ἐν τῷ ἱερῷ. (2) βλέπουσι τὸν ἄγγελον ἀπὸ τοῦ θεοῦ. (3) οἱ νόμοι γράφονται ἐν λίθῳ ὑπὸ τοῦ θεοῦ. (4) ὁ θεὸς παρὰ οὐρανοῦ λαλεῖ τὸν νόμον διὰ τοῦ ἀγγέλου. (5) ὁ υἱὸς πέμπει τὰ δῶρα πρὸς τὸ ἱερόν. (6) ἀπὸ τῶν τέκνων λαμβάνομεν τὸν ἄρτον. (7) οἱ ὄχλοι καλοῦνται ἐν τῷ λόγῳ τοῦ θεοῦ. (8) οἱ ἀπόστολοι μένουσιν ἐν τῷ κόσμῳ. (9) ὁ θεὸς πέμπει ἀγγέλους εἰς τὸν κόσμον. (10) μένει ἐν τῷ οἴκῳ μετὰ τῶν ἀποστόλων.

§53.2. *Translate into Greek*:

(1) Because of the law he is speaking a word to the men. (2) We are leading the men into the temple. (3) The apostle is teaching the slaves and the brothers. (4) The brother is writing the laws on stone. (5) The brothers are being judged by the apostles

in the house. (6) Because of the law of God we are being saved. (7) According to the angel the word is being preached in the world through the apostles. (8) He is throwing stones out of the temple. (9) God is leading the slaves and the apostles into the house. (10) The apostles are calling each other out of the world and into heaven.

Lesson 9

First Declension Nouns

§54. *Vocabulary*.
ἀγάπη, ἡ, *love*
ἀλήθεια, ἡ, *truth*
ἁμαρτία, ἡ, *sin*
βασιλεία, ἡ, *kingdom*
γλῶσσα, ἡ, *tongue*
διδαχή, ἡ, *teaching*
ἐκκλησία, ἡ, *church*
ἐντολή, ἡ, *commandment*
ἡμέρα, ἡ, *day*
μαθητής, ὁ, *disciple*
μεσσίας, ὁ, *messiah*
προφήτης, ὁ, *prophet*

§55. *Inflection*. The second declension nouns (§28) consist mainly of masculine with some neuter nouns. The o sound predominates in the second declension. The first declension consists mainly of feminine nouns (those whose stems end in α or η) with some masculine (those whose stems end in ας or ης). The α sound predominates in the first declension.

In the first declension there are three systems for declining the feminine nouns and two for declining the masculine nouns *in the singular*; all plural forms of all first declension nouns are the same.

§56. *Endings*. First declension feminine nouns end with either α or η in the nominative singular. First declension masculine nouns end with either ας or ης in the nominative singular. You can find the stem of any first declension noun by removing the α, η, ας, or ης from the nominative singular form.

§57. *Declension of Feminine Nouns*.

§57.1. *Feminine nouns ending in ε, ι, or ρ.* Those first declension feminine nouns whose stems end in ε, ι, or ρ in the nominative singular (lexical form): [only the *singular* form will be given here because *all first declension nouns have the same plural forms* (see §59)].

CASE		SINGULAR	ENDING
Nom	ἡ	ἐκκλησία	-α
Gen	τῆς	ἐκκλησίας	-ας
Abl	τῆς	ἐκκλησίας	-ας
Dat	τῇ	ἐκκλησίᾳ	-ᾳ
Loc	τῇ	ἐκκλησίᾳ	-ᾳ
Inst	τῇ	ἐκκλησίᾳ	-ᾳ
Acc	τὴν	ἐκκλησίαν	-αν

§ 57.2. *Feminine nouns ending in σ, λλ, or one of the double consonants.* Those first declension feminine nouns ending in σ, λλ, or one of the double consonants (§10.5) in the nominative singular (lexical form):

CASE		SINGULAR	ENDING
Nom	ἡ	γλῶσσα	-α
Gen	τῆς	γλώσσης	-ης
Abl	τῆς	γλώσσης	-ης
Dat	τῇ	γλώσσῃ	-ῃ
Loc	τῇ	γλώσσῃ	-ῃ
Inst	τῇ	γλώσσῃ	-ῃ
Acc	τὴν	γλῶσσαν	-αν

§57.3. *Feminine nouns ending in any other letter.* First declension nouns whose stems end in letter other than ε, ι, ρ, σ, λλ or one of the double consonants in the nominative singular (lexical form):

CASE		SINGULAR	ENDING
Nom	ἡ	διδαχή	-ή
Gen	τῆς	διδαχῆς	-ῆς
Abl	τῆς	διδαχῆς	-ῆς
Dat	τῇ	διδαχῇ	-ῇ
Loc	τῇ	διδαχῇ	-ῇ
Inst	τῇ	διδαχῇ	-ῇ
Acc	τὴν	διδαχήν	-ήν

§58. *Declension of Masculine Nouns.*

58.1. *Masculine nouns ending in ε, ι, or ρ.* Those first declension nouns whose stems end in ε, ι or ρ in the nominative singular (lexical form):

CASE		SINGULAR	ENDING
Nom	ὁ	μεσσίας	-ας
Gen	τοῦ	μεσσίου	-ου
Abl	τοῦ	μεσσίου	-ου
Dat	τῷ	μεσσίᾳ	-ᾳ
Loc	τῷ	μεσσίᾳ	-ᾳ
Inst	τῷ	μεσσίᾳ	-ᾳ
Acc	τὸν	μεσσίαν	-αν

§58.2. *Masculine nouns ending in any other letter.* Those first declension masculine nouns whose stems end in any letter other than ε, ι, or ϱ in the nominative singular (lexical form):

CASE		SINGULAR	ENDING
Nom	ὁ	μαθητής	-ής
Gen	τοῦ	μαθητοῦ	-οῦ
Abl	τοῦ	μαθητοῦ	-οῦ
Dat	τῷ	μαθητῇ	-ῇ
Loc	τῷ	μαθητῇ	-ῇ
Inst	τῷ	μαθητῇ	-ῇ
Acc	τὸν	μαθητήν	-ήν

§59. *Plural Endings.* Plural endings for *all* first declension nouns are the same. This is true in all varieties, both feminine and masculine. Note that the definite article reflects the *gender as well as the number of the noun with which it is associated.*

§59.1. *Feminine nouns ending in ε, ι, or ϱ:*

CASE		PLURAL	ENDING
Nom	αἱ	ἐκκλησίαι	-αι
Gen	τῶν	ἐκκλησιῶν	-ῶν
Abl	τῶν	ἐκκλησιῶν	-ῶν
Dat	ταῖς	ἐκκλησίαις	-αις
Loc	ταῖς	ἐκκλησίαις	-αις
Inst	ταῖς	ἐκκλησίαις	-αις
Acc	τὰς	ἐκκλησίας	-ας

§59.2. *Feminine nouns ending in σ, λλ, ψ, ξ, or ζ*

CASE		PLURAL	ENDING
Nom	αἱ	γλῶσσαι	-αι
Gen	τῶν	γλωσσῶν	-ῶν
Abl	τῶν	γλωσσῶν	-ῶν
Dat	ταῖς	γλώσσαις	-αις

Loc	ταῖς	γλώσσαις	-αις
Inst	ταῖς	γλώσσαις	-αις
Acc	τὰς	γλώσσας	-ας

§59.3. *Feminine nouns ending in any other letter.*

CASE		PLURAL	ENDING
Nom	αἱ	διδαχαί	-αί
Gen	τῶν	διδαχῶν	-ῶν
Abl	τῶν	διδαχῶν	-ῶν
Dat	ταῖς	διδαχαῖς	-αῖς
Loc	ταῖς	διδαχαῖς	-αῖς
Inst	ταῖς	διδαχαῖς	-αῖς
Acc	τὰς	διδαχάς	-άς

§59.4. *Masculine nouns ending in ε, ι, ρ.*

CASE		PLURAL	ENDING
Nom	οἱ	μεσσίαι	-αι
Gen	τῶν	μεσσιῶν	-ῶν
Abl	τῶν	μεσσιῶν	-ῶν
Dat	τοῖς	μεσσίαις	-αις
Loc	τοῖς	μεσσίαις	-αις
Inst	τοῖς	μεσσίαις	-αις
Acc	τοὺς	μεσσίας	-ας

§59.5. *Masculine nouns ending in any other letter*:

CASE		PLURAL	ENDING
Nom	οἱ	μαθηταί	-αί
Gen	τῶν	μαθητῶν	-ῶν
Abl	τῶν	μαθητῶν	-ῶν
Dat	τοῖς	μαθηταῖς	-αῖς
Loc	τοῖς	μαθηταῖς	-αῖς
Inst	τοῖς	μαθηταῖς	-αῖς
Acc	τοὺς	μαθητάς	-άς

§60. *Definite Article.* The complete declension of the definite article is:

SINGULAR

CASE	MASCULINE	FEMININE	NEUTER
Nom	ὁ	ἡ	τό
Gen	τοῦ	τῆς	τοῦ
Abl	τοῦ	τῆς	τοῦ

Dat	τῷ	τῇ	τῷ
Loc	τῷ	τῇ	τῷ
Inst	τῷ	τῇ	τῷ
Acc	τόν	τήν	τό

PLURAL

CASE	MASCULINE	FEMININE	NEUTER
Nom	οἱ	αἱ	τά
Gen	τῶν	τῶν	τῶν
Abl	τῶν	τῶν	τῶν
Dat	τοῖς	ταῖς	τοῖς
Loc	τοῖς	ταῖς	τοῖς
Inst	τοῖς	ταῖς	τοῖς
Acc	τούς	τάς	τά

Note that the nominative forms in the masculine and feminine singular and plural (ὁ, οἱ, ἡ, αἱ) are pronounced so closely with the word that follows that they have no accent of their own. These *unaccented articles* are called *proclitics* (§71.1).

§61. *Exercises.*

§61.1. *Translate into English*:

(1) ἄγομεν τοὺς μαθητὰς εἰς τὴν ἐκκλησίαν. (2) οἱ μαθηταὶ ἄγονται εἰς τὴν ἐκκλησίαν ὑπὸ τοῦ ὄχλου. (3) ὁ προφήτης βλέπει τὸν μεσσίαν καὶ γινώσκει τὴν ἀγάπην τοῦ θεοῦ. (4) ἡ βασιλεία τοῦ θεοῦ κηρύσσεται ὑπὸ τοῦ μεσσίου καὶ τῶν μαθητῶν. (5) ἡ ἀγάπη τοῦ θεοῦ καλεῖ τοὺς ὄχλους εἰς τὴν βασιλείαν. (6) διὰ ἁμαρτίαν ὁ λόγος τοῦ θεοῦ κηρύσσεται ὑπὸ τῶν μαθητῶν πρὸς τὸν κόσμον. (7) οἱ μαθηταὶ διδάσκονται νόμους καὶ ἐντολάς. (8) οἱ μαθηταὶ καὶ οἱ προφῆται σῴζονται ὑπὸ τοῦ μεσσίου καὶ δοξάζουσι τὸν θεόν. (9) ὁ δοῦλος λαμβάνει ἄρτον καὶ καρπὸν ἀπ' ἀδελφοῦ. (10) οἱ ἀδελφοὶ λέγουσιν λόγους ἀληθείας ὄχλοις ἀνθρώπων.

§61.2. *Translate into Greek*:

(1) The law of the kingdom is being taught by the disciples. (2) The sons are knowing the commandments and are teaching a law to the crowd. (3) The disciple knows sin and is speaking the truth. (4) The servant is seeing the prophet in the church. (5) The apostle is being taught the law. (6) The kingdom of God is being preached by the disciples. (7) God's love is saving the world from sin. (8) The crowds are being led into the temple. (9) The law of marriage is being written by the apostles. (10) A man is receiving a gift from the slave.

Lesson 10
Adjectives

§62. *Vocabulary.*

ἀγαθός, ἀγαθή, ἀγαθόν, *good*

ἀγαπητός, ἀγαπητή, ἀγαπητόν, *beloved*

ἀλλά, *but* (stronger than δέ)

βασιλικός, βασιλική, βασιλίκον, *royal*

γραφή, ἡ, *writing*

δέ, *but, and*

δίκαιος, δικαία, δίκαιον, *righteous, just*

δόξα, ἡ, *glory*

εἰρήνη, ἡ, *peace*

ἔσχατος, ἐσχάτη, ἔσχατον, *last*

ἕτερος, ἑτέρα, ἕτερον, *another* (of a different kind)

καινός, καινή, καινόν, *new*

κακός, κακή, κακόν, *bad*

καλός, καλή, καλόν, *good*

παραβολή, ἡ, *parable*

§63. *Inflection.* Adjectives, like nouns, have *gender, number,* and *case.* To locate an adjective these three bits of information must be provided. ὁ ἀγαθὸς ἀπόστολος = *the good apostle.* Notice that ἀγαθός agrees with the noun it modifies (ἀπόστολος) in *all three respects*: ἀγαθός is written in the *masculine, singular, nominative* form.

All adjectives in §62 are inflected like second declension nouns in the masculine and neuter and like first declension nouns in the feminine. In the feminine, if the stem of the adjective ends in ε, ι, or ρ, the feminine *singular* will have an α throughout instead of an η.

§64. *Forms.*

§64.1. *Adjectives ending in ε, ι, or ϱ.*

SINGULAR

CASE	MASCULINE	FEMININE	NEUTER
Nom	μικϱός	μικϱά	μικϱόν
Gen	μικϱοῦ	μικϱᾶς	μικϱοῦ
Abl	μικϱοῦ	μικϱᾶς	μικϱοῦ
Dat	μικϱῷ	μικϱᾷ	μικϱῷ
Loc	μικϱῷ	μικϱᾷ	μικϱῷ
Inst	μικϱῷ	μικϱᾷ	μικϱῷ
Acc	μικϱόν	μικϱάν	μικϱόν

§64.2. *Adjectives ending in any other letter.*

SINGULAR

CASE	MASCULINE	FEMININE	NEUTER
Nom	ἀγαθός	ἀγαθή	ἀγαθόν
Gen	ἀγαθοῦ	ἀγαθῆς	ἀγαθοῦ
Abl	ἀγαθοῦ	ἀγαθῆς	ἀγαθοῦ
Dat	ἀγαθῷ	ἀγαθῇ	ἀγαθῷ
Loc	ἀγαθῷ	ἀγαθῇ	ἀγαθῷ
Inst	ἀγαθῷ	ἀγαθῇ	ἀγαθῷ
Acc	ἀγαθόν	ἀγαθήν	ἀγαθόν

§64.3. *Plural Forms.* The plural forms for all adjectives are the same regardless of the letter with which the stem ends.

PLURAL

CASE	MASCULINE	FEMININE	NEUTER
Nom	ἀγαθοί	ἀγαθαί	ἀγαθά
Gen	ἀγαθῶν	ἀγαθῶν	ἀγαθῶν
Abl	ἀγαθῶν	ἀγαθῶν	ἀγαθῶν
Dat	ἀγαθοῖς	ἀγαθαῖς	ἀγαθοῖς
Loc	ἀγαθοῖς	ἀγαθαῖς	ἀγαθοῖς
Inst	ἀγαθοῖς	ἀγαθαῖς	ἀγαθοῖς
Acc	ἀγαθούς	ἀγαθάς	ἀγαθά

§65. *Agreement.* Adjectives (and the articles that precede them, if present) reflect the same *gender, number, and case* as the nouns they modify. This process is called *agreement.* Study these examples closely: (1) ὁ ἀγαθὸς λόγος = *the good word.* (2) ἡ κακὴ ἡμέρα = *the bad day.* (3) ἀκούω τὸν ἀγαθὸν λόγον = *I hear the good word*. In all instances notice that the adjective *agrees* with its noun in *gender, case,* and *number*.

·In the first two cases the adjectives are nominative singular because the noun is nominative singular. The first example is built upon a masculine noun, the second a feminine noun; therefore, the adjective in example one is masculine; in example two it is feminine.

In the third example the noun being modified functions as the direct object of the sentence. It is thus in the *accusative* case *as is the adjective*.

Consider one final example: οἱ προφῆται κηρύσσουσιν περὶ τῆς κακῆς ἡμέρας = *the prophets are preaching concerning the bad day*. In this case the preposition περί used with the ablative case means *concerning*. Notice that the definite article, the adjective, and the noun *all* occur in the *ablative* case: τῆς κακῆς ἡμέρας. ἡμέρα is *feminine singular*, therefore the adjective (and the definite article) is *feminine singular*.

§66. *Uses of the Adjective.*

§66.1. *Attributive.* The attributive use of the adjective occurs frequently in the New Testament. Here the adjective *attributes* a quality to the noun (i.e., the adjective *modifies* the noun). Study these two examples: (1) ὁ ἀγαθὸς ἄνθρωπος (2) ὁ ἄνθρωπος ὁ ἀγαθός. Both phrases are to be translated *the good man*. While the position of the adjective varies with reference to the noun, notice that in *both* instances the *article precedes the adjective*.

§66.2. *Predicative.* The predicative use of the adjective makes an assertation about the noun. Study these two examples: ὁ ἄνθρωπος ἀγαθός (2) ἀγαθὸς ὁ ἄνθρωπος. Both examples should be translated *the man is good*. Unlike the attributive usage mentioned above, in the predicative use of the adjective the definite article *never* precedes the adjective.

§66.3. *Substantive.* Sometimes the adjective functions as a noun (or substantive). Thus ὁ ἀγαθός could mean *the good man* or τὸ ἀγαθόν *the good thing*. Notice that there is no *noun* expressed in either example. The substantive use of the adjective suggests that the adjective itself carries the force of a noun.

§67. *Adversatives.* δέ is a *postpositive* conjunction; it cannot stand first in its clause. Its usual place is *second*, though it may occur elsewhere. Usually it is used to indicate a *slight contrast* between what it separates in the sentence. δέ may be translated *and* though often it is translated *but*. δέ is thus *weaker* than ἀλλά (*but*) which expresses a *strong* contrast usually to the degree of *opposition*. Examples: ὁ ἀποστόλος γινώσκει τὸν κύριον, ὁ δὲ κύριος γινώσκει τὸν ἀπόστολον = *the apostle is knowing the Lord, and* (or *but*) *the Lord is knowing the apostle*. A *stronger contrast* may be indicated with ἀλλά: ὁ ἀπόστολος διδάσκει τὸν νόμον, ἀλλὰ ὁ κύριος διδάσκει ἀγάπην = *the apostle is teaching the law, but the Lord is teaching love.*

§68. *Exercises.*

§68.1. *Transalate into English*:

(1) ὁ ἀγαθὸς ἀπόστολος γινώσκει τὸν δίκαιον νόμον. (2) οἱ κακοὶ γινώσκουσιν ἁμαρτίαν. (3) ὁ θεὸς ὁ δίκαιος καλεῖ τοὺς μαθητὰς καὶ τοὺς ἀποστόλους εἰς τὴν βασιλείαν. (4) οἱ δίκαιοι υἱοὶ τῆς βασιλείας διδάσκουσι τοὺς ἀγαπητοὺς ἀδελφούς. (5) διὰ ἁμαρτίαν ἡ ἐκκλησία μένει ἐν κακῷ κόσμῳ. (6) ἡ ἀγαπητὴ ἀκούει τὴν κακὴν διδαχήν. (7) οἱ ἀγαθοὶ ἄνθρωποι ἀκούουσι τὰς παραβολὰς τῆς βασιλείας. (8) οἱ δοῦλοι οἱ κακοὶ λύουσι τὰ ἱερά. (9) οἱ δίκαιοι λέγουσι τοὺς ἀγαθοὺς λόγους ταῖς δικαίαις. (10) ὁ ἀγαθὸς μαθητὴς ἐγείρει τοὺς ἀνθρώπους.

§68.2. *Translate into Greek*:

(1) The houses are bad and the temple is good. (2) The disciples are teaching a parable to the men. (3) The royal law is being taught by the disciple. (4) The messiah is raising up the other apostles. (5) They are eating the bad fruit and the good bread. (6) The righteous disciples are hearing the last law. (7) The disciple is knowing the righteous men and the righteous women. (8) Because of the good word, God is saving the prophets. (9) The other man is saying bad things in the last days. (10) The good people are being raised up by the messiah.

Lesson 11

Personal
and Demonstrative Pronouns

§69. *Vocabulary.*

§69.1. *Personal pronouns*
ἐγώ, *I*
σύ, *you* (sing)
αὐτός, αὐτή, αὐτό, *he, she, it*
ἡμεῖς, *we*
ὑμεῖς, *you* (pl)
αὐτοί, αὐταί, αὐτά, *they*

§69.2. *Demonstrative pronouns.*
ἐκεῖνος, ἐκείνη, ἐκεῖνο, *that*
ἐκεῖνοι, ἐκεῖναι, ἐκεῖνα, *those*
οὗτος, αὕτη, τοῦτο, *this*
οὗτοι, αὗται, ταῦτα, *these*

§70. *Inflection.*

§70.1. *Personal pronouns.*

FIRST PERSON

CASE	SINGULAR	PLURAL
Nom	ἐγώ, *I*	ἡμεῖς, *we*
Gen	ἐμοῦ (or μου), *of me*	ἡμῶν, *of us*
Abl	ἐμοῦ (or μου), *from me*	ἡμῶν, *from us*
Dat	ἐμοί (or μοι), *to* or *for me*	ἡμῖν, *to* or *for us*
Loc	ἐμοί (or μοι), *in me*	ἡμῖν, *in us*
Inst	ἐμοί (or μοι), *by me*	ἡμῖν, *by us*

| Acc | ἐμέ (or με), *me* | ἡμᾶς, *us* |

SECOND PERSON

CASE	SINGULAR	PLURAL
Nom	σύ, *you*	ὑμεῖς, *you*
Gen	σοῦ, *of you*	ὑμῶν, *of you*
Abl	σοῦ, *from you*	ὑμῶν, *from you*
Dat	σοί, *to* or *for you*	ὑμῖν, *to* or *for you*
Loc	σοί, *in you*	ὑμῖν, *in you*
Inst	σοί, *by you*	ὑμῖν, *by you*
Acc	σέ, *you*	ὑμᾶς, *you*

THIRD PERSON - SINGULAR

CASE	MASCULINE	FEMININE	NEUTER
Nom	αὐτός, *he*	αὐτή, *she*	αὐτό, *it*
Gen	αὐτοῦ, *of him*	αὐτῆς, *of her*	αὐτοῦ, *of it*
Abl	αὐτοῦ, *from him*	αὐτῆς, *from her*	αὐτοῦ, *from it*
Dat	αὐτῷ, *to* or *for him*	αὐτῇ, *to* or *for her*	αὐτῷ, *to* or *for it*
Loc	αὐτῷ, *in him*	αὐτῇ, *in her*	αὐτῷ, *in it*
Inst	αὐτῷ, *by him*	αὐτῇ, *by her*	αὐτῷ, *by it*
Acc	αὐτόν, *him*	αὐτήν, *her*	αὐτό, *it*

THIRD PERSON - PLURAL

CASE	MASCULINE	FEMININE	NEUTER
Nom	αὐτοί, *they*	αὐταί, *they*	αὐτά, *they*
Gen	αὐτῶν, *of them*	αὐτῶν, *of them*	αὐτῶν, *of them*
Abl	αὐτῶν, *from them*	αὐτῶν, *from them*	αὐτῶν, *from them*
Dat	αὐτοῖς, *to* or *for them*	αὐταῖς, *to* or *for them*	αὐτοῖς, *to* or *for them*
Loc	αὐτοῖς, *in them*	αὐταῖς, *in them*	αὐτοῖς, *in them*
Inst	αὐτοῖς, *by them*	αὐταῖς, *by them*	αὐτοῖς, *by them*
Acc	αὐτούς, *them*	αὐτάς, *them*	αὐτά, *them*

§70.2. *Demonstrative pronouns.* The declension of οὗτος, αὕτη, and τοῦτο is virtually identical to the 3rd person of the personal pronoun; the endings applied to ἐκειν- are also regular (see definite article, §60).

SINGULAR

	THIS - NEAR			THAT - REMOTE		
CASE	MASCULINE	FEMININE	NEUTER	MASCULINE	FEMININE	NEUTER
Nom	οὗτος	αὕτη	τοῦτο	ἐκεῖνος	ἐκείνη	ἐκεῖνο
Gen	τούτου	ταύτης	τούτου	ἐκείνου	ἐκείνης	ἐκείνου
Abl	τούτου	ταύτης	τούτου	ἐκείνου	ἐκείνης	ἐκείνου
Dat	τούτῳ	ταύτῃ	τούτῳ	ἐκείνῳ	ἐκείνῃ	ἐκείνῳ

Loc	τούτῳ	ταύτῃ	τούτῳ	ἐκείνῳ	ἐκείνῃ	ἐκείνῳ
Inst	τούτῳ	ταύτῃ	τούτῳ	ἐκείνῳ	ἐκείνῃ	ἐκείνῳ
Acc	τοῦτον	ταύτην	τοῦτο	ἐκεῖνον	ἐκείνην	ἐκεῖνο

PLURAL

	THESE - NEAR			THOSE - REMOTE		
CASE	MASCULINE	FEMININE	NEUTER	MASCULINE	FEMININE	NEUTER
Nom	οὗτοι	αὗται	ταῦτα	ἐκεῖνοι	ἐκεῖναι	ἐκεῖνα
Gen	τούτων	ταύτων	τούτων	ἐκείνων	ἐκείνων	ἐκείνων
Abl	τούτων	ταύτων	τούτων	ἐκείνων	ἐκείνων	ἐκείνων
Dat	τούτοις	ταύταις	τούτοις	ἐκείνοις	ἐκείναις	ἐκείνοις
Loc	τούτοις	ταύταις	τούτοις	ἐκείνοις	ἐκείναις	ἐκείνοις
Inst	τούτοις	ταύταις	τούτοις	ἐκείνοις	ἐκείναις	ἐκείνοις
Acc	τούτους	ταύτας	ταῦτα	ἐκείνους	ἐκείνας	ἐκεῖνα

§71. *Enclitics and Proclitics.* Enclitics are pronounced with the word that *precedes* them; proclitics are pronounced with the word that *follows* them. Neither is accented except in special cases (see §203.6).

§71.1. *Enclitics.* The enclitics that occur in the New Testament are τις, τι (indefinite pronouns, §177.4); μου, μοι, με, σου, σοι, σε (unaccented forms of the personal pronouns (§70.1); πού, ποτέ, πώς (indefinite adverbs); τε (conjunction); γε and the verb εἰμί (§76).

§71.2 *Proclitics.* The proclitics that occur in the New Testament are ὁ, ἡ, οἱ, and αἱ (forms of the definite article); οὐ, οὐκ, οὐχ (the negative); εἰς, ἐν, ἐκ (prepositions); εἰ and ὡς (conjunctions).

§72. *Use of Pronouns.*

§72.1. *Use of personal pronouns.* Personal pronouns are used in Greek generally the same way as they are in English, i.e., to replace nouns to avoid monotony. The noun that the pronoun stands for is called its *antecedent.* A pronoun agrees with its antecedent in *gender* and *number*; the *case* of a pronoun, however, is determined by its use in the sentence in which it occurs. Example: ὁ νόμος γράφεται καὶ διδάσκομεν αὐτόν. The gender and number of αὐτόν is the same as νόμος—masculine singular. But notice that the *case* of αὐτόν is *accusative.* This is so because αὐτόν is the direct object of διδάσκομεν. In the sentence γινώσκω τὸν νόμον καὶ μένω ἐν αὐτῷ, the gender and number agree with the antecedent νόμον but the case is *locative* because the preposition ἐν requires that case.

While the pronoun *them* does not reflect gender in English, it does in Greek. The sentence γινώσκω τὰ τέκνα καὶ διδάσκω αὐτά = *I am knowing the children and*

I am teaching them has the *neuter* form αὐτά because its antecedent, τὰ τέκνα, is neuter.

Unlike English, Greek uses the personal pronouns as subjects *only* if special emphasis is intended. βλέπομεν translates *we see* <u>without</u> the help of a personal pronoun. ἡμεῖς βλέπομεν also translates *we see* but <u>with</u> the pronoun the *we see* is used to indicate a contrast: ἡμεῖς βλέπομεν, ὑμεῖς δὲ ἀκούετε = *we are seeing, but you are hearing*. Note that the use of the *third person* personal pronoun (αὐτός, αὐτή, αὐτό) in the nominative is distinct from its function as a personal pronoun (see §73).

Note the unemphatic forms (enclitics, §71) of the personal pronouns in the first and second persons singular (these forms may be found in parentheses in the paradigm at §70.1.). These are used regularly to indicate possession: ὁ λόγος μου is translated *my word* and not literally as *the word of me*. Emphatic forms are usually found after a preposition: ἀπ᾽ ἐμοῦ (the final vowel o of ἀπό drops before a vowel and is replaced by an apostrophe—see §52).

§72.2. *Use of demonstrative pronouns.* The near demonstrative (sometimes called the "proximate") is used to refer to something that is relatively *close* to the speaker; the remote demonstrative (sometimes called the "distant") is used to refer to something relatively *far* from the speaker. There are both singular and plural forms for the demonstrative pronouns in all genders. Examples:

this	βλέπω τοῦτον ἄνθρωπον
	ἀκούω ταύτην ἀλήθειαν
that	βλέπω ἐκεῖνον ἄνθρωπον
	ἀκούω ἐκείνην ἀλήθειαν
these	ἀκούω ταύτας γλώσσας
	βλέπω ταῦτα ἱερά
those	ἀκούω ἐκείνας γλώσσας
	βλέπω ἐκεῖνα ἱερά

Both οὗτος and ἐκεῖνος are frequently used with nouns. When they are, the noun has the article and the demonstrative pronoun is in the *predicate* position: οὗτος ὁ ἀγαθὸς λόγος or ὁ ἀγαθὸς λόγος οὗτος = *this good word*.

Both οὗτος and ἐκεῖνος are frequently used as *substantives* so that, alone, ἐκεῖναι might mean "those women" or τοῦτο "this thing."

§73. *Special Uses of αὐτός, αὐτή, αὐτό.* The uses of the third person *personal pronouns* in the *nominative case* are *distinct* from their function as personal pronouns (when used as a personal pronoun αὐτός, etc. are translated *his, her, him, their, them, etc.*). The following instances *are distinct from these regular usages*:

§73.1. When αὐτός, αὐτή, αὐτό are used with a noun, in any case, and when these appear in the attributive position (§66.1), they must be translated "same." Thus ὁ αὐτὸς νόμος = *the same law* [cf. τὸν αὐτὸν λόγον, Matthew 26:44].

§73.2. When used with a noun in the predicate position (§66.2) αὐτός, αὐτή, αὐτό are translated *intensively*. Thus ὁ νόμος αὐτός or αὐτὸς ὁ νόμος = *the law itself* [cf. αὐτὸ τὸ πνεῦμα, Romans 8:16].

§73.3. Sometimes αὐτός is found *together with* another personal pronoun (expressed or unexpressed). The latter personal pronoun serves as the subject of the verb and agrees with the verb in person and number. The presence of a form of αὐτός *together with* the other personal pronoun calls for the *intensive* translation: αὐτὸς σὺ ἀκούεις or αὐτὸς ἀκούεις = *you yourself are hearing*.

§74. *Exercises.*

§74.1. *Translate into English*:
(1) γινώσκω τοὺς ἀδελφούς μου καὶ διδάσκομεν αὐτούς. (2) οἱ δοῦλοι ὑμῶν λαμβάνουσιν ἡμᾶς εἰς τοὺς οἴκους αὐτῶν. (3) ὁ ἀδελφός μου βλέπει τὸ ἱερὸν μεθ'[1] ὑμῶν. (4) οἱ μαθηταί μου ἀκούουσι τὸν λόγον τοῦ ἀδελφοῦ. (5) οὗτος ὁ μαθητὴς γινώσκει ἐκεῖνον τὸν μαθητήν. (6) ὁ ἀπόστολος ὁ αὐτὸς κηρύσσει ταύτας τὰς παραβολὰς περὶ ἁμαρτίας καὶ θανάτου. (7) οἱ ἀδελφοὶ ἡμῶν βαπτίζουσι τὰ τέκνα εἰς τὴν βασιλείαν τοῦ οὐρανοῦ. (8) ἐκεῖνοι οἱ μαθηταὶ ἄγουσι τοὺς δούλους αὐτῶν πρὸς τὴν ἀλήθειαν. (9) λαμβάνω τοὺς λόγους αὐτῶν ἀπὸ τοῦ ἀποστόλου. (10) ἐγὼ λέγω, σὺ δὲ γράφεις.

§74.2. *Translate into Greek*:
(1). We are hearing the words of the apostle. (2) Because of me you (pl) are teaching the truth. (3) Your brothers are leading us into their houses. (4) We are hearing the words of the disciples and these are leading us to the truth. (5) But in the last days the apostles are preaching the commandment of love. (6) In love you (sing) are speaking the good words. (7) The righteous words of your good son are being heard by the crowds. (8) These good men are seeing the kingdom of heaven in the world. (9) God is raising these apostles. (10) The brothers are judging the righteous disciples and are leading them to the kingdom.

---

[1]μετά elides its final vowel before a word beginning with a vowel (§52); in this case, τ becomes θ before a rough breathing.

Lesson 12
Εἰμί and Deponent Verbs

§75. *Vocabulary* [verbs noted D are discussed in §78].

ἄλλος, ἄλλη, ἄλλο, *other, another* [cf §62, ἕτερος]

ἀποκρίνομαι (D), *I answer*

ἄρχομαι (D), *I begin*

γίνομαι (D), *I become*

διέρχομαι (D), *I come through*

εἰμί, *I am*

εἰσέρχομαι (D), *I come into, I enter*

ἐξέρχομαι (D), *I come out of*

ἔρχομαι (D), *I come, I go*

κατέρχομαι (D), *I come down*

κύριος, ὁ, *Lord, the Lord*

μικρός, μικρά, μικρόν, *small*

μόνος, μόνη, μόνον, *only*

νεκρός, νεκρά, νεκρόν, *dead*

οὐ, *not* (οὐκ before vowels; οὐχ before a rough breathing)

πιστεύω, *I believe*

πιστός, πιστή, πιστόν, *faithful*

πονηρός, πονηρά, πονηρόν, *evil*

πρῶτος, πρώτη, πρῶτον, *first*

συνέρχομαι (D), *I come with*

§76. *Present of εἰμί.* The Greek verb εἰμί does *not* have voice because it does not indicate action, rather *a state of being*. It is located as follows: ἐσμέν = present indicative, 1st person plural, from εἰμί.

The forms for the present indicative of εἰμί are:

	SINGULAR	PLURAL
1st per	εἰμί, *I am*	ἐσμέν, *we are*

| 2nd per | εἶ, *you are* | ἐστέ, *you are* |
| 3rd per | ἐστί(ν), *he is* | εἰσί(ν), *they are* |

Note that all the forms of εἰμί are *enclitic* (§71.1) except εἶ. The *circumflex* accent distinguishes this form from the the Greek word *if* (εἰ).

§77. *Usage of εἰμί.* εἰμί is a linking verb, i.e., it "links" the subject to a *predicate nominative* in order to complete, or extend, the meaning of the subject. Remember: when there is a word in the predicate position (with the verb εἰμί) that word will tell something about the subject. The predicate nominative is *never* a direct object (accusative case) but *always* the *nominative case*. Example: ὁ προφήτης ἐστὶν ἀγαθός = *the prophet is good* (review §66). Also note that *the prophet is good* could have been written ἀγαθὸς ὁ προφήτης *without* any form of εἰμί.

Usually the New Testament writers prefer to *express* εἰμί; but in cases where they do not, you must be able to recognize the *predicative use* (see §66.2).

§78. *Deponent Verbs.* Doponent verbs (indicated with a D in §75 and all other subsequent vocabularies) are verbs whose lexical form is *middle* or *passive* but whose function is *active.* Example: γίνομαι appears in §75 in the *middle/passive* form, yet it is translated *I am becoming,* i.e., in the *active* voice. Compare the translation of λύομαι, *I am loosing myself* or *I am being loosed* with γίνομαι, *I am becoming* and you will see that deponent verbs must be mastered to avoid confusion in translating the New Testament.

§79. *Use of the Negative.* The negative particle οὐ is generally placed *before* the word it negates. Example: οὐ γινώσκω αὐτόν = *I am not knowing him.*

§80. *Verbs with Prepositions.* Vocabulary §75 contains several verbs in combination with a preposition (review §50).

§81. *Various Cases with Verbs.* Some Greek verbs may take more than one case, or may take a case different from the case that same verb in English might take. εἰμί (§77) takes the *nominative* case as does γίνομαι. Examples: εἰμὶ ἄνθρωπος = *I am a man;* γίνομαι ἄνθρωπος = *I am becoming a man.*

ἀποκρίνομαι, however, takes the *dative* case: οἱ ἄνθρωποι ἀποκρίνονται τοῖς ἀποστόλοις = *the men are answering the apostles.*

ἀκούω (§15) may take either the *accusative* (*to hear* "with understanding") or the *genitive* (*to hear* "without understanding").

πιστεύω takes the *dative* case. Thus πιστεύω τῷ ἀποστόλῳ = *I am believing the apostle* is correct. Hereafter in the vocabularies at the beginning of each lesson look for a C (and then see accompanying note) to indicate verbs that may require some case other than the accusative.

§82. *Exercises*.

§82.1. Translate into English:

(1) τῷ ἀγαθῷ λόγῳ τοῦ ἀποστόλου εἰσέρχεται εἰς τὴν βασιλείαν τοῦ θεοῦ. (2) οἱ υἱοὶ τοῦ δούλου γίνονται ἄνθρωποι τοῦ θεοῦ. (3) γινώσκω τοὺς ἀδελφούς μου καὶ διδάσκω αὐτούς. (4) ἐκεῖνοι οἱ πονηροὶ ἔρχονται πρὸς τὸν κύριον καὶ λαμβάνουσι δόξαν ἀπ᾽ αὐτοῦ. (5) σῳζόμεθα ἀπὸ τῶν ἁμαρτιῶν ἡμῶν ὑπὸ τοῦ κυρίου τοῦ οὐρανοῦ. (6) οἱ ἀπόστολοι διέρχονται διὰ τῶν κακῶν τόπων καὶ εἰσέρχονται εἰς τοὺς ἀγαθοὺς οἴκους. (7) διδάσκεται ὑπὸ τοῦ πιστοῦ μαθητοῦ τοῦ κυρίου. (8) ὁ δοῦλος οὐκ ἔχει ἄρτον καὶ οὐκ ἔχει καρπόν. (9) ὁ ἀπόστολος αὐτὸς βαπτίζει τὰ τέκνα. (10) εἶ μαθητὴς τοῦ θεοῦ καὶ ἄγγελος ἀγάπης.

§82.2. *Translate into Greek*:

(1) The little children are going down into the house of that man. (2) We are believing in the son of God and we are having peace. (3) The righteous God is being known in this world. (4) The good apostles are answering the Lord. (5) The prophet is receiving the bread and the fruit from the apostle. (6) We are coming out of the evil temple and are entering into the church of the Lord. (7) The good gifts are being brought to the crowd. (8) The apostles are answering us and speaking parables to us. (9) We were receiving these commandments from the Lord and we were teaching them to the others. (10) We are hearing these words of the faithful apostles of our Lord.

Imperfect Indicative

§83. *Vocabulary*.

ἀναγινώσκω, *I read*

ἀποστέλλω, *I send* (with a message)

ἄρχω (C), *I rule* (usually takes dative case)

ἔρημος, ἡ, *desert*

ζωή, ἡ, *life*

καρδία, ἡ, *heart*

λαός, ὁ, *people*

νῦν, *now*

ὁδός, ἡ, *way*

πορεύομαι (D), *I go*

συνάγω, *I gather together*

τότε, *then*

φωνή, ἡ, *voice*

χριστός, ὁ, *Christ*

§84. *Inflection*. The imperfect indicative forms are:

   §84.1. *Active voice*.

	SINGULAR	PLURAL
1st per	ἔλυον[1], *I was loosing*	ἐλύομεν, *we were loosing*
2nd per	ἔλυες, *you were loosing*	ἐλύετε, *you were loosing*
3rd per	ἔλυε, *he, she, it was loosing*	ἔλυον[1], *they were loosing*

   §84.2. *Middle voice*.

SINGULAR	PLURAL

---

[1]The context, or the explicit nominative, must dictate whether ἔλυον is to be translated first singular or third plural.

1st per ἐλυόμην, *I was loosing myself*   ἐλυόμεθα, *we were loosing ourselves*
2nd per ἐλύου, *you were loosing yourself*   ἐλύεσθε, *you were loosing yourselves*
3rd per ἐλύετο, *he was loosing himself*   ἐλύοντο, *they were loosing themselves*

§84.3. Passive voice.

	SINGULAR	PLURAL
1st per	ἐλυόμην, *I was being loosed*	ἐλυόμεθα, *we were being loosed*
2nd per	ἐλύου, *you were being loosed*	ἐλύεσθε, *you were being loosed*
3rd per	ἐλύετο, *he, she, it was being loosed*	ἐλύοντο, *they were being loosed*

§84.4. Imperfect indicative of εἰμί.

	SINGULAR	PLURAL
1st per	ἤμην, *I was*	ἦμεν, *we were*
2nd per	ἦς, *you were*	ἦτε, *you were*
3rd per	ἦν, *he, she, it was*	ἦσαν, *they were*

§84.5. Imperfect of εω verbs [review §21, 22].

ACTIVE

	SINGULAR	PLURAL
1st per	ἐκάλουν, *I was calling*	ἐκαλοῦμεν, *we were calling*
2nd per	ἐκάλεις, *you were calling*	ἐκαλεῖτε, *you were calling*
3rd per	ἐκάλει, *he, she, it was calling*	ἐκάλουν, *they were calling*

MIDDLE

	SINGULAR	PLURAL
1st per	ἐκαλούμην, *I was calling myself*	ἐκαλούμεθα, *we were calling ourselves*
2nd per	ἐκαλοῦ, *you were calling yourself*	ἐκαλεῖσθε, *you were calling yourselves*
3rd per	ἐκαλεῖτο, *he was calling himself*	ἐκαλοῦντο, *they were calling themselves*

PASSIVE

	SINGULAR	PLURAL
1st per	ἐκαλούμην, *I was being called*	ἐκαλούμεθα, *we were being called*
2nd per	ἐκαλοῦ, *you were being called*	ἐκαλεῖσθε, *you were being called*
3rd per	ἐκαλεῖτο, *he, she, it was being called*	ἐκαλοῦντο, *they were being called*

§85. *Augment.* The initial ε in paradigm §84 is called an *augment*. It is a tense sign that indicates a *secondary tense*, i.e., a tense that indicates action that occurred in *past time* (review §18.2). Only secondary tenses in the *indicative mood* have an augment. There are two such tenses: the imperfect and the aorist.

§85.1. *Syllabic augment*. Since the secondary tense sign is an ε, when added, it creates an additional syllable. The *syllabic augment* occurs only with verbs that begin with a *consonant*. Examples: ἐλάμβανον = *I was receiving*; ἔβλεπον = *I was seeing*.

§85.2. *Temporal augment*. When the secondary tense sign is added to a verb that begins with a *vowel* the addition of the initial ε will lengthen the beginning vowel of the verb as follows:

TENSE SIGN	VERB BEGINS WITH	RESULTS IN
ε	ε	η
ε	ο	ω
ε	α	η

Examples: ἐγείρω, *I am raising up*; ἤγειρον, *I was raising up.* ὁμολογῶ, *I am confessing*; ὡμολόγουν, *I was confessing.* ἄγω, *I am leading;* ἦγον, *I was leading.*

§85.3. *Augment with compound verbs*. Verbs that are compounded with a preposition take the augment *after* the preposition and *before* the verb stem. If the preposition ends in a vowel, that vowel elides (except for περί and πρό) when the augment is attached to the verb stem. If the verb *begins* with a vowel, the elision takes place *before* the stem is lengthened. Examples: ἀναβαίνω = ἀνέβαινον; καταβαίνω = κατέβαινον; ἀποστέλλω = ἀπέστελλον; συνάγω = συῆγον; ἐκβάλλω = ἐξέβαλλον (ἐκ becomes ἐξ before vowels).

§86. *Deponent Verbs in the Imperfect*. Verbs that are deponent in the present will be deponent in the imperfect.

§87. *The Uses of the Imperfect Tense*. Review §18.2 on the uses of the present tense as well as the other terms defined in §18.

As a secondary tense, the imperfect describes *durative* action that is occurring in *past time*. Examples: ἄγω, *I am leading* (today); ἦγον, *I was leading* (yesterday). Think of the imperfect tense *exactly* as you do the present tense, except the imperfect translates action that is *past time*. The imperfect is the present tense *moved into past time*.

§88. *Exercises*.

§88.1. *Translate into English*:
(1) διδασκόμεθα νῦν ὑπὸ τοῦ χριστοῦ, τότε δὲ ἐδιδάσκομεν τοὺς ἀλλήλους. (2) ὁ ἀπόστολος ἐλάλει παραβολὴν τοῖς πιστοῖς δούλοις τοῦ κυρίου. (3) οἱ πονηροὶ ἄνθρωποι ἐπορεύοντο εἰς τὴν ἐκκλησίαν. (4) ὁ κύριος ἦν ἐν τῷ κόσμῳ, ἀλλὰ ὁ κόσμος οὐκ ἐγίνωσκεν αὐτόν. (5) οἱ ἄνθρωποι

οἱ νεκροὶ ἠγείροντο ἐκ θανάτου. (6) τὰ καλὰ δῶρα ἐφέρετο τοῖς ἀνθρώποις ἐν τῷ ἱερῷ. (7) ἀνηγίνωσκον τοὺς λόγους τοῦ προφήτου καὶ ἤκουον τὴν φωνὴν τοῦ θεοῦ. (8) ὁ ὄχλος ἀπεστέλλετο ὑπὸ τοῦ χριστοῦ εἰς τὸν αὐτὸν οἶκον. (9) ἐν ἐκείναις ταῖς ἡμέραις ἐπορευόμεθα πρὸς τὸ ἱερὸν τοῦ θεοῦ, νῦν δὲ οὐκ εἰσερχόμεθα εἰς αὐτό. (10) σὺ ἦς κακός, νῦν δὲ σὺ εἶ ἀγαθός.

§88.2. *Translate into Greek*:

(1) He was in the world and the world was not knowing him. (2) The prophet was receiving the bread of life from the Lord. (3) The Lord is walking about in these days but now evil men and evil women are not knowing him. (4) The people were hearing the voice of the Lord through the apostles of God. (5) We were gathering together the same apostles in the temple. (6) I am glorifying Christ in heaven. (7) The way of the Lord was being taught by the disciples of God. (8) I was being sent to the people of the world. (9) You (pl) were reading the laws of God. (10) Christ was ruling the kingdoms of the world.

Lesson 14
Infinitives
Additional Uses of Καί

§89. *Vocabulary.*

ἁμαρτάνω, *I sin*

ἁμαρτωλός, ὁ, *sinner*

ἀναβαίνω, *I go up*

ἄρχομαι (D), *I begin* (usually followed by the infinitive)

βαίνω, *I go*

βιβλίον, τό, *book*

γάρ, *for* (postpositive)

διδάσκαλος, ὁ, *teacher*

ἐπαγγέλια, ἡ, *promise*

εὐαγγέλιον, τό, *gospel*

καταβαίνω, *I go down*

ὅτι, *because, that*

χαρά, ἡ, *joy*

§90. *Present Infinitives.*

§90.1. *Forms of the present infinitive.*

§90.1.1. *Regular verbs.*

ACTIVE	MIDDLE	PASSIVE
λύειν	λύεσθαι	λύεσθαι
to loose	*to loose myself*	*to be loosed*

§90.1.2. *εω verbs.*

ACTIVE	MIDDLE	PASSIVE
λαλεῖν	λαλεῖσθαι	λαλεῖσθαι
to speak	*to speak myself*	*to be spoken*

§90.1.3. The present infinitive of εἰμί is εἶναι. εἶναι is located *present infinitive* since εἰμί has no *voice* (see §76).

§90.2. *Syntactical study.* Infinitives, like participles (§124), are verbal nouns. That is, they reflect something of the nature of a verb and something of that of a noun. The infinitive is *infinite* in that it is not limited by a subject (as a verb is); neither does it have personal endings. Thus the infinitive has voice and tense but not person or number. Infinitives are located as follows:

Present active infinitive   ἄρχομαι <u>διδάσκειν</u> τὰ τέκνα
                                 I am beginning to teach the children

Present middle infinitive   ἀρχόμεθα <u>διδάσκεσθαι</u>
                                 we are begining to teach ourselves

Present passive infinitive   ἄρχεται <u>διδάσκεσθαι</u> ὑπὸ τοῦ κυρίου
                                 he is beginning to be taught by the Lord

§91. *Other Uses of καί.* The most common conjunction in Greek is καί. In addition to being translated *and*, καί may also be translated in a number of other ways depending upon the context: (1) καί may be translated *also* as in the sentence καὶ γὰρ ἐγὼ ἄνθρωπός εἰμι ὑπὸ ἐξουσίαν = *for I also am a man under authority* (Matthew 8:9). (2) καί may also be translated *and yet* as in the sentence καὶ ὁ θεὸς τρέφει αὐτούς = *and yet God feeds them* (Luke 12:24). (3) καί may also be translated *even* as in the sentence γινώσκουσι καὶ ἁμαρτωλοὶ τὸν νόμον = *even sinners know the law.* (4) καί may also be translated *but* as in the sentence καὶ ἐφοβήθησαν τὸν λαόν = *but they feared the people* (Luke 20:19). (5) καί . . . καί may also be translated *both . . . and* as in the sentence καὶ οἱ μαθηταὶ καὶ οἱ προφῆται γινώσκουσι τοῦτο = *both the disciples and the prophets know this.*

§92. *Exercises.*

§92.1. *Translate into English*:
(1) ἄρχομαι ἀναγινώσκειν τὸ βιβλίον τῆς ζωῆς καὶ δοξάζειν τὸν θεόν. (2) οἱ μαθηταὶ τοῦ χριστοῦ διδάσκουσι τοὺς ἀνθρώπους ἀκούειν τὴν φωνὴν τοῦ θεοῦ. (3) οἱ διδάσκαλοι ἄρχονται διδάσκειν τὸ εὐαγγέλιον τῷ τέκνῳ. (4) ὁ κύριος ἔπεμπε τὰ τέκνα ἐκ τοῦ ἱεροῦ καὶ εἰς τὴν ἐκκλησίαν. (5) τὸ εὐαγγέλιον τῆς βασιλείας ἐκηρύσσετο ἐν τῷ κόσμῳ ὑπὸ τῶν μαθητῶν τοῦ χριστοῦ. (6) ἐκεῖνος ὁ δίκαιος δοῦλος διδάσκει τοὺς ἀδελφοὺς αὐτοῦ καὶ διδάσκουσι τοὺς ἁμαρτωλούς. (7) ἐν ἐκείνῃ τῇ ἡμέρᾳ ἤρχοντο ἀκούειν τὸ εὐαγγέλιον τῆς βασιλείας. (8) ἡ χαρὰ τοῦ χριστοῦ ἐκηρύσσετο ἐν ἐκείναις ταῖς πονηραῖς ἡμέραις. (9) ἡ ἐπαγγελία τοῦ θεοῦ ἠκούετο ὑπὸ τῶν τέκνων τούτων. (10) ἄρχομαι διδάσκεσθαι τὸ εὐαγγέλιον τῆς βασιλείας ὑπὸ τοῦ κύριου.

§92.2. *Translate into Greek*:

(1) Those men were not knowing the laws of Christ. (2) The apostles were receiving the good bread from the apostles of the Lord and they were eating it. (3) The righteous brothers were going down to the temple in those days. (4) The messiah was casting the sinners out of the temple and baptizing them into the kingdom. (5) The gospel of Christ is being preached to the crowds. (6) These teachers are going down into the houses of the slaves. (7) The gospel of joy is being heard by the men. (8) These words of the prophet were beginning to be written by the apostles. (9) Because of the word of God the apostles were being saved out of this world. (10) In those days the messiah was preaching to the children.

Lesson 15

Future Active
and Middle Indicative

§93. *Vocabulary.*
ἄξω, *I shall lead* (future of ἄγω, §42)
ἀκούσω, *I shall hear* (future of ἀκούω, §15)
βλέψω, *I shall see* (future of βλέπω, §15)
γνώσομαι (D), *I shall know* (future of γινώσκω, §15)
γενήσομαι (D), *I shall become* (future of γίνομαι, §75)
διδάξω, *I shall teach* (future of διδάσκω, §15)
δοξάσω, *I shall glorify* (future of δοξάζω, §42)
ἕξω, *I shall have* (future of ἔχω, §15)
ἐλεύσομαι (D), *I shall come, I shall go* (future of ἔρχομαι, §75)
κηρύξω, *I shall proclaim* (future of κηρύσσω, § 36)
λήμψομαι (D), *I shall take* (future of λαμβάνω, §15)
λύσω, *I shall loose* (future of λύω, §15)
οἴσω, *I shall bring* (future of φέρω, §36)
πιστεύσω, *I shall believe* (future of πιστεύω, §75)
σώσω, *I shall save* (future of σῴζω, §36)

§94. *Formation of the Future Tense.* Both the future active and middle indicative forms are built by adding a -σ plus the primary personal ending to verb stem. Because the future tense is a *primary* tense, the same primary active (§17) and middle (§38) endings already learned are used. Hence, the stem of λύω is λύ. Add to this stem the tense sign (σ) plus the first person singular ending ω and the future form is λύσω = *I shall loose*.

Unfortunately, all verbs do not form the future tense so simply as does λύω. In fact, there is such variety at this point, the student should carefully observe the second form in the verb chart (§205) or in the Greek vocabulary at the back of the book. In both places the first person future active will be the second form given. The other forms (forms 3-6) will be studied later.

§95. *Future Active Indicative Forms of ω Verbs.* The identifying sign for the future tense is a σ. It occurs between the verb stem and the personal ending. When the verb stem ends in a vowel the future is easy to form: for the verb ἀκούω, the stem is ἀκου. To form the future add a σ and then the *primary* personal endings:

ACTIVE

	SINGULAR	PLURAL
1st per	ἀκούσω, *I shall hear*	ἀκούσομεν, *we shall hear*
2nd per	ἀκούσεις, *you will hear*	ἀκούσετε, *you will hear*
3rd per	ἀκούσει, *he, she, it will hear*	ἀκούσουσι, *they will hear*

MIDDLE[1]

	SINGULAR	PLURAL
1st per	ἀκούσομαι, *I shall hear myself*	ἀκουσόμεθα, *we shall hear ourselves*
2nd per	ἀκούσῃ, *you will hear yourself*	ἀκούσεσθε, *you will hear yourselves*
3rd per	ἀκούσεται, *he will hear himself*	ἀκούσονται, *they will hear themselves*

When the verb stem ends in a consonant, the addition of the tense sign σ causes certain changes to occur in the final letter of the stem:

$$\pi \quad \beta \quad \varphi \quad + \quad \sigma \quad = \quad \psi$$
$$\varkappa \quad \gamma \quad \chi \quad + \quad \sigma \quad = \quad \xi$$
$$\tau \quad \delta \quad \theta \quad + \quad \sigma \quad = \quad \sigma$$

Hence the future active of βλέπω is βλέψω, of ἄγω it is ἄξω, etc. The future middle of βλέπω is βλέψομαι, of ἄγω it is ἄξομαι.

Some verb stems cannot be found by removing the ω from the present form: the stem of βαπτίζω is βαπτιδ rather than βαπτιζ. Thus the future form is βαπτίσω. The *only way to be certain* is to check the principal parts of the verb in the back of the book.

§96. *Future Active and Middle Indicative of εω Verbs* (review §21 and §38). The contraction that occurs in the present, imperfect, and infinitives, does *not* occur in the future tense because the tense sign σ separates the stem vowel from the initial vowel of the personal ending. The stem vowel, however, usually lengthens before the tense

---

[1]While the *present* middle and passive forms are identical, the *future* middle and passive have *different* forms (see §115).

sign is added. The future active of εὐλογέω is εὐλογήσω. The middle is εὐλογή-
σομαι.

ACTIVE

	SINGULAR	PLURAL
1st per	λαλήσω, *I shall speak*	λαλήσομεν, *we shall speak*
2nd per	λαλήσεις, *you will speak*	λαλήσετε, *you will speak*
3rd per	λαλήσει, *he, she, it will speak*	λαλήσουσι, *they will speak*

MIDDLE

	SINGULAR	PLURAL
1st per	λαλήσομαι, *I shall speak myself*	λαλησόμεθα, *we shall loose ourselves*
2nd per	λαλήσῃ, *you will speak yourself*	λαλήσεσθε, *you will speak yourselves*
3rd per	λαλήσεται, *he will speak himself*	λαλήσονται, *they will speak themselves*

§97. *Deponent Verbs* [review §78]. Some verbs will have a deponent form in the future *even when* the present form is *not* deponent. Examples:

	PRESENT	FUTURE
	γινώσκω	γνώσομαι
	λαμβάνω	λήμψομαι

§98. *Future Indicative of εἰμί.*

	SINGULAR	PLURAL
1st per	ἔσομαι, *I shall be*	ἐσόμεθα, *we shall be*
2nd per	ἔσῃ, *you will be*	ἔσεσθε, *you will be*
3rd per	ἔσται, *he, she, it will be*	ἔσονται, *they will be*

§99. *Uses of the Future Tense.* The *time* of action in the future tense is obviously *future*. The *kind* of action in the future is either *durative* or *point*, and only the context
will indicate which it is.

There are several specific uses of the future tense in the New Testament. Some
examples includes:

(1) Futuristic. This is the most common usage. It expresses an action that will
occur in future time. ἐκεῖνος ὑμᾶς διδάξει = *that man will teach you.*

(2) Imperative future. This usage employs the future tense to express an imperative (this usage is distinct from the imperative mood). καλέσεις τὸ ὄνομα αὐτοῦ
Ἰησοῦν = *you shall call his name Jesus* (Luke 1:31).

(3) Rhetorical future. This usage employs the future tense to pose a rhetorical
question concerning a possible course of action. πρὸς τίνα ἀπελευσόμεθα; = *to
whom shall we go?* (John 6:68).

§100. *Exercises.*

§100.1. *Translate into English*:

(1) γινώσκω τὸν κύριον καὶ γενήσομαι ὁ μαθητὴς αὐτοῦ. (2) ὁ χριστὸς ἐλεύσεται ἀπὸ τῶν οὐρανῶν μετὰ τῶν ἀγγέλων αὐτοῦ. (3) ἁμαρτωλοὶ ἄξουσι τοὺς πιστοὺς εἰς τὸν οὐρανὸν διὰ τὴν ἀγάπην τοῦ θεοῦ. (4) ἔσονται ἐν τῇ βασιλείᾳ τοῦ θεοῦ ἐν ταῖς ἐσχάταις ἡμέραις. (5) ἐκεῖνος ὁ δίκαιος ἄνθρωπος διδάξει τοὺς ἀδελφοὺς αὐτοῦ καὶ διδάξουσι τοὺς ἄλλους. (6) οἱ κακοὶ ἔβαλλον λίθους εἰς τὸ ἱερόν. (7) ἀρξόμεθα γινώσκεσθαι ὑπὸ τοῦ κυρίου ἐν τῇ ἐκκλησίᾳ αὐτοῦ. (8) κηρύξουσιν ἀπόσολοι τοῦ θεοῦ τὴν ὁδὸν εἰρήνης καὶ ἀγάπης. (9) ἡ ἐπαγγελία τοῦ χριστοῦ ἐστιν ἀπὸ τοῦ θεοῦ διὰ τῆς γραφῆς. (10) τὰ τέκνα βλέψει τὸν ἄγγελον τῇ ἐκκλησίᾳ.

§100.2. *Translate into Greek*:

(1) The apostles were seeing the Lord in the desert. (2) Both the slaves and the brothers will hear the words of life. (3) An evil tongue is a bad thing. (4) His disciples will see each other in the last days. (5) The good men will teach each other the parables of the kingdom. (6) The kingdom of God will be in you (pl). (7) The Lord will write those good words in the book of life. (8) They will hear the voice of the prophets and they will believe their teachings. (9) His slaves will receive good gifts and will bring them into the temple. (10) In the last days you (sing) will know the word of God.

Lesson 16
First Aorist Active and Middle Indicative

§101. *Vocabulary*.

δαιμόνιον, τό, *demon*

ἔβλεψα, *I saw* (1st aorist of βλέπω, §15)

ἔγραψα, *I wrote* (1st aorist of γράφω, §15)

ἐκήρυξα, *I preached* (1st aorist of κηρύσσω, §36).

ἔπεμψα, *I sent* (1st aorist of πέμπω §15)

ἐπίστευσα, *I believed* (first aorist of πιστεύω, §75).

ἔσωσα, *I saved* (1st aorist of σῴζω §36)

ἤκουσα, *I heard* (1st aorist of ἀκούω §15)

καθαρίζω, καθαριῶ, ἐκαθάρισα, *I cleanse, I shall cleanse, I cleansed*[1]

οὐκέτι, *no longer*

πείθω, πείσω, ἔπεισα, *I persuade, I shall persuade, I persuaded*

πλοῖον, τό, *boat*

ὑποστρέφω, ὑποστρέψω, ὑπέστρεψα, *I return, I shall return, I returned*

§102. Syntactical Study. Greek has two past tenses: imperfect (§84) and the aorist. Since both relate to past time the difference between them is seen in the *kind of action* that each represents. The imperfect tense represents *continuous* action in past time while the aorist represents *point* action in past time. Point action means that the action is viewed as *finished* (the imperfect represents action that *continues* over a period of time). Examples: ὁ ἀπόστολος ἔλυε τὸν δοῦλον = *the apostle was loosing the slave* (continuous action in past time); ὁ ἀπόστολος ἔλυσε τὸν δοῦλον = *the apostle loosed the slave* (point action in past time).

---

[1]All verbs listed for the first time in this, and subsequent vocabularies, will include the present, future, and aorist forms.

§103. *Inflection.*

§103.1. *Forms for first aorist active.* Because the aorist is a *secondary tense* (just as the *imperfect*), it takes an augment—either temporal or syllabic. The *tense sign* for the aorist is a σ that stands between the stem and the secondary ending.[2] As in the future tense the addition of this σ causes some alteration to the stem. Usually these changes are the same as in the future, <u>but not always</u>. *To be certain of the formation of the aorist tense refer to a lexicon or check the verb in the vocabularies in the back of this book.*

	SINGULAR	PLURAL
1st per	ἔλυσα, *I loosed*	ἐλύσαμεν, *we loosed*
2nd per	ἔλυσας, *you loosed*	ἐλύσατε, *you loosed*
3rd per	ἔλυσε (ν), *he, she, it loosed*	ἔλυσαν, *they loosed*

103.2. *Forms for first aorist middle.* The first aorist middle is formed like the active, i.e., add the augment, the tense sign, and the personal ending to the stem of the verb. Of course, the same changes result with the addition of the σ. Unlike the imperfect the aorist has *different* forms for the middle and passive.

	SINGULAR	PLURAL
1st per	ἐλυσάμην, *I loosed myself*	ἐλυσάμεθα, *we loosed ourselves*
2nd per	ἐλύσω, *you loosed yourself*	ἐλύσασθε, *you loosed yourselves*
3rd per	ἐλύσατο, *he loosed himself*	ἐλύσαντο, *they loosed themselves*

§104. *Translation of the Aorist.* Usually the Greek aorist is translated into English with the simple past tense. ἔλυσα = *I loosed.* The aorist may also, however, be translated into English with the use of the *perfect tense* (§152) provided there is no emphasis upon the *resulting state of being* described by the verb. ἐπιστεύσατε τοὺς λόγους μου = *you have believed my words.* Here the aorist tense is translated into English to indicate an event that occurred at some indefinite past time. Had the emphasis been upon a past action and the *resulting state of being* the Greek *perfect tense* (see §154) would have been employed.

§105. *Exercises.*

§105.1. *Translate into English:*
(1) τὰ δαιμόνια ὑπέστρεψε τῷ ἁμαρτωλῷ. (2) οἱ ἄνθρωποι ἐπίστευσαν τὴν διδαχὴν τοῦ χριστοῦ καὶ ἐκήρυξαν τὸ εὐαγγέλιον. (3) ἔπεισα τοὺς

---

[2]The first aorist active and middle forms of liquid verbs (§10.3) are formed by adding α rather than σα to the stem and by making certain other changes such as lengthening the stem vowel. μένω has an aorist form of ἔμεινα.

ἁμαρτωλοὺς ὁμολογεῖν τὰς ἁμαρτίας αὐτῶν καὶ ζητεῖν τὸ εὐαγγέλιον. (4) ἐσόμεθα σὺν αὐτῷ ἐν τῇ βασιλείᾳ αὐτοῦ. (5) οἱ ἀπόστολοι ἔλυσαν τοὺς δούλους αὐτῶν. (6) ὁ μεσσίας ἐκαθάρισε τὰς καρδίας τοῦ μαθητοῦ αὐτοῦ. (7) οἱ ἀπόστολοι ἐδιδάξαντο ἐν τῷ ἱερῷ καὶ ἐν τῷ οἴκῳ. (8) ἀκούσουσι τῆς φωνῆς αὐτοῦ καὶ πιστεύσουσι. (9) ὁ κύριος ἔσωσέ με ἀπὸ τῶν ἁμαρτιῶν μου. (10) ἐπέμψατε τὰ τέκνα ἐκ τοῦ οἴκου καὶ εἰς τὸ ἱερόν.

§105.2. *Translate into Greek*:

(1) In those days they were hearing his voice, now they are no longer hearing it. (2) You (pl) sent the children into the temple. (3) God saved me from my sins through the Lord. (4) The Lord loosed the slaves and began to teach them. (5) We will hear the voice of Christ in the last day. (6) The men were teaching parables to the children. (7) These good apostles are being taught the laws of God. (8) The Lord will send commandments to his disciples. (9) The word of God will remain in those faithful men. (10) Christ saved the evil men from their sins.

Lesson 17

Second Aorist
Active and Middle

§106. *Vocabulary.*

ἔβαλον, *I threw* (2nd aorist of βάλλω, §36)

εἶπον, *I said* (2nd aorist of λέγω, §15)

ἔλαβον, *I took* (2nd aorist of λαμβάνω, §15)

ἔσχον, *I had* (2nd aorist of ἔχω, §15)

εὑρίσκω, εὑρήσω, εὗρον, *I find, I shall find, I found*

ἔφαγον, *I ate* (2nd aorist of ἐσθίω, §42)

ἤγαγον, *I led* (2nd aorist of ἄγω, §42)

ἤνεγκα[1], *I bore, I brought* (1st κ aorist of φέρω, §36)

ἦλθον[2], *I came, I went* (2nd aorist of ἔρχομαι, §75)

λείπω, λείψω, ἔλιπον, *I leave, I shall leave, I left*

πάσχω, _____ ,[3] ἔπαθον, *I suffer,* _____ , *I suffered*

§107. *The Second Aorist.* The distinction between the first and second aorist is one of *form only*; each *functions* in exactly the same way, i.e., to indicate point action that occurred in past time.

The second aorist is formed on the *second aorist stem*. This stem must be learned as part of the vocabulary. Once the stem is learned the formation of the second aorist

---

[1]This verb is referred to as a κ first aorist because the usual σ is replaced by the κ. A few verbs have both a first and a second aorist form, e.g., ἤνεγκον.

[2]While ἔρχομαι is deponent in the present system, it has active forms in the aorist—ἦλθον not ἠλθόμην, εἰσῆλθον not εἰσηλθόμην.

[3]The future form is deponent and does not occur in the New Testament.

is a simple matter: the stem is first augmented and then the secondary endings are appended. *The σ tense sign is not used.*

English also has two ways of forming the past tense of its verbs: in addition to the common *ed* (*talked, loved, moved*) the past tense of some verbs is formed by *changing* the stem (*I wrote, I ran, I taught*). The second aorist is roughly equivalent to the formation of these verbs because *a change in the stem occurs*. The first aorist is analogous to those English verbs that form their past tense in a more regularized way, i.e., by adding *ed*. The Greek, of course, adds the augment and the tense sign σ.

§108. *Inflection.*

§108.1. *Forms for the second aorist active.*

	SINGULAR	PLURAL
1st per	ἔλαβον, *I took*	ἐλάβομεν, *we took*
2nd per	ἔλαβες, *you took*	ἐλάβετε, *you took*
3rd per	ἔλαβε (ν), *he, she, it took*	ἔλαβον, *they took*

§108.2. *Forms for the second aorist middle.*

	SINGULAR	PLURAL
1st per	ἐλαβόμην, *I took myself*	ἐλαβόμεθα, *we took ourselves*
2nd per	ἐλάβου, *you took yourself*	ἐλάβεσθε, *you took yourselves*
3rd per	ἐλάβετο, *he took himself*	ἐλάβοντο, *they took themselves*

§109. *Principal Parts of a Verb.* All verb entries in the vocabulary in the back of this book contain six (6) principal parts (all of which are expressed in the indicative mood). An entry looks like this: λύω, λύσω, ἔλυσα, λέλυκε, λέλυμαι, ἐλύθην. The sequence of the forms may be seen in the following chart:

PRESENT ACTIVE	FUTURE ACTIVE	AORIST ACTIVE	PERFECT ACTIVE	PERFECT MIDDLE/ PASSIVE	AORIST PASSIVE
λύω	λύσω	ἔλυσα	λέλυκε	λέλυμαι	ἐλύθην
I loose	*I will loose*	*I loosed*	*I have loosed*	*I have loosed myself (been loosed)*	*I was loosed*

If _____ appears, the missing form *does not occur* in the New Testament. Example: βλέπω, βλέψω, ἔβλεψα, _____, _____, _____. This means that the *perfect active, perfect middle/passive, and the aorist passive* forms of βλέπω do not occur in the New Testament.

§110. *Exercises.*

§110.1. *Translate into English*:

(1) ὁ χριστὸς ἐξέβαλε τὰ δαιμόνια τῷ εὐαγγελίῳ. (2) οἱ ἀπόστολοι ἐλάβοντο ἄρτον καὶ καρπόν. (3) ἡ καλὴ διδαχὴ ἐπιστεύετο ὑπὸ τοῦ μαθητοῦ τοῦ χριστοῦ. (4) ὁ μικρὸς ἄνθρωπός ἐστι νῦν ἀπόστολος τῆς βασιλείας. (5) ὁ πιστὸς ἀδελφὸς ἤγαγε τοὺς δούλους αὐτοῦ εἰς τὴν ὁδὸν τῆς εἰρήνης. (6) καὶ ἤκουσε τὸν κύριον καὶ ἐπίστευσε αὐτόν. (7) τὰ τέκνα ἔλαβε τὰ καλὰ δῶρα ἀπὸ τῶν ἀποστόλων. (8) οἱ ἄνθρωποι οἱ πιστοὶ ἐλάμβανον δῶρα καὶ ἔπεμπον αὐτὰ τοῖς ἀποστόλοις. (9) ἤλθομεν εἰς τὸν οἶκον τοῦ δικαίου ἀνθρώπου. (10) ὁ διδάσκαλος αὐτῶν διδάξει τὰ τέκνα περὶ τῆς ἀγάπης τοῦ θεοῦ.

§110.2. *Translate into Greek*:

(1) The righteous slaves took bread to the good disciple of the Lord. (2) Those good men threw the stones out of the temple. (3) The good disciples were teaching each other about the love of Christ. (4) The brother brought the sinner to the Lord. (5) Christ suffered evil on behalf of us. (6) The apostle went into the temple and took gifts of bread and fruit. (7) The children brought stones and threw them into the house of the prophet. (8) The Lord will not leave us in this world. (9) In that day we saw the Lord and we heard his parables. (10) They received the message of Christ through the apostles.

Lesson 18

Aorist Passive
and Future Passive

§111. *Vocabulary.*

ἀπεστάλην, *I was sent* (2nd aorist passive of ἀποστέλλω, §83)
ἐβλήθην, *I was thrown* (1st aorist passive of βάλλω, §36)
ἐγνώσθην, *I was known* (1st aorist passive of γινώσκω, §15)
ἐγράφην, *I was written* (2nd aorist passive of γράφω, §15)
ἐδιδάχθην, *I was taught* (1st aorist passive of διδάσκω, §15)
ἐκηρύχθην, *I was proclaimed* (1st aorist passive of κηρύσσω, §36)
ἐλήμφθην, *I was taken* (1st aorist passive of λαμβάνω, §15)
ἐλύθην, *I was loosed* (1st aorist passive of λύω, §15)
ἔργον, τό, *work*
ἤχθον, *I was led* (1st aorist passive of ἄγω, §42)
πίνω, πίομαι, ἔπιον, *I drink, I shall drink, I drank*
σκοτία, ἡ, *darkness*

§112. *Formation of the Aorist Passive.* Unlike the imperfect tense where the middle/passive forms are identical, the aorist tense has *different* forms for the middle and the passive. As a secondary tense the aorist passive is augmented in the usual way (§85). The secondary *active* endings are used even though the form is *aorist passive*.

§112.1. *Formation of the first aorist passive.* In the first aorist passive the tense sign θη is added between the aorist passive stem and the secondary *active* personal endings (the aorist passive stem is the sixth principal part of the verb [§109]). When the verb stem ends in a consonant, certain changes occur when the tense suffix θη is added.

§112.1.1. *Liquid consonants.* ν drops out before θ (κρίνω becomes ἐκρίθην); λ and ρ retained before θ (ἀγγέλλω becomes ἠγγέλθην); μ has η inserted before θ (νέμω becomes ἐνεμήθην).

§112.1.2. *Mute consonants.*

(1) *Palatals.* κ and γ change to χ before θ (ἄγω becomes ἤχθην); χ is retained before θ (διδαχ [stem of διδάσκω] becomes ἐδιδάχθην).

(2) *Labials.* π and β change to φ before θ (πέμπω becomes ἐπέμφθην); θ drops out after φ (γράφω becomes ἐγράφην, second aorist [see §112.2]).

(3) *Dentals.* τ, δ, and θ change to σ before θ (πείθω becomes ἐπείσθην).

§112.1.3. *Sibilants.* ζ, ξ, σ, and ψ change to σ before θ (σῴζω becomes ἐσώθην).

FIRST AORIST PASSIVE

	SINGULAR	PLURAL
1st per	ἐλύθην, *I was loosed*	ἐλύθημεν, *we were loosed*
2nd per	ἐλύθης, *you were loosed*	ἐλύθητε, *you were loosed*
3rd per	ἐλύθη, *he, she, it was loosed*	ἐλύθησαν, *they were loosed*

§112.2. *Formation of the second aorist passive.* The second aorist passive is formed exactly as the first except the tense sign θ is not employed. Again, you must check the sixth principal part of the verb in order to be certain of the aorist passive stem (§109).

SECOND AORIST PASSIVE

	SINGULAR	PLURAL
1st per	ἐγράφην, *I was written*	ἐγράφημεν, *we were written*
2nd per	ἐγράφης, *you were written*	ἐγράφητε, *you were written*
3rd per	ἐγράφη, *he, she, it was written*	ἐγράφησαν, *they were written*

§113. *Function of the Aorist Passive.* The function of the aorist passive (both *first* and *second* aorist) is to indicate completed action that is received by the subject in past time. Study the following chart and the significance will become clear:

PRESENT PASSIVE	IMPERFECT PASSIVE	AORIST PASSIVE
λύομαι	ἐλυόμην	ἐλύθην
I am being loosed	*I was being loosed*	*I was loosed*

§114. *Deponent Verbs in the Aorist.* Usage at this point varies widely, and you are advised to check the sixth principal part in the verb vocabularies in the back of this book. Some verbs that are deponent in the aorist passive will appear in the *middle voice* with an active function: ἐγενόμην, *I became* (from γίνομαι). These verbs are referred to as *middle deponents*. But γίνομαι also appears in the passive form ἐγεν-ήθην, *I became*. In this instance it is referred to as a *passive deponent*. Some verbs like πορεύομαι, *I go*, have both an aorist active and aorist passive form yet *both* forms are given an active translation: ἐπορευσάμην = *I went*; and ἐπορεύθην = *I went*.

§115. *The Future Passive*. The future passive indicative is based upon the aorist passive stem. Because the future tense is a *primary* tense it has no augment. It uses the tense sign θη between the unaugmented aorist passive stem and the *primary* personal endings. Note the presence of the σ (tense sign for the future, §94).

FUTURE PASSIVE

	SINGULAR	PLURAL
1st per	λυθήσομαι, *I shall be loosed*	λυθησόμεθα, *we shall be loosed*
2nd per	λυθήσῃ, *you will be loosed*	λυθήσεσθε, *you will be loosed*
3rd per	λυθήσεται, *he, she, it will be loosed*	λυθήσονται, *they will be loosed*

§116. *Exercises*.

§116.1. *Translate into English*:

(1) ὁ χριστὸς ἀπεστάλη εἰς τὸν κόσμον σῴζειν ἁμαρτωλούς. (2) μετὰ ταῦτα ὁ χριστὸς ἔβλεψε τοὺς ἀποστόλους. (3) οἱ δοῦλοι λυθήσονται ἐν ταῖς ἡμέραις ταῖς ἐσχάταις. (4) ἐδιδάχθην τοὺς λόγους τοῦ νόμου ὑπὸ ἀποστόλου τοῦ χριστοῦ. (5) ὁ νόμος ἐγράφη ὑπὸ τῶν προφήτων καὶ τῶν ἀποστόλων. (6) τῶν ἁμαρτωλῶν πρῶτός εἰμι, καὶ δὲ ἐγὼ ἐσώθην ὑπὸ τῇ ἀγάπῃ τοῦ θεοῦ. (7) αἱ ἐντολαὶ τοῦ κυρίου ἐγράφησαν ἐν τῷ βιβλίῳ. (8) τὸ εὐαγγέλιον τοῦ χριστοῦ κηρυχθήσεται τοῖς μαθηταῖς αὐτοῦ. (9) οἱ λίθοι ἐξεβλήθησαν ἐκ τοῦ ἱεροῦ καὶ ἐλήμφθησαν εἰς ἄλλον τόπον. (10) κατὰ τὴν ἐπαγγελίαν τοῦ κυρίου τόπος ἑτοιμασθήσεται ἡμῖν ἐν οὐρανῷ.

116.2. *Translate into Greek*:

(1) The righteous brother will be loosed from sin by the teachings of scripture. (2) Evil words were being said against those men. (3) Christ destroyed the darkness of sin. (4) The disciples of Christ were sent to save sinners. (5) These good messengers were sent by God into an evil world. (6) The disciple was cast out of the temple because he did not know the Lord. (7) The same disciple was being taught by the Lord. (8) Because of the love of God evil men will be saved. (9) The voice of the Lord was heard in the desert. (10) The children were brought into the church by the disciples of the Lord.

Lesson 19
αω **Contract Verbs**

§117. *Vocabulary.*

ἀγαπάω, ἀγαπήσω, ἠγάπησα, *I love, I will love, I loved*

ἁγιάζω, _____, ἡγίησα, *I sanctify,* _____, *I sanctified*

γεννάω, γεννήσω, ἐγέννησα, *I give birth to, I will give birth to, I gave birth to*

διώκω, διώξω, ἐδίωξα, *I persecute, I will persecute, I persecuted*

ἐξουσία, ἡ, *authority*

ἐπερωτάω, ἐπερωτήσω, ἐπηρώτησα, *I ask a question of, I shall ask a question of, I asked a question of*

ἐρωτάω, ἐρωτήσω, ἠρώτησα, *I ask, I shall ask, I asked*

ζάω, ζήσω, ἔζησα, *I live, I shall live, I lived*

θάλασσα, ἡ, *sea*

θαυμάζω, θαυμάσω, ἐθαύμασα, *I marvel, I shall marvel, I marvelled*

τιμάω, τιμήσω, ἐτίμησα, *I honor, I shall honor, I honored*

§118. *Inflection* [review §21]. The αω contract verbs form a special class of the ω conjugation. This lesson deals with those contract verb whose stems end in αω. The following contractions occur *in the present and imperfect tenses only*. Because of the addition of the tense sign in the aorist, future, perfect, pluperfect, and future perfect passive tenses, this contraction does not occur in these tenses.

PRESENT ACTIVE

	SINGULAR	PLURAL
1st per	τιμάω = τιμῶ	τιμάομεν = τιμῶμεν
2nd per	τιμάεις = τιμᾷς	τιμάετε = τιμᾶτε
3rd per	τιμάει = τιμᾷ	τιμάουσι(ω) = τιμῶσι (ν)

IMPERFECT ACTIVE

SINGULAR	PLURAL

1st per   ἐτιμάον = ἐτιμῶν   ἐτιμάομεν = ἐτιμῶμεν
2nd per   ἐτιμάες = ἐτιμᾶς   ἐτιμάετε = ἐτιμᾶτε
3rd per   ἐτιμάε = ἐτιμᾶ   ἐτιμάον = ἐτιμῶν

§119. *Rules for Contraction in αω.* Rules for contraction for verbs ending in αω:

α	+	ω	=	ω	(1st person sing)
α	+	ει	=	ᾳ	(2nd person sing)
α	+	ει	=	ᾳ	(3rd person sing)
α	+	ο	=	ω	(1st person pl)
α	+	ε	=	α	(2nd person pl)
α	+	ο	=	ω	(3rd person pl)

§120. The εω verbs are listed in their lexical vocabulary form (§117) in the *un*contracted form so the student may recognize the type of configuration readily (the uncontracted form is given only for the present tense, i.e., the *first* form).

§121. *Exercises.*[1]

(1) ἀγαπήσω τὸν κύριον καὶ τὴν βασιλείαν αὐτοῦ ὅτι ὁ θεὸς ἠγάπησε ἡμᾶς. (2) ἡ ἐξουσία τοῦ χριστοῦ μενεῖ ἐν τῷ κόσμῳ. (3) οἱ ἀπόστολοι ἀπεστάλησαν ὑπὸ τοῦ κυρίου εἰς τὸν κόσμον. (4) ἐπηρώτησα περὶ τοῦ λόγου τοῦ θεοῦ. (5) γεννήσω τέκνον καὶ ἄρξει ὑπὲρ τὸν κόσμον. (6) ὁ μεσσίας λέγει παραβολὴν παρὰ τὴν θάλασσαν. (7) ὁ χριστὸς ἔπαθε πονηρὰ ὑπὲρ ἁμαρτωλῶν. (8) διὰ τοὺς λόγους ὑμῶν ἐβλέψαμεν τὴν πονηρὰν ὁδὸν τοῦ κόσμου. (9) ἀγαπήσω τὸν κύριον μετὰ πάσης τῆς καρδίας μου. (10) ἡ ἐξουσία τοῦ χριστοῦ ἐστιν ἀπὸ θεός.

---

[1]The English to Greek exercises will be discontinued with this lesson.

Lesson 20
Present Participles

§122. *Vocabulary.*
ἀποκτείνω, ἀποκτενῶ, ἀπέκτεινα, *I kill, I shall kill, I killed*
θεραπεύω, θεραπεύσω, ἐθεράπευσα, *I heal, I shall heal, I healed*
᾿Ιησοῦς, ὁ, *Jesus*[1]
λύων, λύουσα, λῦον, present active participle of λύω, §15
μέν . . . δέ, (conj.) *on the one hand . . . on the other hand*
οὐδέ, (conj.) *and not, nor, not even*
σημεῖον, τό, *miracle*
σκάνδαλον, τό, *stumbling block*
φαίνω, φανοῦμαι, _____, *I shine, I shall shine,* _____
χαίρω, χαρήσομαι, _____, *I rejoice, I shall rejoice,* _____
ψεύδομαι, _____, ἐψευσάμην, *I lie,* _____, *I lied*
ψεύστης, ὁ, *liar*
ὤν, οὖσα, ὄν, present participle of εἰμί, §75

§123. *Grammatical Study.*

§123.1. *Nature of the participle.* The participle is a verbal adjective. Because of its hybrid nature, the participle partakes of the qualities of a verb (it has voice and tense) and those of an adjective (it has gender, case, and number). As a verb, the participle may take an object or be used as an adverbial modifier. As an adjective, it may be used substantively or it may be used an adjective modifier.

---

[1]The proper noun ᾿Ιησοῦς, ὁ, *Jesus,* exhibits a mixed declension like many other proper names. ᾿Ιησοῦς is declined as follows:
Nom   ᾿Ιησοῦς
Gen/Abl   ᾿Ιησοῦ
Dat/Loc/Inst   ᾿Ιησοῦ
Acc   ᾿Ιησοῦν

Only four of the Greek tenses have participles: present, aorist, future, and perfect. You will remember that in the indicative mood, *tense* refers to *kind of action* and *time of action* (§18.2). In the participle, there is no relation to *time* of action, only to *kind* of action. The time of action in the participle is indicated by the tense of the main verb in the sentence. The present participle, for example, indicates action that is simultaneous with the action of the main verb. The future participle, on the other hand, indicates action that is subsequent to that of the main verb. Example: ταῦτα γραφῶν ὁ ἀπόστολος ἀκούει τὴν φωνήν = *while writing these things the apostle is hearing the voice*. The key to translating participles accurately lies in understanding that you must determine the *time of action* described by a participle by <u>noting the tense of the main verb</u>. *Participles are related to the main verbs as follows:*

§123.1.1. *Aorist participles*. Aorist participles descibe action that occurred *before* the action of the main verb. Example: ὁ ἀπόστολος <u>λύσας</u> τὸν δοῦλον βλέπει τὸν κύριον = *the apostle, <u>having loosed</u> the slave, is seeing the Lord*. Notice that the action described by the participle is *antecedent* to that of the main verb, i.e., the *seeing* is occurring in the *present*; therefore, given the presence of the aorist participle, *the action of the participle must precede that of the main verb*. Had the main verb itself been a secondary tense the example would look like this: ὁ ἀπόστολος <u>λύσας</u> τὸν δοῦλον ἔβλεψε τὸν κύριον = <u>when the apostle had loosed the slave, he saw the Lord</u>. Thus in both examaples the action of the *aorist* participle precedes that of the main verb.

§123.1.2. *Present participles*. Present participles describe action that occurs *simultaneous* to that of the main verb. Example: ὁ ἀπόστολος <u>λύων</u> τὸν δοῦλον βλέπει τὸν κύριον = <u>*while loosing*</u> *the slave, the apostle is seeing the Lord*.

§123.1.3. *Future participles*. Future participles describe action that occurs *subsequent* to that of the main verb. Because this construction is rare in the New Testament paradigms for the future participle are not included in this text.

§123.1.4. *Perfect participles*. Perfect participles betray the distinctive character of the perfect tense, i.e., completed action that has produced a state of being that exists at the time of the main verb. Example: ὁ ἀπόστολος <u>λελυκὼς</u> τὸν δοῦλον ἔβλεψε τὸν κύριον = <u>*after*</u> *the apostle had loosed the slave* (and the slave stands *loosed*) *he saw the Lord*.

§123.2. *Attributive participles*. Because of its adjectival nature, a participle may stand in the attributive position (occurring *with* the definite article) modifying another substantive. Example: ἤκουσα τὸν ἄνθρωπον <u>τὸν λέγοντα</u> ταῦτα = *I heard the man <u>who was saying</u> these things*. Had the participle been in the *aorist*, the translation would have been *I heard the man <u>who had said</u> these things. Generally, when the par-*

ticiple occurs in the attributive position it is translated relatively, i.e., *the one who, he who, she who,* or *the bread which,* etc.

§123.3. *Predicative participles.* Because of its adverbial nature, a participle may stand in the predicate position (occurring *without* the definite article) modifying the verb. In this regard the participle indicates something about the verb itself, i.e., the participle may indicate *where, how, under what circumstances,* the action of the main verb took place. Usually temporal helping words such as *while* or *as* are supplied to assist the participle in expressing its meaning. Example: ἀναβαίνων ἔβλεψε τὸν κύριον = *as he was coming he saw the Lord* or *while he was coming he saw the Lord.*

§124. *Inflection.*

§124.1. *Present active participle.*

SINGULAR

CASE	MASCULINE	FEMININE	NEUTER
Nom	λύων	λύουσα	λῦον
Gen	λύοντος	λυούσης	λύοντος
Abl	λύοντος	λυούσης	λύοντος
Dat	λύοντι	λυούσῃ	λύοντι
Loc	λύοντι	λυούσῃ	λύοντι
Inst	λύοντι	λυούσῃ	λύοντι
Acc	λύοντα	λύουσαν	λῦον

PLURAL

CASE	MASCULINE	FEMININE	NEUTER
Nom	λύοντες	λύουσαι	λύοντα
Gen	λυόντων	λυουσῶν	λυόντων
Abl	λυόντων	λυουσῶν	λυόντων
Dat	λύουσι (ν)	λυούσαις	λύουσι (ν)
Loc	λύουσι (ν)	λυούσαις	λύουσι (ν)
Inst	λύουσι (ν)	λυούσαις	λύουσι (ν)
Acc	λύοντας	λυούσας	λύοντα

§124.2. *Present middle/passive participle.*

SINGULAR

CASE	MASCULINE	FEMININE	NEUTER
Nom	λυόμενος	λυομένη	λυόμενον
Gen	λυομένου	λυομένης	λυομένου
Abl	λυομένου	λυομένης	λυομένου
Dat	λυομένῳ	λυομένη	λυομένῳ

Loc	λυομένῳ	λυομένη	˙λυομένῳ
Inst	λυομένῳ	λυομένη	λυομένῳ
Acc	λυόμενον	λυομένην	λυόμενον

PLURAL

CASE	MASCULINE	FEMININE	NEUTER
Nom	λυόμενοι	λυόμεναι	λυόμενα
Gen	λυομένων	λυομένων	λυομένων
Abl	λυομένων	λυομένων	λυομένων
Dat	λυομένοις	λυομέναις	λυομένοις
Loc	λυομένοις	λυομέναις	λυομένοις
Inst	λυομένοις	λυομέναις	λυομένοις
Acc	λυομένους	λυομένας	λυόμενα

§124.3. *Future active participle.*

SINGULAR

CASE	MASCULINE	FEMININE	NEUTER
Nom	λύσων	λύσουσα	λῦσον
Gen	λύσοντος	λυσούσης	λύσοντος
Abl	λύσοντος	λυσούσης	λύσοντος
Dat	λύσοντι	λυσούσῃ	λύσοντι
Loc	λύσοντι	λυσούσῃ	λύσοντι
Inst	λύσοντι	λυσούσῃ	λύσοντι
Acc	λύσοντα	λύσουσαν	λῦσον

PLURAL

CASE	MASCULINE	FEMININE	NEUTER
Nom	λύσοντες	λύσουσαι	λύσοντα
Gen	λυσόντων	λυσουσῶν	λυσόντων
Abl	λυσόντων	λυσουσῶν	λυσόντων
Dat	λύσουσι (ν)	λυσούσαις	λύσουσι (ν)
Loc	λύσουσι (ν)	λυσούσαις	λύσουσι (ν)
Inst	λύσουσι (ν)	λυσούσαις	λύσουσι (ν)
Acc	λύσοντας	λυσούσας	λύσοντα

§124.4. *Future middle participle.*

SINGULAR

CASE	MASCULINE	FEMININE	NEUTER
Nom	λυσόμενος	λυσομένη	λυσόμενον
Gen	λυσομένου	λυσομένης	λυσομένου
Abl	λυσομένου	λυσομένης	λυσομένου
Dat	λυσομένῳ	λυσομένη	λυσομένῳ

Loc	λυσομένῳ	λυσομένη	λυσομένῳ
Inst	λυσομένῳ	λυσομένη	λυσομένῳ
Acc	λυσόμενον	λυσομένην	λυσόμενον

PLURAL

CASE	MASCULINE	FEMININE	NEUTER
Nom	λυσόμενοι	λυσόμεναι	λυσόμενα
Gen	λυσομένων	λυσομένων	λυσομένων
Abl	λυσομένων	λυσομένων	λυσομένων
Dat	λυσομένοις	λυσομέναις	λυσομένοις
Loc	λυσομένοις	λυσομέναις	λυσομένοις
Inst	λυσομένοις	λυσομέναις	λυσομένοις
Acc	λυσομένους	λυσομένας	λυσόμενα

§124.5. *Future passive participle.*

SINGULAR

CASE	MASCULINE	FEMININE	NEUTER
Nom	λυθησόμενος	λυθησομένη	λυθησόμενον
Gen	λυθησομένου	λυθησομένης	λυθησομένου
Abl	λυθησομένου	λυθησομένης	λυθησομένου
Dat	λυθησομένῳ	λυθησομένη	λυθησομένῳ
Loc	λυθησομένῳ	λυθησομένη	λυθησομένῳ
Inst	λυθησομένῳ	λυθησομένη	λυθησομένῳ
Acc	λυθησόμενον	λυθησομένην	λυθησόμενον

PLURAL

CASE	MASCULINE	FEMININE	NEUTER
Nom	λυθησόμενοι	λυθησόμεναι	λυθησόμενα
Gen	λυθησομένων	λυθησομένων	λυθησομένων
Abl	λυθησομένων	λυθησομένων	λυθησομένων
Dat	λυθησομένοις	λυθησομέναις	λυθησομένοις
Loc	λυθησομένοις	λυθησομέναις	λυθησομένοις
Inst	λυθησομένοις	λυθησομέναις	λυθησομένοις
Acc	λυθησομένους	λυθησομένας	λυθησόμενα

§124.6. *Present participle of* εἰμί.

SINGULAR

CASE	MASCULINE	FEMININE	NEUTER
Nom	ὤν	οὖσα	ὄν
Gen	ὄντος	οὔσης	ὄντος
Abl	ὄντος	οὔσης	ὄντος
Dat	ὄντι	οὔσῃ	ὄντι

Loc	ὄντι	οὔσῃ	ὄντι
Inst	ὄντι	οὔσῃ	ὄντι
Acc	ὄντα	οὖσαν	ὄν

PLURAL

CASE	MASCULINE	FEMININE	NEUTER
Nom	ὄντες	οὖσαι	ὄντα
Gen	ὄντων	οὐσῶν	ὄντων
Abl	ὄντων	οὐσῶν	ὄντων
Dat	οὖσι (ν)	οὔσαις	οὖσι (ν)
Loc	οὖσι (ν)	οὔσαις	οὖσι (ν)
Inst	οὖσι (ν)	οὔσαις	οὖσι (ν)
Acc	ὄντας	οὔσας	ὄντα

§125. *Exercises*.

(1) ὁ Ἰησους ἦλθεν παρὰ τὴν θάλασαν καὶ ἐκήρυξεν τὴν βασιλείαν τοῦ θεοῦ. (2) ταῦτα εἶπον ὑμῖν ἐν τῷ ἱερῷ. (3) ταύτας τὰς ἐντολὰς ἔλαβον ἀπὸ τοῦ ἀποστόλου τοῦ κυρίου. (4) ἐν ἐκείναις ταῖς ἡμέραις οὐ ἔγνω τὴν ὁδὸν τοῦ χριστοῦ. (5) ὁ χριστὸς ἐθεράπευσεν τοὺς πονηρούς. (6) οὗτος ὁ ἄνθρωπός ἐστιν ψεύστης καὶ σκάνδαλον. (7) ἔβλεψα τὸν ἀπόστολον λέγοντα ταῦτα. (8) οὗτός ἐστιν ὁ χριστὸς ὁ λέγων τοῖς ἀποστόλοις. (9) τὸ εὐαγγέλιον ἔσται σκάνδαλον. (10) ἡ ἐντολὴ τοῦ θεοῦ διδάσκει ἡμῖν τὴν ὁδὸν τῆς ζωῆς.

Lesson 21
Aorist Active and Middle Participles

§126. *Vocabulary*.

ἀδικία, ἡ, *unrighteousness*

ἀποθνήσκω, ἀποθανοῦμαι, ἀπέθανον, *I die, I shall die, I died*

ἐλπίζω, ἐλπιῶ, ἤλπισα, *I hope, I shall hope, I hoped*

ἔτι, *still, yet*

ἑτοιμάζω, ἑτοιμάσω, ἡτοίμασα, *I prepare, I shall prepare, I prepared*

λιπών, λιποῦσα, λιπόν, 2nd aorist participle of λείπω, §106.

λύσας, λύσασα, λύσαν, 1st aorist participle of λύω, §15

παράκλητος, ὁ, *advocate*

παρρησία, ἡ, *boldness*

Πέτρος, ὁ, *Peter*

σοφία, ἡ, *wisdom*

§127. *Formation of the Aorist Participles*. There is no augment in the aorist participle since the augment occurs *only* in the indicative mood. The aorist participle, however, is built upon the aorist stem. The first aorist active has the tense suffix σα added to the stem λυ plus the ending. Note that the first aorist participle is very close in form to the present participle (cf. §124.1)

The first aorist middle consists of the stem λυ, the tense suffix σα, the middle participle suffix μεν plus the ending. The first aorist middle is exactly like the present middle/passive except the first aorist adds the tense suffix (cf. §124.2).

The second aorist participle is built upon the second aorist stem. The second aorist active and middle participles are declined exactly like the present participle except that the second aorist participle is built on the second aorist stem. Thus the present active participle, nominative, masculine, singular of λείπω is λείπων. The second aorist active participle, nominative, masculine, singular of the same verb is λιπών.

§128. *Grammatical Study*. The aorist participle translates action that is *point* in nature. This is the kind of action already discussed in connection with the aorist tense (§102). The aorist participle translates point action that is antecedent to the action ascribed to the main verb of the sentence.

The use of the aorist participles with or without the definite article is the same as with the present participles (see §123.2 and §123.3).

§129. *Inflection of Aorist Participle*.

§129.1. *First aorist active participle*.

SINGULAR

CASE	MASCULINE	FEMININE	NEUTER
Nom	λύσας	λύσασα	λῦσαν
Gen	λύσαντος	λυσάσης	λύσαντος
Abl	λύσαντος	λυσάσης	λύσαντος
Dat	λύσαντι	λυσάσῃ	λύσαντι
Loc	λύσαντι	λυσάσῃ	λύσαντι
Inst	λύσαντι	λυσάσῃ	λύσαντι
Acc	λύσαντα	λύσασαν	λῦσαν

PLURAL

CASE	MASCULINE	FEMININE	NEUTER
Nom	λύσαντες	λύσασαι	λύσαντα
Gen	λυσάντων	λυσασῶν	λυσάντων
Abl	λυσάντων	λυσασῶν	λυσάντων
Dat	λύσασι (ν)	λυσάσαις	λύσασι (ν)
Loc	λύσασι (ν)	λυσάσαις	λύσασι (ν)
Inst	λύσασι (ν)	λυσάσαις	λύσασι (ν)
Acc	λύσαντας	λυσάσας	λύσαντα

§129.2. *First aorist middle participle*.

SINGULAR

CASE	MASCULINE	FEMININE	NEUTER
Nom	λυσάμενος	λυσαμένη	λυσάμενον
Gen	λυσαμένου	λυσαμένης	λυσαμένου
Abl	λυσαμένου	λυσαμένης	λυσαμένου
Dat	λυσαμένῳ	λυσομένη	λυσαμένῳ
Loc	λυσαμένῳ	λυσαμένη	λυσαμένῳ
Inst	λυσαμένῳ	λυσαμένη	λυσαμένῳ
Acc	λυσάμενον	λυσαμένην	λυσάμενον

PLURAL

CASE	MASCULINE	FEMININE	NEUTER
Nom	λυσάμενοι	λυσάμεναι	λυσάμενα
Gen	λυσαμένων	λυσαμένων	λυσαμένων
Abl	λυσαμένων	λυσαμένων	λυσαμένων
Dat	λυσαμένοις	λυσαμέναις	λυσαμένοις
Loc	λυσαμένοις	λυσαμέναις	λυσαμένοις
Inst	λυσαμένοις	λυσαμέναις	λυσαμένοις
Acc	λυσαμένους	λυσαμένας	λυσάμενα

§129.3. *Second aorist active participle.*

SINGULAR

CASE	MASCULINE	FEMININE	NEUTER
Nom	λιπών	λιποῦσα	λιπόν
Gen	λιπόντος	λιπούσης	λιπόντος
Abl	λιπόντος	λιπούσης	λιπόντος
Dat	λιπόντι	λιπούση	λιπόντι
Loc	λιπόντι	λιπούση	λιπόντι
Inst	λιπόντι	λιπούση	λιπόντι
Acc	λιπόντα	λιποῦσαν	λιπόν

PLURAL

CASE	MASCULINE	FEMININE	NEUTER
Nom	λιπόντες	λιποῦσαι	λιπόντα
Gen	λιπόντων	λιπουσῶν	λιπόντων
Abl	λιπόντων	λιπουσῶν	λιπόντων
Dat	λιποῦσι (ν)	λιπούσαις	λιποῦσι (ν)
Loc	λιποῦσι (ν)	λιπούσαις	λιποῦσι (ν)
Inst	λιποῦσι (ν)	λιπούσαις	λιποῦσι (ν)
Acc	λιπόντας	λιπούσας	λιπόντα

§129.4. *Second aorist middle participle.*

SINGULAR

CASE	MASCULINE	FEMININE	NEUTER
Nom	λιπόμενος	λιπομένη	λιπόμενον
Gen	λιπομένου	λιπομένης	λιπομένου
Abl	λιπομένου	λιπομένης	λιπομένου
Dat	λιπομένῳ	λιπομένη	λιπομένῳ
Loc	λιπομένῳ	λιπομένη	λιπομένῳ
Inst	λιπομένῳ	λιπομένη	λιπομένῳ
Acc	λιπόμενον	λιπομένην	λιπόμενον

PLURAL

CASE	MASCULINE	FEMININE	NEUTER
Nom	λιπόμενοι	λιπόμεναι	λιπόμενα
Gen	λιπομένων	λιπομένων	λιπομένων
Abl	λιπομένων	λιπομένων	λιπομένων
Dat	λιπομένοις	λιπομέναις	λιπομένοις
Loc	λιπομένοις	λιπομέναις	λιπομένοις
Inst	λιπομένοις	λιπομέναις	λιπομένοις
Acc	λιπομένους	λιπομένας	λιπόμενα

§130. *Exercises.*

(1) ἔβλεψε τὸν ἀπόστολον βαπτίζοντα τὸν ἁμαρτωλὸν εἰς τὴν ὁδὸν τοῦ κυρίου. (2) βλέψομεν τὴν δόξαν τοῦ κυρίου, καὶ ἐν τῇ ἡμέρᾳ ἐκείνῃ σωθησόμεθα. (3) ἤκουσα τὸν μαθητὴν τὸν λέγοντα ταῦτα. (4) κατὰ τὸν προφήτην ἀγαθὸς ὁ νόμος. (5) τὰ καλὰ τέκνα ἄγεται ὑπὸ τοῦ πονηροῦ προφήτου πρὸς τὴν ὁδὸν αὐτοῦ. (6) οἱ μαθηταὶ βαπτίσουσιν τὰ τέκνα ὅτι ἐξέρχονται ἐκ τοῦ πονηροῦ κόσμου. (7) τὸ ἅγιον πνεῦμα ἤγαγε τοὺς ἀνθρώπους εἰς τὸ φῶς. (8) κηρύσσομεν περὶ τοῦ σώσαντος ἡμᾶς ἀπὸ τῶν ἁμαρτιῶν ἡμῶν. (9) ἀκούσαντες τῶν λεγομένων ὑπὸ τοῦ μαθητοῦ τοῦ κυρίου, ἐπίστευσαν εἰς αὐτὸν καὶ ἐβαπτίσθησαν. (10) γράφομεν ὑμῖν περὶ τοῦ αὐτοῦ νόμου.

Lesson 22
Aorist
Passive Participle

§131. *Vocabulary.*

ἀγγελία, ἡ, *message*

ἀποσταλείς, ἀποσταλεῖσα, ἀποσταλέν, second aorist passive participle of
    ἀποστέλλω, §83

ἀρχή, ἡ, *beginning*

δέχομαι, δέξομαι, ἐδεξάμην (D), *I receive, I shall receive, I received*

διακονία, ἡ, *ministry*

κεφαλή, ἡ, *head*

κοινωνία, ἡ, *fellowship*

λυθείς, λυθεῖσα, λυθέν, first aorist passive participle of λύω, §15

σωτηρία, ἡ, *salvation*

ὀφθαλμός, ὁ, *eye*

§132. *Formation of Aorist Passive Participles.* All aorist passive participles will be
declined like λύω in the paradigm in §134. The first aorist passive participles like λύω
will have the aorist passive participle tense sign θ; the second aorist passive participles
like ἀποστέλλω will *not* have the tense sign θ.

§133. *Grammatical Study.* The aorist passive participles are to be translated like any
other aorist participle, i.e., it indicates action that is antecedent to that of the main
verb. Since it is an aorist <u>passive</u> participle, it indicates that the subject receives the
action. Example: ὁ λυθείς δοῦλος ἤκουσε τὸν κύριον = *the slave who was
loosed heard the Lord* or *the slave who had been loosed heard the Lord.*

§134. *Inflection of Aorist Passive Participle.*

  §134.1 *First aorist passive participle.*

SINGULAR

CASE	MASCULINE	FEMININE	NEUTER
Nom	λυθείς	λυθεῖσα	λυθέν
Gen	λυθέντος	λυθείσης	λυθέντος
Abl	λυθέντος	λυθείσης	λυθέντος
Dat	λυθέντι	λυθείσῃ	λυθέντι
Loc	λυθέντι	λυθείσῃ	λυθέντι
Inst	λυθέντι	λυθείσῃ	λυθέντι
Acc	λυθέντα	λυθεῖσαν	λυθέν

PLURAL

CASE	MASCULINE	FEMININE	NEUTER
Nom	λυθέντες	λυθεῖσαι	λυθέντα
Gen	λυθέντων	λυθεισῶν	λυθέντων
Abl	λυθέντων	λυθεισῶν	λυθέντων
Dat	λυθεῖσι (ν)	λυθείσαις	λυθεῖσι (ν)
Loc	λυθεῖσι (ν)	λυθείσαις	λυθεῖσι (ν)
Inst	λυθεῖσι (ν)	λυθείσαις	λυθεῖσι (ν)
Acc	λυθέντας	λυθείσας	λυθέντα

§134.2. *Second aorist passive participle*.

SINGULAR

CASE	MASCULINE	FEMININE	NEUTER
Nom	ἀποσταλείς	ἀποσταλεῖσα	ἀποσταλέν
Gen	ἀποσταλέντος	ἀποσταλείσης	ἀποσταλέντος
Abl	ἀποσταλέντος	ἀποσταλείσης	ἀποσταλέντος
Dat	ἀποσταλέντι	ἀποσταλείσῃ	ἀποσταλέντι
Loc	ἀποσταλέντι	ἀποσταλείσῃ	ἀποσταλέντι
Inst	ἀποσταλέντι	ἀποσταλείσῃ	ἀποσταλέντι
Acc	ἀποσταλέντα	ἀποσταλεῖσαν	ἀποσταλέν

PLURAL

CASE	MASCULINE	FEMININE	NEUTER
Nom	ἀποσταλέντες	ἀποσταλεῖσαι	ἀποσταλέντα
Gen	ἀποσταλέντων	ἀποσταλεισῶν	ἀποσταλέντων
Abl	ἀποσταλέντων	ἀποσταλεισῶν	ἀποσταλέντων
Dat	ἀποσταλεῖσι (ν)	ἀποσταλείσαις	ἀποσταλεῖσι (ν)
Loc	ἀποσταλεῖσι (ν)	ἀποσταλείσαις	ἀποσταλεῖσι (ν)
Inst	ἀποσταλεῖσι (ν)	ἀποσταλείσαις	ἀποσταλεῖσι (ν)
Acc	ἀποσταλέντας	ἀποσταλείσας	ἀποσταλέντα

§135. *Genitive Absolute*. The *genitive absolute* is very common in the New Testament. The *genitive absolute* refers to the adverbial use of the participle in which it has *no specific grammatical connection with the main clause*. The adverbial use of the participle is very common in Greek: Example, εἰσελθὼν εἰς τὸν οἶκον, ἔβλεψε τὸ τέκνον = *when he had come into the house he saw the children*. Notice that the participle εἰσελθών agrees in gender, number and case with the subject (*he*) of the main verb ἔβλεψε. But this is not the case with the *genitive absolute*. The genitive absolute is always in the genitive case as well as the subject of the participle which is always expressed. Thus the subject of a *genitive absolute* participle is not derived from that of the main clause as it is with the regular use of an adverbial participle. Instead the subject of a genitive absolute construction is always expressed and is always in the genitive case. Example: λέγοντος τοῦ δούλου ταῦτα, οἱ μαθηταὶ διδάσκουσιν = *while the slave is saying these things, the disciples are teaching*.

§136. *Exercises*.

   (1) ἡ ἀγγελία ἀπὸ θεοῦ ἐκηρύσσετο τοῖς ὄχλοις ὑπὸ τῶν μαθητῶν τοῦ χριστοῦ. (2) δεξόμεθα τὴν ἀγγελίαν τῆς σωτηρίας ὅτι ὁ θεὸς ἠγάπησα ἡμᾶς ἐν τῷ χριστῷ. (3) ὁ χριστὸς ἐθεράπευσα τὰ τέκνα τὰ ἀκούοντα τὸ εὐαγγέλιον. (4) οἱ ἀπόστολοι ἀπεστάλησαν εἰς τὰς συναγωγάς, οἱ δὲ μαθηταὶ μένουσιν ἐν τῇ ἐκκλησίᾳ. (5) αὕτη ἐστὶν ἡ ἀγάπη ἡ κηρυχθεῖσα ἐν τῇ ἐκκλησίᾳ ὑπὸ τῶν ἀκουόντων τὸ εὐαγγέλιον. (6) ἀκουθέντος τοῦ λόγου τὸ ὄνομα τοῦ χριστοῦ ἐδοξάσθη ἐν τῷ κόσμῳ. (7) οἱ διδαχθέντες τὴν ἀλήθειαν τοῦ θεοῦ ἐπίστευσαν καὶ ἐβαπτίσθησαν εἰς τὴν ἐκκλησίαν. (8) ἐκεῖναι αἱ ἐκκλησίαι ἔλαβον τὴν διακονίαν ἀπὸ τῆς ἀρχῆς. (9) ὁ χριστός ἐστιν ἡ κεφαλὴ τῆς ἐκκλησίας. (10) λέγοντος τοῦ δούλου ταῦτα οἱ μαθηταὶ διδάσκουσιν.

Lesson 23
οω Contract Verbs

§137. *Vocabulary*.
βίος, ὁ, *life*
δηλόω, δηλώσω, ἐδήλωσα, *I show, I shall show, I showed*
ἐπιθυμία, ἡ, *lust*
ἱλασμός, ὁ, *propitiation*
πληρόω, πληρώσω, ἐπλήρωσα, *I fulfill, I shall fulfill, I fulfilled*
σταυρόω, σταυρώσω, ἐσταύρωσα, *I crucify, I shall crucify, I crucified*

§138. *Inflection* [review §21, 118]. The οω contract verbs form a special class of the
ω conjugation. This lesson deals with those contract verb whose stems end in οω. The
following contractions occur *in the present and imperfect tenses only*. Because of the
addition of the tense sign in the aorist, future, perfect, pluperfect, and future perfect
passive tenses, this contraction does not occur in these tenses.

PRESENT ACTIVE

	SINGULAR	PLURAL
1st per	δηλόω = δηλῶ	δηλόομεν = δηλοῦμεν
2nd per	δηλόεις = δηλοῖς	δηλόετε = δηλοῦτε
3rd per	δηλόει = δηλοῖ	δηλόουσι (ν) = δηλοῦσι (ν)

IMPERFECT ACTIVE

	SINGLUAR	PLURAL
1st per	ἐδηλόον = ἐδηλοῦν	ἐδηλόομεν = ἐδηλοῦμεν
2nd per	ἐδηλόες = ἐδηλοῦς	ἐδηλόετε = ἐδηλοῦτε
3rd per	ἐδηλόε = ἐδηλοῦ	ἐδηλόον = ἐδηλοῦν

§139. *Rules for Contraction in* αω. Rules for contraction for verbs ending in οω:

o	+	ω	=	ω	(1st person sing)
o	+	ει	=	οι	(2nd person sing)
o	+	ει	=	οι	(3rd person sing)
o	+	o	=	ου	(1st person pl)
o	+	ε	=	ου	(2nd person pl)
o	+	o	=	ου	(3rd person pl)

§140. The οω verbs are listed in their lexical vocabulary form (§137) in the *un*contracted form so the student may recognize the type of configuration readily (the uncontracted form is given only in the present tense, i.e., the *first* form).

§141. *Exercises.*

(1) ἐν τῇ ἀρχῇ ὁ θεὸς ἐπλήρωσε τὴν ἐπαγγελίαν αὐτοῦ. (2) ζητῶ τὴν βασιλείαν τοῦ θεοῦ καὶ τὴν δικαιοσύνην αὐτῆς. (3) εὐαγγελιζόμεθα ἐν παραβολαῖς τοῖς δούλοις περὶ ᾽Ιησοῦ. (4) ὁ κύριος τῆς ζωῆς ἐσταυροῦτο ὑπὸ τῶν πονηρῶν. (5) τὸ εὐαγγέλιον τῆς βασιλείας κηρυχθήσεται τοῖς λαοῖς. (6) ἐδιδάχθημεν ὑπὸ τῶν μαθητῶν ἐν ἐκείναις ταῖς ἡμέραις. (7) ὁ χριστὸς οὐκ ἔστιν ἁμαρτωλός· ἀπέθανε ὑπὲρ ἁμαρτωλῶν. (8) ὁ λέγων ὅτι ἔχει κοινωνίαν μετὰ τοῦ θεοῦ ἀλλὰ μένει ἐν τῇ σκοτίᾳ ἁμαρτίας ἐστὶ ψεύστης. (9) εἰσελθόντων τῶν μαθητῶν εἰς τὸ ἱερόν, ὁ κύριος ἐπορεύσατο εἰς τὴν ἔρημον. (10) οἱ ἅγιοι συνάγουσι τοὺς ἁμαρτωλοὺς εἰς τὴν ἐκκλησίαν.

Lesson 24

Third Declension
Liquid and Mute Nouns

§142. *Vocabulary*.
αἰών, αἰῶνος, ὁ, *age*
ἄρχων, ἄρχοντος, ὁ, *ruler*
εἰς τὸν αἰῶνα, *for ever*
εἰς τοὺς αἰῶνας τῶν αἰώνων, *for ever and ever*
ἐλπίς, ἐλπίδος, ἡ, *hope*
μήτηρ, μητρός, ἡ, *mother*
νύξ, νυκτός, ἡ, *night*
πατήρ, πατρός, ὁ, *father*
πᾶς, πᾶσα, πᾶν, *all, whole*[1]
σάρξ, σαρκός, ἡ, *flesh*
χάρις, χάριτος, ἡ, *grace*

§143. *Introduction to the Third Declension* [review first declension nouns, §57-59 and second declension nouns, §28]. There are three declension systems for Greek nouns:

   1st declension = stem ends with an α sound
   2nd declension = stem ends with an o sound
   3rd declension = stem ends with a consonant, ι, υ or a diphthong

The third declension is often called the consonant declension because of the predominance of nouns that have stems ending in consonants though some stems do end with vowels.

   Since there are masculine, feminine and neuter nouns in the third declension, the article must be learned as part of the vocabulary. It is often the *only* clue to the gender

---

[1]The masculine and neuter forms (πᾶς and πᾶν) are declined like a third declension noun; the feminine form (πᾶσα) is declined like a first declension feminine noun (see §191.3).

of the noun.

There are four types of third declension nouns (each has several sub-categories):

        (1) Liquid
        (2) Mute
        (3) Vowels
        (4) Neuter

In all four types the same ending are applied:

SINGULAR

CASE	MASCULINE[2]	FEMININE[2]	NEUTER
Nom	ς or none	ς or none	none
Gen	ος	ος	ος
Abl	ος	ος	ος
Dat	ι	ι	ι
Loc	ι	ι	ι
Inst	ι	ι	ι
Acc	α or ν	α or ν	none

PLURAL

CASE	MASCULINE	FEMININE	NEUTER
Nom[3]	ες	ες	α
Gen[4]	ων	ων	ων
Abl	ων	ων	ων
Dat	σι	σι	σι
Loc	σι	σι	σι
Inst	σι	σι	σι
Acc	ας	ας	α

In the third declension the stem of the noun is determined by the genitive singular. This form is included as a part of the lexical form for each third declension noun, i.e., both the nominative and the genitive forms appear.

The dative, locative and instrumental forms of all third declension nouns will be altered with the addition of the σι *if the stem ends in a consonant.* These alterations will occur as follows [review §95]:

        π, β, or φ + σι = ψι
        κ, γ, or χ + σι = ξι
        τ, δ or θ drops out leaving σι

---

[2]Masculine and feminine nouns have the same endings in the third declension.
[3]All third declension nouns have the same form in the nominative and in the accusative plural.
[4]The genitive and ablative plural is the same for all third declension nouns.

ν drops out before σι[5]

ϱ will be retained before σι

§144. *Liquid Stem Nouns.* These nouns are mostly masculine with a few feminine. The stems may be found by removing the final ος in the genitive singular. There are two varieties of the liquid third declension nouns:

§144.1. *Stems ending in λ, μ, ν, or ϱ.*

CASE	SINGULAR		PLURAL	
Nom	ὁ	αἰών	οἱ	αἰῶνες
Gen	τοῦ	αἰῶνος	τῶν	αἰώνων
Abl	τοῦ	αἰῶνος	τῶν	αἰώνων
Dat	τῷ	αἰῶνι	τοῖς	αἰῶσι (ν)
Loc	τῷ	αἰῶνι	τοῖς	αἰῶσι (ν)
Inst	τῷ	αἰῶνι	τοῖς	αἰῶσι (ν)
Acc	τὸν	αἰῶνα	τοὺς	αἰῶνας

§144.2. *Stems ending in εϱ[6].* These nouns are both masculine and feminine. To find the stem remove the ος from the genitive singular and insert an ε before the ϱ:

CASE	SINGULAR		PLURAL	
Nom	ὁ	πατήϱ	οἱ	πατέϱες
Gen	τοῦ	πατϱός	τῶν	πατέϱων
Abl	τοῦ	πατϱός	τῶν	πατέϱων
Dat	τῷ	πατϱί	τοῖς	πατϱάσι (ν)
Loc	τῷ	πατϱί	τοῖς	πατϱάσι (ν)
Inst	τῷ	πατϱί	τοῖς	πατϱάσι (ν)
Acc	τὸν	πατέϱα	τοὺς	πατέϱας

The genitive/abalative and the dative/locative/instrumental singular forms drop the stem vowel ε while the dative/locative/instrumental plural forms drop the stem vowel ε and insert an α before the σι ending.

§145. *Mute Stem Nouns* [review §10.4]. This type has both masculine and feminine nouns. The stem may be found by removing the ος from the genitive singular. This type also has two sub-categories:

§145.1. *Monosyllabic mute stem nouns.*

CASE	SINGULAR	PLURAL

---

[5]When ν is followed by τ, the ντ will drop out before σι and the vowel will lengthen from o to ου. Example: dative, locative, instrumental plural of ἄϱχων, ἄϱχοντος is ἄϱχουσι(ν)

[6]This anaylsis does not hold with the noun ἀνήϱ. It is so *irregular* that it is omitted here; its forms are best learned by observation in the Greek New Testament.

Nom	ἡ	νύξ		αἱ	νύκτες
Gen	τῆς	νυκτός		τῶν	νυκτῶν
Abl	τῆς	νυκτός		τῶν	νυκτῶν
Dat	τῇ	νυκτί		ταῖς	νυξί (ν)
Loc	τῇ	νυκτί		ταῖς	νυξί (ν)
Inst	τῇ	νυκτί		ταῖς	νυξί (ν)
Acc	τὴν	νύκτα		τὰς	νύκτας

The nominative singular form is derived by finding the stem (genitive singular νυκτός minus ος = νυκτ) and adding a ς. The τ drops out before ς and the κς combines to yield ξ, hence νυκτς = νύξ. This same phenomenon occurs in the dative/locative/instrumental plural.

§145.2. *Other mute stem nouns.*

CASE		SINGULAR			PLURAL
Nom	ἡ	ἐλπίς		αἱ	ἐλπίδες
Gen	τῆς	ἐλπίδος		τῶν	ἐλπίδων
Abl	τῆς	ἐλπίδος		τῶν	ἐλπίδων
Dat	τῇ	ἐλπίδι		ταῖς	ἐλπίσι (ν)
Loc	τῇ	ἐλπίδι		ταῖς	ἐλπίσι (ν)
Inst	τῇ	ἐλπίδι		ταῖς	ἐλπίσι (ν)
Acc	τὴν	ἐλπίδα[7]		τὰς	ἐλπίδας

CASE		SINGULAR			PLURAL
Nom	ὁ	ἄρχων[8]		οἱ	ἄρχοντες
Gen	τοῦ	ἄρχοντος		τῶν	ἀρχόντων
Abl	τοῦ	ἄρχοντος		τῶν	ἀρχόντων
Dat	τῷ	ἄρχοντι		τοῖς	ἄρχουσι (ν)
Loc	τῷ	ἄρχοντι		τοῖς	ἄρχουσι (ν)
Inst	τῷ	ἄρχοντι		τοῖς	ἄρχουσι (ν)
Acc	τὸν	ἄρχοντα		τοὺς	ἄρχοντας

§146. *Exercises.*

(1) ἐκήρυξαν τὸ εὐαγγέλιον ἐκείνοις τοῖς ἀνθρώποις τοῖς κακοῖς καὶ ἐπίστευσαν αὐτό. (2) ἐν τῇ σαρκὶ ἡμῶν οὐ γινώσκομεν αὐτὸν ἀλλὰ

---

[7]When a mute stem noun has a stem that ends in τ, δ, or θ preceded by an ι or an υ and *not* accented on the last syllable (of the stem), the accusative singular ends in a ν instead of an α. Example: χάρις, χάριτος. The stem is χάριτ which ends in ατ preceeded by an ι and *not* accented on the last syllable. The accusative singular form is χάριν.

[8]There is no ending added to the stem in the nominative; therefore, the final τ drops and the preceeding o lengthens to ω.

γνωσόμεθα αὐτὸν ἐν τῷ καινῷ αἰῶνι. (3) ἐν ἐνείνῃ τῇ ἡμέρᾳ πονηροὶ γνώσονται τὴν χάριν τοῦ χριστός. (4) ὁ θεός ἐστιν ἀγαθὸς καὶ ὁ υἱὸς αὐτοῦ μενεῖ ἐν ταῖς καρδίαις ἡμῶν εἰς τοὺς αἰῶνας τῶν αἰώνων. (5) ἐλπίδα οὐκ ἔχομεν ὅτι οὐ ἀγαπῶμεν τὸν κύριον. (6) ἡ γραφή διδάσκει ὅτι ὁ θεός ἐστιν ὁ πατὴρ παντός τοῦ κόσμου. (7) ἡ μήτηρ καὶ ὁ πατὴρ βαπτίζουσι τὸν υἱὸν αὐτῶν. (8) ὁ μαθητὴς οὐκέτι γινώσκει Ἰησοῦ κατὰ τὴν σάρκα. (9) ὁ χριστὸς ἐδίδαξε ὅτι ὁ λόγος αὐτοῦ μενεῖ εἰς τὸν αἰῶνα. (10) οἱ ἄρχοντες ἐπίστευσαν εἰς τὸν κύριον καὶ οἱ ἄλλοι ἤχθησαν πρὸς αὐτὸν ὑπ' αὐτῶν.

Lesson 25

Third Declension
Vowel and Neuter Nouns

§147. Vocabulary.
αἷμα, αἷματος, τό, *blood*
ἀνάστασις, ἀναστάσεως, ἡ, *resurrection*
βασιλεύς, βασιλέως, ὁ, *king*
γένος, γένους, τό, *race*
γνῶσις, γνώσεως, ἡ, *judgment*
γραμματεύς, γραμματέως, ὁ, *scribe*
δύναμις, δυνάμεως, ἡ, *power*
ἔθνος, ἔθνους, τό, *nation*
ἔλεος, ἐλέους, τό, *mercey*
θέλημα, θελήματος, τό, *will*
ἱερεύς, ἱερέως, ὁ, *priest*
κρίσις, κρίσεως, τό, *judgment*
ὄνομα, ὀνόματος, τό, *name*
πόλις, πόλεως, τό, *city*
στάχυς, στάχυος, ὁ, *ear of corn*
σῶμα, σώματος, τό, *body*
τέλος, τέλους, τό, *end*

§148. *Neuter Nouns.* There are two sub-categories of this type of third declension noun. Obviously, all nouns of this type are *neuter*. As in the neuter nouns of the second declension, in neuter third declension nouns the nominative and accusative forms are identical in both the singular and the plural.

§148.1. *ματ stem nouns.* The stems of these nouns end in ματ after the final ος is removed from the genitive singular form.

CASE	SINGULAR		PLURAL	
Nom	τὸ	ὄνομα	τὰ	ὀνόματα
Gen	τοῦ	ὀνόματος	τῶν	ὀνομάτων
Abl	τοῦ	ὀνόματος	τῶν	ὀνομάτων
Dat	τῷ	ὀνόματι	τοῖς	ὀνόμασι (ν)
Loc	τῷ	ὀνόματι	τοῖς	ὀνόμασι (ν)
Inst	τῷ	ὀνόματι	τοῖς	ὀνόμασι (ν)
Acc	τὸ	ὄνομα	τὰ	ὀνόματα

The τ of the stem drops out before the σι ending in the dative/locative/instrumental plural.

§148.2. *εϛ stem nouns*.

CASE	SINGULAR		PLURAL	
Nom	τὸ	γένος	τὰ	γένη
Gen	τοῦ	γένους	τῶν	γενῶν
Abl	τοῦ	γένους	τῶν	γενῶν
Dat	τῷ	γένει	τοῖς	γένεσι (ν)
Loc	τῷ	γένει	τοῖς	γένεσι (ν)
Inst	τῷ	γένει	τοῖς	γένεσι (ν)
Acc	τὸ	γένος	τὰ	γένη

The older form for the genitive singular was γένεσος. This form would yield the stem if the οϛ were removed. In Koine Greek, however, the ending contracted with the stem vowel because the final ϛ dropped out. In the resulting contraction the ε was lost except in the dative/locative/instrumental plural forms.

§149. *Vowel Stem Nouns*. The third declension liquid (§144) and the mute (§145) nouns and the neuter nouns (§148) all have stems ending in a consonant. The vowel stem nouns of the third declension consist of those nouns whose stem end in either an ι, an υ, or an ευ. In each type the stem is found by removing the ϛ from the *nominative* singular form.

§149.1 *ι stem nouns*. All the nouns of this variety are feminine.

CASE	SINGULAR		PLURAL	
Nom	ἡ	πόλις	αἱ	πόλεις
Gen	τῆς	πόλεως	τῶν	πόλεων
Abl	τῆς	πόλεως	τῶν	πόλεων
Dat	τῇ	πόλει	ταῖς	πόλεσι (ν)
Loc	τῇ	πόλει	ταῖς	πόλεσι (ν)
Inst	τῇ	πόλει	ταῖς	πόλεσι (ν)
Acc	τὴν	πόλιν	τὰς	πόλεις

The stem of the ι nouns is found by removing the σ from the *nominative* singular. The stem of πόλις is πόλι. An ε replaces the ι in all forms except the nominative and accusative singular. In the nominative and accusative plural the εις is the result of the contraction of ε + ες and the ε + ας respectively.

§149.2. *υ stem nouns*. This type consists mostly of masculine nouns with a few feminine.

CASE	SINGULAR		PLURAL	
Nom	ὁ	στάχυς	οἱ	στάχυες
Gen	τοῦ	στάχυος	τῶν	σταχύων
Abl	τοῦ	στάχυος	τῶν	σταχύων
Dat	τῷ	στάχυι	τοῖς	στάχυσι (ν)
Loc	τῷ	στάχυι	τοῖς	στάχυσι (ν)
Inst	τῷ	στάχυι	τοῖς	στάχυσι (ν)
Acc	τὸν	στάχυν	τοὺς	στάχυας

The stem of the υ nouns is found by removing the ς from the *nominative* singular. The stem of στάχυς is στάχυ. Notice that in the accusative singular the ν is used instead of the α.

§149.3. *ευ stem nouns*. All of the nouns of this type are masculine.

CASE	SINGULAR		PLURAL	
Nom	ὁ	βασιλεύς	οἱ	βασιλεῖς
Gen	τοῦ	βασιλέως	τῶν	βασιλέων
Abl	τοῦ	βασιλέως	τῶν	βασιλέων
Dat	τῷ	βασιλεῖ	τοῖς	βασιλεῦσι (ν)
Loc	τῷ	βασιλεῖ	τοῖς	βασιλεῦσι (ν)
Inst	τῷ	βασιλεῖ	τοῖς	βασιλεῦσι (ν)
Acc	τὸν	βασιλέα	τοὺς	βασιλεῖς

The stem of the ευ nouns is found by removing the ς from the nominative singular. The stem of βασιλεύς is βασιλεύ. The υ of the final ευ diphthong drops out before an ending that begins with a vowel. The εις in the nominative and accusative plural results from the contraction of the ε + εσ and the ε + ας.

§150. *Exercises*.

(1) τοῦτο γάρ ἐστιν τὸ θέλημα τοῦ πατρός μου. (2) ἡ κρίσις τοῦ θεοῦ ἐλεύσεται ἐπὶ τῶν ἐθνῶν ἐν τῷ τέλει. (3) ὁ θεὸς ἔσωσε ἡμᾶς διὰ τῆς δυνάμεως τοῦ αἵματος τοῦ χριστοῦ. (4) ἐν ἐκείνῃ τῇ νυκτὶ ὁ μαθητὴς ἔβλεψε τὸν χριστὸν ἐν τῇ ἀναστάσει αὐτοῦ. (5) ἡ ἀγάπη τοῦ θεοῦ δι-δάξει ὑπὸ τῶν ἀποστόλων καὶ ὑπὸ τοῦ ἱερέως. (6) ἔχω γνῶσιν τοῦ θεοῦ διὰ τοῦ ἐλέους τοῦ υἱοῦ αὐτοῦ. (7) ὁ Ἰησοῦς ἔβλεψε τοὺς γραμματεῖς

διδάσκοντας τοὺς μαθητάς. (8) ὁ ἱερεὺς καὶ ὁ βασιλεὺς γινώσκουσιν τὸ θέλημα τοῦ θεοῦ. (9) τὸ σῶμα τοῦ χριστοῦ λαμβάνεται ἀπὸ τῆς πόλεως ὑπὸ τῶν ἀποστόλων. (10) λημψόμεθα τὴν δύναμιν ἀπὸ τοῦ θεοῦ ἐν ἐκείνῃ τῇ ἡμέρᾳ.

Lesson 26
Perfect Tense
Pluperfect Tense

§151. *Vocabulary.*

ἀκήκοα, *I have heard* (2nd perfect active of ἀκούω, §15)

ἀληθινός, ἀληθινή, ἀληθινόν, *true*

ἁλιεύς, ἁλιέως, ὁ, *fisherman*

ἀρχιερεύς, ἀρχιερέως, ὁ, *high priest*

βάθος, βάθους, τό, *depth*

βέβληκα, *I have thrown* (perfect active of βάλλω, §36)

γέγραφα, *I have written* (perfect active of γράφω, §15)

ἔγνωκα, *I have known* (perfect active of γινώσκω, §15)

ἠγάπηκα, *I have loved* (perfect active of ἀγαπάω, §117)

λέλυκα, *I have loosed* (perfect active of λύω, §15)

συναγωγή, ἡ, *synagogue*

χείρ, χειρός, ἡ, *hand*

§152. *Forms of the Perfect.*

§152.1. *Perfect active indicative.*

	SINGULAR	PLURAL
1st per	λέλυκα, *I have loosed*	λελύκαμεν, *we have loosed*
2nd per	λέλυκας, *you have loosed*	λελύκατε, *you have loosed*
3rd per	λέλυκε, *he, she, it has loosed*	λελύκασι, *they have loosed*

152.2. *Perfect middle/passive indicative.*

	SINGULAR	PLURAL

1st per λέλυμαι, *I have loosed myself*[1]   λελύμεθα, *we have loosed ourselves*
2nd per λέλυσαι, *you have loosed*   λέλυσθε, *you have loosed yourselves*
          yourself
3rd per λέλυται, *he has loosed himself*   λέλυνται, *they have loosed themselves*

§152.3. *Perfect active participle.*

SINGULAR

CASE	MASCULINE	FEMININE	NEUTER
Nom	λελυκώς	λελυκυῖα	λελυκός
Gen	λελυκότος	λελυκυίας	λελυκότος
Abl	λελυκότος	λελυκυίας	λελυκότος
Dat	λελυκότι	λελυκυίᾳ	λελυκότι
Loc	λελυκότι	λελυκυίᾳ	λελυκότι
Inst	λελυκότι	λελυκυίᾳ	λελυκότι
Acc	λελυκότα	λελυκυῖαν	λελυκός

PLURAL

CASE	MASCULINE	FEMININE	NEUTER
Nom	λελυκότες	λελυκυῖαι	λελυκότα
Gen	λελυκότων	λελυκυιῶν	λελυκότων
Abl	λελυκότων	λελυκυιῶν	λελυκότων
Dat	λελυκόσι (ν)	λελυκυίαις	λελυκόσι (ν)
Loc	λελυκόσι (ν)	λελυκυίαις	λελυκόσι (ν)
Inst	λελυκόσι (ν)	λελυκυίαις	λελυκόσι (ν)
Acc	λελυκότας	λελυκυίας	λελυκότα

§152.4. *Perfect middle/passive participle.*

SINGULAR

CASE	MASCULINE	FEMININE	NEUTER
Nom	λελυμένος	λελυμένη	λελυμένον
Gen	λελυμένου	λελυμένης	λελυμένου
Abl	λελυμένου	λελυμένης	λελυμένου
Dat	λελυμένῳ	λελυμένη	λελυμένῳ
Loc	λελυμένῳ	λελυμένη	λελυμένῳ
Inst	λελυμένῳ	λελυμένη	λελυμένῳ
Acc	λελυμένον	λελυμένην	λελυμένον

PLURAL

CASE	MASCULINE	FEMININE	NEUTER

---

[1]Since the Greek forms for the perfect middle and passive are identical, they are given only once; in this paradigm these forms are given middle translation. The passive would be translated *I have been loosed*, etc.

Nom	λελυμένοι	λελυμέναι	λελυμένα
Gen	λελυμένων	λελυμένων	λελυμένων
Abl	λελυμένων	λελυμένων	λελυμένων
Dat	λελυμένοις	λελυμέναις	λελυμένοις
Loc	λελυμένοις	λελυμέναις	λελυμένοις
Inst	λελυμένοις	λελυμέναις	λελυμένοις
Acc	λελυμένους	λελυμένας	λελυμένα

§152.5. *Perfect infinitive.*

Perfect active infinitive
  ἄρχομαι λελυκέναι τὰ τέκνα
  I am beginning to have loosed the children

Perfect middle infinitive
  ἀρχόμεθα λελύσθαι
  we are begining to have loosed ourselves

Perfect passive infinitive
  ἄρχεται λελύσθαι ὑπὸ τοῦ κυρίου
  he is beginning to have been loosed by the Lord

§153. *Formation of the Perfect Tense.*

§153.1. *Reduplication..* The fourth principal part of the verbs listed in the back of this book is the *perfect active indicative*. The fifth is the *perfective middle/passive indicative. The most striking feature of these forms is the reduplication*, or doubling of the initial consonant. The reduplicated consonant is separated from the initial consonant by the vowel ε, i.e., λύω = present, λέλυκα = perfect; κρίνω = present, κέκρικα = perfect. This phenomenon occurs in all verbs that begin with a consonant, with the following exceptions:

(1) Verbs beginning with φ, θ, χ reduplicate with correspondingly smooth consonants π, τ, κ. As above, these are separated by an ε. Thus the perfect of φιλέω is πεφίληκα.

(2) Verbs beginning with two consonants, one of the double consonants (see §10.5), or a ρ reduplicates *usually* by placing an ε onto the front of the word. This initial ε is in all respects the same as the augment employed in the imperfect and aorist tenses. Thus the perfect of γινώσκω is ἔγνωκα.

When the verb begins with a vowel or a diphthong, reduplication occurs by the *lengthening* of that initial vowel or diphthong to its corresponding longer form. Thus the perfect of ἐλπίζω is ἤλπικα.

These "rules" are intended to provide some guidance for understanding the process of duplication. The only sure method for determining the form of the perfect for a given verb is to look it up in the back of this book, or in a lexicon.

§153.2. *Tense sign.* The tense sign of the perfect is a κ though there are a few *second* perfects that do not employ the κ (γέγονα is the second perfect of γίνομαι). *The tense sign κ occurs only in the perfect active and aorist active; it does* not *occur in the middle and passive forms.* The additon of the κ causes certain changes when the stem ends in a consonant:

(1) In contract verbs the contract vowel (α, ε, ο) is lengthened before the tense sign κ. Thus the perfect of ἀγαπάω is ἠγάπηκα.

(2) A τ, δ, θ will drop out when the κ is added. Thus the perfect of ἐλπίζω is ἤλπικα (remember that the stem of ἐλπίζω is ἐλπίδ).

§154. *The Use of the Perfect Tense* [review §18.2]. In Greek the perfect tense describes action that is completed while its English translation often makes it appear as a "past" tense; the perfect tense in Greek is not a secondary, but a primary tense. Indeed, it is often called the "present perfect." This is so because its emphasis is upon action that has been completed and continues to the present in that "completed" state. Example: ἐλήλυθα (perfect active indicative, first person singular from ἔρχομαι) = *I came (and I am still here!).* Thus the emphasis in the perfect tense is upon the resultant state of being.

Remember the distinction drawn between the kind of action described as durative (§87) and point (§l02). The perfect tense blends both of these notions in a unique way. The combination of point and linear action in the perfect tense may signal a state of completion that continues into the present (●_____) or an action that has just come to a state of completion (_____●).

Often the Greek perfect can be translated by using forms of the English *have.* Keep in mind, however, that the English language contains no corresponding tense adequate for expressing the significance of the Greek perfect. All attempts in English are at best accommodations, and often you will simply have to remember that, despite any necessary English circumlocutions, the Greek perfect describes the present state result of a past action.

§155. *Forms of the Pluperfect.* The formation of the pluperfect tense employs as a prefix the reduplication principle found in the perfect tense (§153). In addition, there is a ε augment added so that the resulting sequence is ε-λε-λυ. Also, as in the perfect, the pluperfect adds the tense sign κ *in the active voice only.*

§155.1. *Pluperfect active indicative.*

SINGULAR	PLURAL
1st per ἐλελύκειν, *I had loosed*[2]	ἐλελύκειμεν, *we had loosed*
2nd per ἐλελύκεις, *you had loosed*	ἐλελύκειτε, *you had loosed*
3rd per ἐλελύκει, *he, she, it had loosed*	ἐλελύκεισαν, *they had loosed*

---

[2]See note 1 above.

§155.2. *Pluperfect middle/passive indicative.*

	SINGULAR	PLURAL
1st per	ἐλελύμην, *I had loosed myself*	ἐλελύμεθα, *we had loosed ourselves*
2nd per	ἐλέλυσο, *you had loosed yourself*	ἐλέλυσθε, *you had loosed yourselves*
3rd per	ἐλέλυτο, *he had loosed himself*	ἐλέλυντο, *they had loosed themselves*

§156. *The Use of the Pluperfect.* The <u>kind</u> of actions described by the pluperfect is the same as that of the perfect (see §154). The <u>time</u> of the action in the pluperfect, however, is in <u>past</u> time. In other words, the pluperfect is the perfect tense ''moved'' into past time. Compare the following:

$$\lambda έλυκα = I \underline{have} loosed$$
$$\dot{\epsilon}λελύκειν = I \underline{had} loosed$$

§157. *Tenses in Greek.* You will remember that in the indicative mood, tense indicates two things about verbs: <u>time</u> of action and <u>kind</u> of action. In each case there are three possibilities in Greek. Reducing these possibilities to a chart reveals nine possible tense ideas in Greek. Of these nine possibilities, two have no distinct forms (note that future durative action may be occasionally represented by the use of the future tense and that present point action may be indicated by the present tense). One of these, the future perfect, is virtually extinct in the New Testament and is therefore omitted from this study. There remain six tenses to be learned. Of these six, the pluperfect is used in the New Testament only rarely.

Note that the six tenses that you must learn can be readily divided into two categories: secondary tenses (imperfect, aorist and pluperfect); primary tenses (present, perfect, and future).

INDICATIVE MOOD

	SECONDARY	PRIMARY	
	PAST	PRESENT	FUTURE
DURATIVE ___	Imperfect	Present	No distinct form
POINT •	Aorist	No distinct form	Future
COMPLETED •___ ___•	Pluperfect	Perfect	Future Perfect

§158. *Exercises.*

(1) ὁ ἁλιεὺς βέβληκε τοὺς λίθους ἐκ τοῦ πλοίου. (2) ἀκήκοα ὅτι ὁ ἀρχιερεὺς λύσει τὸ ἱερὸν ἐν τῷ τέλει. (3) τὰ γεγραμμένα ἐν τῷ βιβλίῳ τῆς ζωῆς ἐστιν ἀληθινά. (4) ἡ χεὶρ τοῦ θεοῦ ἐστιν ἐπὶ τῶν μαθητῶν. (5) οἱ ἄρχοντες ἐπίστευσαν εἰς αὐτὸν καὶ οἱ ἄλλοι ἤχθησαν πρὸς αὐτὸν ὑπ' αὐτῶν. (6) οἱ ἀπόστολοι ἐγνώκασι τὸν κύριον ἐν τῇ σαρκὶ, ἀλλὰ γνώσομαι ἐν τῷ βάθει τῆς καρδίας μου. (7) ἔγνωκε τὸ θέλημα τοῦ θεοῦ καὶ ἄξει τοὺς ἀδελφοὺς εἰς αὐτό. (8) ἐν ἐκείνῃ τῇ νυκτὶ βλέψομεν τὸν ἄγγελον τοῦ κυρίου. (9) ὁ λέγων ὅτι γινώσκει τὸν κύριον μένων ἐν σκοτίᾳ ἐστὶν ψεύστης. (10) ἔλεγον ταῦτα τοῖς πορευομένοις εἰς τὸ ἱερόν.

Lesson 27
Subjunctive Mood

§159. *Vocabulary.*
δικαιοσύνη, ἡ, *righteousness*
ἐάν, *if* (with moods other than the indicative)
εἰ, *if, whether*
θυγάτηρ, θυγατρός, ἡ, *daughter*
ἵνα, *in order that* (used with subjunctive)
ἰχθύς, ἰχθύος, ὁ, *fish*
λύω, 1st person, present, active, subjunctive of λύω, §15
μαρτυρία, ἡ, *witness*
πίστις, πίστεως, ἡ, *faith*
πνεῦμα, πνεύματος, τό, *spirit*
ῥῆμα, ῥήματος, τό, *word*
σκότος, σκότους, τό, *darkness*
στόμα, στόματος, τό, *mouth*
ὦ, 1st person, present, subjunctive of εἰμί, §75

§160. *Mood* [review §18.1]. Mood is that quality of the verb that indicates the relationship of the assertion being made to reality from the vantage point of the perception of the speaker. Up to this point all of the tenses that have been studied are instances of the *indicative* mood, i.e., the mood that indicates that the action being spoken about is really occurring (from the point of view of the speaker). There are four moods in Koine Greek. In addition to the indicative, there are subjunctive, imperative and optative moods. These three are sometimes referred to as *potential* moods since all of them refer to action that is *potential*, but action that has not been *actualized* from the point of view of the speaker.

§160.1 *Subjunctive mood.* This mood describes action as potential, often under certain conditions. Example: *If the child were to die, I will come home.* Except for a few instances where the subjunctive occurs in the perfect, all instances of it in the New Testament are in the present or the aorist. The subjunctive may be translated in one of four ways: hortatory, imperative, rhetorical, or final.

§160.2. *Imperative mood*. This mood describes action that is in the form of a command, request, exhortation, or prohibition. The imperative in the New Testament occurs in the second and third person forms. This third person form has no exact English translation. We can approximate the thrust of the expression by using the verb *let*: *Let him (her, it, them) learn Greek!*

§160.3. *Optative mood*. The optative mood is used to describe action that is not taking place but action that *is subjectively possible from the vantage point of the speaker*. The optative is one step further removed from reality than the subjunctive. In contradistinction to the subjunctive mood (the mood of probability), the optative is sometimes referred to as the mood of *possibility*. Example: *Oh, that the student would learn Greek!*

§161. *Forms of the Subjunctive.*[1]

§161.1. *Present active subjunctive.*

	SINGULAR	PLURAL
1st per	λύω	λύωμεν
2nd per	λύῃς	λύητε
3rd per	λύῃ	λύωσι (ν)

§161.2. *Present middle/passive subjunctive.*

	SINGULAR	PLURAL
1st per	λύωμαι	λυώμεθα
2nd per	λύῃ	λύησθε
3rd per	λύηται	λύωνται

§161.3. *First aorist active subjunctive*[2].

	SINGULAR	PLURAL
1st per	λύσω	λύσωμεν
2nd per	λύσῃς	λύσητε
3rd per	λύσῃ	λύσωσι (ν)

§161.4. *First aorist middle subjunctive.*

---

[1]No English translation for the subjunctive forms is given because any such translation depends upon the context, i.e., the tense of the main verb.

[2]Notice that there is no augment in the aorist forms of the subjunctive. This is because there is no time significance for any verb in Greek *except in* the indicative mood.

	SINGULAR	PLURAL
1st per	λύσωμαι	λυσώμεθα
2nd per	λύσῃ	λύσησθε
3rd pcr	λύσηται	λύσωνται

§161.5. *Second aorist active subjunctive.*

	SINGULAR	PLURAL
1st per	λάβω	λάβωμεν
2nd per	λάβῃς	λάβητε
3rd per	λάβῃ	λάβωσι (ν)

§161.6. *Second aorist middle subjunctive.*

	SINGULAR	PLURAL
1st per	λάβωμαι	λαβώμεθα
2nd per	λάβῃ	λάβησθε
3rd per	λάβηται	λάβωνται

§161.7. *First aorist passive subjunctive.*

	SINGULAR	PLURAL
1st per	λυθῶ	λυθῶμεν
2nd per	λυθῆς	λυθῆτε
3rd per	λυθῇ	λυθῶσι (ν)

§161.8. *Second aorist passive subjunctive.*

	SINGULAR	PLURAL
1st per	γραφῶ	γραφῶμεν
2nd per	γραφῆς	γραφῆτε
3rd per	γραφῇ	γραφῶσι (ν)

§161.9. *Present subjunctive of* εἰμί.

	SINGULAR	PLURAL
1st per	ὦ	ὦμεν
2nd per	ᾖς	ἦτε
3rd per	ᾖ	ὦσι (ν)

§162. *The Function of the Subjunctive Mood.*

§162.1 *Tense in the subjunctive.* In the indicative mood, tense indicates time of action and kind of action. Outside of the indicative mood tense indicates only kind of action, i.e., in the subjunctive mood tense describes the kind of action which is occurring and does not indicate anything about the time of the action. As in the case of the participle, in the subjunctive mood, the time of action is relative to that of the main verb.

The present subjunctive indicates action that is linear or durative in nature while the aorist subjunctive indicates action that is completed or point action.

§162.2. *Uses of the subjunctive.*

§162.2.1. *Hortatory subjunctive.* The New Testament contains many examples of these "exhortations." Often these are expressed in the first person plural of the subjunctive. The exhortation is an invitation extended to others to join the speaker in a particular action. ἀγαπητοί, ἀγαπῶμεν ἀλλήλους = *beloved, let us love one another* (1 John 4:7).

§162.2.2. *Imperative subjunctive.* The subjunctive may be used to express a prohibition when the speaker wishes to prohibit the <u>beginning</u> of an action. This prohibitive subjunctive requires the second person aorist (never the present): μή νομίσητε = *don't begin to think* (Matthew 5:17).

The subjunctive is also used with the double negative οὐ μή to indicate emphatic negation. Because this construction employs the double negative the resulting translation is much stronger than that assigned to the simple οὐ with the indicative mood. οὐ μὴ φάγω = *I shall by no means eat.*

§162.2.3. *Rhetorical subjunctive.* This usage of the subjunctive the speaker expresses a question which may be a mere rhetorical device, in which case no answer at all is expected. On the other hand, if an answer is anticipated, it will be given in the imperative mood. τί εἴπω ὑμῖν = *what shall I say to you?*

§162.2.4. *Final subjunctive.* The subjunctive may be utilized in a subordinate clause to indicate purpose. This construction usually involves the use of ἵνα. ἔρχομαι ἵνα λύσω τοὺς δούλους = *I come in order that I may loose the slaves.*

§163. *Conditional Sentences.* There are four classes of conditional sentences in Greek. A conditional sentence consists of (1) a conjunction (such as εἰ or ἐάν); (2) an <u>if</u> clause (called the protasis); (3) a <u>result</u> clause (called the apodosis). The mood used determines the class of the condition.

CLASS	CHARACTER	PROTASIS	APODOSIS
1st	affirms reality	εἰ = indicative	any mood
2nd	contrary to fact	εἰ = indicative	ἄν = indicative
3rd	probable future	ἐάν = subjunctive	any mood
4th	possible future	εἰ = optative	ἄν = optative

§163.1. *First class conditional sentences.* The first class conditional sentence affirms the reality of the condition and is therefore expressed with the indicative mood (the indicative mood is the mood of reality) in the protasis and almost any mood in the apodosis. εἰ ἀπόστολόι ἐσμεν τοῦ χριστοῦ γνώσεται ἡμᾶς = *if (since) we are apostles of Christ he will know us.*

§163.2. *Second class conditional sentences.* The second class conditional sentence is a *contrary to fact* statement. Even though a contrary to fact sentence is expressed in *English* in the subjunctive, it is expressed in *Greek* with a secondary tense of the indicative. Example: εἰ ἔσχες πίστιν, ἐπίστευσας ἂν ταῦτα = *if you had faith, you would believe these things.*

§163.3. *Third class conditional sentences.* The third class conditional sentence is a *probable future* statement. It describes a condition that does not now exist but which will *probably* take place in the future. It is expressed with ἐάν plus the subjunctive in the protasis and any form needed in the apodosis. Example: ἐάν τις ἀγαπᾷ τὸν κόσμον, οὐκ ἔστιν ἡ ἀγάπη τοῦ πατρὸς ἐν αὐτῷ = *if anyone loves the world, the love of the father is not in him* (1 John 2:15).

§163.4. *Fourth class conditional sentences.* The fourth class conditional sentence is the more remote *possible future* condition. While the third class sentence is one that expresses a condition not yet fulfilled, but probable, you can see that the fourth class condition is much less likely of being actualized. The fourth class conditional sentence describes a condition that has like likelihood of becoming *reality*. There is no complete example of the fourth class conditional sentence in the New Testament.

§164. *Negative with the Subjunctive.* All moods other than the indicative require the negative particle μή. It is also used with participles and infinitives.

§165. *Exercises*:
(1) ὁ κύριος λέγει τὰ ῥήματα τῆς ζωῆς τοῖς μαθηταῖς αὐτοῦ. (2) λαμβάνω τὸν λόγον τοῦ χριστοῦ ἵνα γινώσκω τὸ θέλημα τοῦ θεοῦ. (3) τὸ πνεῦμα τοῦ θεοῦ ἐστὶν ἡ μαρτυρία τῆς ἀγάπης αὐτοῦ. (4) ἐὰν εἰσέλθητε εἰς τὸ ἱερόν, ὁ ἱερεὺς διδάξει ὑμῖν ῥήμασι τῆς ζωῆς. (5) λάβωμεν τοὺς ἀποστόλους εἰς τὸν οἶκον ἡμῶν. (6) ὁ ἀπόστολος διδάσκει ὅτι ὁ ἔχων τὸν υἱὸν ἔχει τὴν ζωήν. (7) ἡ δικαιοσύνη τοῦ θεοῦ ἐδιδάσκετο ὑπὸ τῶν μαθητῶν τοῦ κυρίου. (8) ὁ υἱὸς τοῦ θεοῦ ἦλθεν ἐν τῷ κόσμῳ ἵνα σώσῃ ἁμαρτωλοὺς ἀπὸ τῶν ἁμαρτιῶν αὐτῶν. (9) ταῦτα γράφω ὑμῖν ἵνα μὴ ἁμάρτητε. (10) οἱ μὴ πιστεύοντες τὸ εὐαγγέλιον οὐ μὴ σωθῶσιν ἐν τῇ ἐσχάτῃ τῇ ἡμέρᾳ.

Lesson 28
Imperative Mood

§166. *Vocabulary*.

αἰτέω, αἰτήσω, ἤτησα, *I ask, I shall ask, I asked*

ἀληθῶς, *truly*

ἀναγγέλλω, ἀναγγελῶ, ἀνήγγειλα, *I announce, I shall announce, I announced*

γῆ, ἡ, *earth*

δικαιόω, δικαιώσω, ἐδικαίωσα, *I justify, I shall justify, I justified*

ἐγγίζω, ἐγγίσω, ἤγγισα, *I come near, I shall come near, I came near*

ἥλιος, ὁ, *sun*

παιδίον, τό, *child*

ποῦ, *where* (interrogative)

σάββατον, τό, *sabbath*

φανερόω, φανερώσω, ἐφανέρωσα, *I make manifest, I shall make manifest, I made manifest*

§167. *The Imperative Mood*. In the New Testament the imperative mood is found in three tenses: present, aorist, and perfect. The perfect tense occurs so rarely that only the present and aorist forms are presented here. The imperative is found only in the second and third persons. Specifically, it is used in the giving of commands where the speaker seeks to exercise his will over that of the hearer. Neither the present nor the aorist imperative has any reference to time (and hence neither is augmented). The present tense refers to action that continues; the aorist refers to simple or point action.

§168. *Uses of the Imperative Mood*.

§168.1. *Positive commands*. The use of the imperative in issuing positive commands is sometimes called the *cohortative imperative*. This construction uses either the present or the aorist imperative. Example: λῦε τὸ ἱερόν = *destroy the temple*. λυέτω τὸ ἱερόν = *let him destroy the temple*.

§168.2. *Negative commands*. This construction requires the use of the present imperative together with the negative particle μή. This use of the imperative prohibits the continuation of an action which is already begun; therefore, it is frequently translated "stop . . ." Example: μὴ λῦε τὸ ἱερόν = *stop destroying the temple* (Review §162.2.2. Remember the second person aorist *subjunctive* is used to prohibit the <u>beginning</u> of an action.)

§168.3. *Permissive imperative*. This usage of the imperative requires the *third* person form and the use of the English auxiliary verb *let* to translate its meaning into English. Example: ὁ ἔχων ὦτα ἀκουέτω = *the one having ears, let him hear* (Matthew 11:15).

§169. *Forms of the Imperative.*

§169.1. *Present active imperative.*

	SINGULAR	PLURAL
2nd per	λῦε, *you loose*	λύετε, *you loose*
3rd per	λυέτω, *let him loose*	λυέτωσαν, *let them loose*

§169.2. *Present middle/passive imperative.*

	SINGULAR	PLURAL
2nd per	λύου, *you loose for yourself*	λύεσθε, *you loose for yourselves*
3rd per	λυέσθω, *let him loose for himself*	λυέσθωσαν, *let them loose for themselves*

§169.3. *First aorist active imperative.*

	SINGULAR	PLURAL
2nd per	λῦσον, *you loose*	λύσατε, *you loose*
3rd per	λυσάτω, *let him loose*	λυσάτωσαν, *let them loose*

§169.4. *First aorist middle imperative.*

	SINGULAR	PLURAL
2nd per	λῦσαι, *you loose yourself*	λύσασθε, *you loose yourselves*
3rd per	λυσάσθω, *let him loose himself*	λυσάσθωσαν, *let them loose themselves*

§169.5. *First aorist passive imperative.*

	SINGULAR	PLURAL
2nd per	λύθητι, *you be loosed*	λύθητε, *you be loosed*
3rd per	λυθήτω, *let him be loosed*	λυθήτωσαν, *let them be loosed*

§169.6. *Second aorist active imperative.*

	SINGULAR	PLURAL
2nd per	λάβε, *you take*	λάβετε, *you take*

3rd per   λαβέτω, *let him take*   λαβέτωσαν, *let them take*

§169.7. *Second aorist middle imperative.*

	SINGULAR	PLURAL
2nd per	λαβοῦ, *you take for yourself*	λάβεσθε, *you take for yourself*
3rd per	λαβέσθω, *let him take for himself*	λαβέσθωσαν, *let them take for themselves*

§169.8. *Second aorist passive imperative.*

	SINGULAR	PLURAL
2nd per	λάβηθι, *you be taken*	λάβητε, *you be taken*
3rd per	λαβήτω, *let him be taken*	λαβήτωσαν, *let them be taken*

§169.9. *Present infinitive of εἰμί.*

	SINGULAR	PLURAL
2nd per	ἴσθι, *you be*	ἔστε, *you be*
3rd per	ἔστω, *let him be*	ἔστωσαν, *let them be*

§170. *Exercises.*

(1) πᾶς ὁ πιστεύων εἰς ἐμὲ οὐ μὴ ἀποθάνῃ. (2) ὁ ἔχων τὸ πνεῦμα ἀκουσάτω τοὺς λόγους τοῦ ἱερέως. (3) τὰ παιδία ἀληθῶς φανερώσει τὴν ἀγάπην τοῦ θεοῦ. (4) οἱ ἀπόστολοι ἀπήγγειλαν τὸ εὐαγγέλιον ἐν πάσῃ τῇ γῇ ὅτι ἀγαπῶσι τὸν κύριον. (5) ὁ λαβὼν τοὺς διωκομένους ὑπὸ τῶν πονηρῶν σωθήσεται ἐν τῇ ἐσχάτῃ ἡμέρᾳ. (6) λυσάτω τὸν δοῦλον ἵνα ἀκούσῃ τοὺς λόγους τοῦ χριστοῦ. (7) ἡ βασιλεία τοῦ θεοῦ ἐγγίζει ὅτι ὁ Ἰησοῦς διδάσκει περὶ αὐτήν. (8) ἡ χάρις τοῦ κυρίου Ἰησοῦ χριστοῦ δικαιοῖ ἡμᾶς καὶ καθαρίζει ἡμᾶς ἀπὸ τῶν ἁμαρτιῶν ἡμῶν. (9) ἁγίασατωσαν τὸ ἱερὸν τοῦ θεοῦ. (10) πᾶν τὸ σῶμά ἐστιν ἱερὸν θεῷ.

Lesson 29
Infinitives

§171. *Vocabulary.*
ἅγιος, ἁγία, ἅγιον, *holy*
εὐαγγελίζομαι, _____, εὐηγγέλισα (D), *I preach the gospel.* _____, *I preached the gospel*
ἐχθρός, ὁ, *enemy*
θέλω, θελήσω, θέλησα,[1] *I wish, I shall wish, I wished*
καλῶς, *well*
πάντοτε, *always*
πειράζω, πειράσω, _____, *I tempt, I will tempt,* _____
πρίν, *before*
χρεία, ἡ, *need*
χρόνος, ὁ, *time*

§172. *Grammatical Study.* The infinitive is a hybrid form—part noun and part verb (see §90.2). Its usage in Greek closely parallels its usage in English. As a verb, it has neither person nor number; as noun it has neither gender nor case.

As with participles, tense does not indicate *time* of action; therefore, as a verb, its aorist form has no augment. The infinitive occurs in three tenses: present, aorist, and perfect. The present tense of the infinitive indicates continuous action; the aorist infinitive indicates point action; the perfect infinitive indicates completed action. Hence, as with the imperative and subjunctive moods, no distinction is made in translation between the present and the aorist infinitive.

§173. *Uses of the Infinitive.*

§173.1. *As a verb.* When the infinitive functions like a verb it may take an object and may be modified by adverbs.

---

[1]The imperfect of θέλω is ἤθελον.

§173.1.1. *Purpose*. The infinitive is often used to express the specific purpose of the main verb. Example: οὐ ἦλθον λῦσαι τοὺς δούλους = *I did not come to loose the slaves*.

§173.1.2. *Time*. It is common to find temporal ideas expressed in Greek with the infinitive. Example: ἐλεύσομαι πρὶν² λυθῆναι τὸ ἱερόν = *I will come before the temple is destroyed*. *"After" may be expressed with* μετὰ τό + *the infinitive*. Example: εἶπεν ταῦτα αὐτοῖς μετὰ τὸ παθεῖν αὐτόν = *he said these things to them after his suffering*. *"While" may be expressed with* ἐν τῷ + *the infinitive*. Example: ἡτοίμαζον τὸν ἱερὸν ἐν τῷ διδάσκειν αυτόν = *they were preparing the temple while he was teaching*.

§173.2. *As a noun*. Actually, the infinitive may be used as a noun in any of the ways "real" nouns are used.

§173.2.1. *Subject of a verb*. Example: δεῖ τὸν υἱὸν τοῦ ἀνθρώπου πολλὰ παθεῖν = *it is necessary for the Son of Man to suffer many things* (Luke 9:22).

§173.2.2. *Predicate nominative*. In this usage the infinitive occurs without the definite article. Example: οὐδεὶς δύναται ἐλθεῖν πρός με = *no one is able to come to me* (John 6:44).

§173.2.3. *Object*. The infinitive may serve to limit the action of the main verb (direct object); in this usage the infinitive occurs *without* the article. Example: ὁ Ἰησοῦς ἤρξατο διδάσκειν τὸν νόμον = *Jesus began to teach the law*.

§174. *Forms of the Infinitive*.

	PRESENT INFINITIVE	
ACTIVE	MIDDLE	PASSIVE
λύειν	λύεσθαι	λύεσθαι
to loose	*to loose oneself*	*to be loosed*
	FUTURE INFINITIVE	
ACTIVE	MIDDLE	PASSIVE
λύσειν	λύσεσθαι	λυθήσεσθαι
to loose	*to loose oneself*	*to be loosed*
	FIRST AORIST INFINITIVE	
ACTIVE	MIDDLE	PASSIVE
λῦσαι	λύσασθαι	λυθῆναι
to loose	*to loose oneself*	*to be loosed*
	SECOND AORIST INFINITIVE	
ACTIVE	MIDDLE	PASSIVE

---

²"Before" may be expressed also with πρὸ τοῦ + the infinitive.

λαβεῖν   λαβέσθαι   λαβῆναι
to take   *to take oneself*   *to be taken*

PERFECT INFINITIVE

ACTIVE   MIDDLE   PASSIVE
λελυκέναι   λελύσθαι   λελύσθαι
to have loosed   *to have loosed oneself*   *to have been loosed*

§175. *Exercises.*

(1) οὐ θέλετε ἐλθεῖν πρός με. (2) οὐ γάρ ἐστιν καλὸν λαβεῖν τὸν ἄρτον τῶν ἁμαρτωλῶν. (3) τὸ πνεῦμα τὸ ἅγιον ἐλαμβάνετο ὑπὸ τῶν ἀποστόλων τοῦ χριστοῦ. (4) εἰ ἀγαπῶμεν τὸν κύριον, τηρῶμεν τὰς ἐντολὰς αὐτοῦ. (5) ὁ ἐχθρὸς τοῦ κυρίου οὐ λαλήσει ταῦτα τοῖς ἀδελφοῖς. (6) οἱ ἄνθρωποι ἄρχονται συνέρχεσθαι ἵνα ὁ θεὸς δοξασθῇ δι᾽ αὐτῶν. (7) τὸ εὐαγγέλιον τοῦ χριστοῦ εὐαγγελισθήσεται ἐν παντὶ τῷ κόσμῳ πρὶν πληροῦν τὸ τέλος τοῦ χρόνου. (8) ὁ μαθητὴς ἄρχεται διδάσκειν τὸ τέκνον τὴν ἀλήθειαν περὶ τῆς βασιλείας τοῦ θεοῦ. (9) ἔβλεψε τὴν χεῖρα τοῦ θεοῦ μετὰ τὸ παθεῖν αὐτόν. (10) λέγει ἀγαθοὺς λόγους ἵνα ἔχωσιν ἀγάπην ἐν ταῖς καρδίαις αὐτῶν.

Lesson 30

Pronouns

§176. *Vocabulary.*

ἀλλήλων, *one another* (reciprocal pronoun)

ἐμαυτοῦ, ἐμαυτῆς, *of myself* (reflexive pronoun)

ἐμός, ἐμή, ἐμόν, *my* (possessive pronoun)

ὅς, ἥ, ὅ, *who, which* (relative pronoun)

ὅστις, ἥτις, ὅτι, *whoever* (indefinite relative pronoun)

οὐδείς, οὐδεμία, οὐδέν, *no one* (negative pronoun)

τις, τις, τι, *somebody* (indefinite pronoun)

τίς, τίς, τί, *who, which* (interrogative pronoun)

τοιοῦτος, τοιαύτη, τοιοῦτο, *such* (correlative demonstrative pronoun)

§177. *Pronouns.* There are twelve distinct classes of pronouns in Greek. You have already studied the personal pronouns (§70.1), the demonstrative pronouns (§70.2), and the intensive pronoun αὐτός (§73). The nine remaining varieties of pronouns are treated in this lesson.

§177.1. *Possessive pronouns.* Sometimes called possessive adjectives, these pronouns agree in gender, case and number with the nouns they modify (just like adjectives). They are found in the attributive position. Examples: ὁ ἐμὸς οἶκος = *my house;* οἱ σοὶ οἶκοι = *your* (sing) *houses. Note that there are no third person forms of these possessive pronouns.*

FIRST PERSON SINGULAR

CASE	SINGULAR			PLURAL		
	MASCULINE	FEMININE	NEUTER	MASCULINE	FEMININE	NEUTER
Nom	ἐμός	ἐμή	ἐμόν	ἐμοί	ἐμαί	ἐμά
Gen	ἐμοῦ	ἐμῆς	ἐμοῦ	ἐμῶν	ἐμῶν	ἐμῶν
Abl	ἐμοῦ	ἐμῆς	ἐμοῦ	ἐμῶν	ἐμῶν	ἐμῶν
Dat	ἐμῷ	ἐμῇ	ἐμῷ	ἐμοῖς	ἐμαῖς	ἐμοῖς
Loc	ἐμῷ	ἐμῇ	ἐμω	ἐμοῖς	ἐμαῖς	ἐμοῖς

| Inst | ἐμῷ | ἐμῇ | ἐμῷ | ἐμοῖς | ἐμαῖς | ἐμοῖς |
| Acc | ἐμόν | ἐμήν | ἐμόν | ἐμούς | ἐμάς | ἐμά |

SECOND PERSON SINGULAR

	SINGULAR			PLURAL		
CASE	MASCULINE	FEMININE	NEUTER	MASCULINE	FEMININE	NEUTER
Nom	σός	σή	σόν	σοί	σαί	σά
Gen	σοῦ	σῆς	σοῦ	σῶν	σῶν	σῶν
Abl	σοῦ	σῆς	σοῦ	σῶν	σῶν	σῶν
Dat	σῷ	σῇ	σῷ	σοῖς	σαῖς	σοῖς
Loc	σῷ	σῇ	σῷ	σοῖς	σαῖς	σοῖς
Inst	σῷ	σῇ	σῷ	σοῖς	σαῖς	σοῖς
Acc	σόν	σήν	σόν	σούς	σάς	σά

FIRST PERSON PLURAL

	SINGULAR			PLURAL		
CASE	MASCULINE	FEMININE	NEUTER	MASCULINE	FEMININE	NEUTER
Nom	ἡμέτερος	ἡμετέρα	ἡμέτερον	ἡμέτεροι	ἡμέτεραι	ἡμέτερα
Gen	ἡμετέρου	ἡμετέρας	ἡμετέρου	ἡμετέρων	ἡμετέρων	ἡμετέρων
Abl	ἡμετέρου	ἡμετέρας	ἡμετέρου	ἡμετέρων	ἡμετέρων	ἡμετέρων
Dat	ἡμετέρῳ	ἡμετέρα	ἡμετέρῳ	ἡμετέροις	ἡμετέραις	ἡμετέροις
Loc	ἡμετέρῳ	ἡμετέρα	ἡμετέρῳ	ἡμετέροις	ἡμετέραις	ἡμετέροις
Inst	ἡμετέρῳ	ἡμετέρα	ἡμετέρῳ	ἡμετέροις	ἡμετέραις	ἡμετέροις
Acc	ἡμέτερον	ἡμετέραν	ἡμέτερον	ἡμετέρους	ἡμετέρας	ἡμέτερα

SECOND PERSON PLURAL

	SINGULAR			PLURAL		
CASE	MASCULINE	FEMININE	NEUTER	MASCULINE	FEMININE	NEUTER
Nom	ὑμέτερος	ὑμετέρα	ὑμέτερον	ὑμέτεροι	ὑμέτεραι	ὑμέτερα
Gen	ὑμετέρου	ὑμετέρας	ὑμετέρου	ὑμετέρων	ὑμετέρων	ὑμετέρων
Abl	ὑμετέρου	ὑμετέρας	ὑμετέρου	ὑμετέρων	ὑμετέρων	ὑμετέρων
Dat	ὑμετέρῳ	ὑμετέρα	ὑμετέρῳ	ὑμετέροις	ὑμετέραις	ὑμετέροις
Loc	ὑμετέρῳ	ὑμετέρα	ὑμετέρῳ	ὑμετέροις	ὑμετέραις	ὑμετέροις
Inst	ὑμετέρῳ	ὑμετέρα	ὑμετέρῳ	ὑμετέροις	ὑμετέραις	ὑμετέροις
Acc	ὑμέτερον	ὑμετέραν	ὑμέτερον	ὑμετέρους	ὑμετέρας	ὑμέτερα

§177.2. *Reflexive pronouns* [review §45.3]. The reflexive pronouns "reflect" the action of the verb back upon the subject. The reflexive pronouns are formed by combining the personal pronouns with the oblique cases (§30) of αὐτός (for the *nominative* reflexive see §73).

FIRST PERSON

	SINGULAR - MYSELF			PLURAL - OURSELVES		
CASE	MASCULINE	FEMININE	NEUTER	MASCULINE	FEMININE	NEUTER
Gen	ἐμαυτοῦ	ἐμαυτῆς	-	ἑαυτῶν	ἑαυτῶν	-

Abl	ἐμαυτοῦ	ἐμαυτῆς	-	ἑαυτῶν	ἑαυτῶν	-
Dat	ἐμαυτῷ	ἐμαυτῇ	-	ἑαυτοῖς	ἑαυταῖς	-
Loc	ἐμαυτῷ	ἐμαυτῇ	-	ἑαυτοῖς	ἑαυταῖς	-
Inst	ἐμαυτῷ	ἐμαυτῇ	-	ἑαυτοῖς	ἑαυταῖς	-
Acc	ἐμαυτόν	ἐμαυτήν	-	ἑαυτούς	ἑαυτάς	-

SECOND PERSON

	SINGULAR - YOURSELF			**PLURAL - YOURSELVES**		
CASE	MASCULINE	FEMININE	NEUTER	MASCULINE	FEMININE	NEUTER
Gen	σεαυτοῦ	σεαυτῆς	-	ἑαυτῶν	ἑαυτῶν	-
Abl	σεαυτοῦ	σεαυτῆς	-	ἑαυτῶν	ἑαυτῶν	-
Dat	σεαυτῷ	σεαυτῇ	-	ἑαυτοῖς	ἑαυταῖς	-
Loc	σεαυτῷ	σεαυτῇ	-	ἑαυτοῖς	ἑαυταῖς	-
Inst	σεαυτῷ	σεαυτῇ	-	ἑαυτοῖς	ἑαυταῖς	-
Acc	σεαυτόν	σεαυτήν	-	ἑαυτούς	ἑαυτάς	-

THIRD PERSON

	SINGULAR - HIMSELF			**PLURAL - THEMSELVES**		
CASE	MASCULINE	FEMININE	NEUTER	MASCULINE	FEMININE	NEUTER
Gen	ἑαυτοῦ	ἑαυτῆς	ἑαυτοῦ	ἑαυτῶν	ἑαυτῶν	ἑαυτῶν
Abl	ἑαυτοῦ	ἑαυτῆς	ἑαυτοῦ	ἑαυτῶν	ἑαυτῶν	ἑαυτῶν
Dat	ἑαυτῷ	ἑαυτῇ	ἑαυτῷ	ἑαυτοῖς	ἑαυταῖς	ἑαυτοῖς
Loc	ἑαυτῷ	ἑαυτῇ	ἑαυτῷ	ἑαυτοῖς	ἑαυταῖς	ἑαυτοῖς
Inst	ἑαυτῷ	ἑαυτῇ	ἑαυτῷ	ἑαυτοῖς	ἑαυταῖς	ἑαυτοῖς
Acc	ἑαυτόν	ἑαυτήν	ἑαυτό	ἑαυτούς	ἑαυτάς	ἑαυτά

There are no distinct forms for the plural, i.e., first, second, third person plural forms are the same.

§177.3. *Interrogative pronouns*[1]. The interrogative pronouns ask the question *who, which* or *what*[2]. They are used to introduce a direct question. Example: τί ἀκού-εις = *what are you hearing?*

	SINGULAR			**PLURAL**		
CASE	MASCULINE	FEMININE	NEUTER	MASCULINE	FEMININE	NEUTER
Nom	τίς	τίς	τί	τίνες	τίνες	τίνα
Gen	τίνος	τίνος	τίνος	τίνων	τίνων	τίνων
Abl	τίνος	τίνος	τίνος	τίνων	τίνων	τίνων
Dat	τίνι	τίνι	τίνι	τίσι (ν)	τίσι (ν)	τίσι (ν)

---

[1] Other interrogative pronouns found in the New Testament include: ποῖος, ποία, ποῖον, the qualitative interrogative pronoun usually translated *of what type?* πηλίκος, πηλίκη, πηλίκον, the quantitative interrogative pronoun is usually translated *how great?*

[2] The accusative neuter singular τί may be used adverbially. In these cases it should be translated *why*.

Loc	τίνι	τίνι	τίνι	τίσι (ν)	τίσι (ν)	τίσι (ν)
Inst	τίνι	τίνι	τίνι	τίσι (ν)	τίσι (ν)	τίσι (ν)
Acc	τίνα	τίνα	τί	τίνας	τίνας	τίνα

Note that all three genders follow the third declension endings (§143) and that the masculine and feminine forms are the same.

§177.4. *Indefinite pronouns*. The indefinite pronouns are formed exactly like the interrogative pronouns except the indefinite pronouns have no accent (see §71.1, enclitics), unless special rules for accenting enclitics apply.

The indefinite pronoun is translated *somebody, something* or *a certain one*.

CASE	SINGULAR			PLURAL		
	MASCULINE	FEMININE	NEUTER	MASCULINE	FEMININE	NEUTER
Nom	τις	τις	τι	τινες	τινες	τινα
Gen	τινος	τινος	τινος	τινων	τινων	τινων
Abl	τινος	τινος	τινος	τινων	τινων	τινων
Dat	τινι	τινι	τινι	τιοι (ν)	τιοι (ν)	τιοι (ν)
Loc	τινι	τινι	τινι	τιοι (ν)	τιοι (ν)	τιοι (ν)
Inst	τινι	τινι	τινι	τιοι (ν)	τιοι (ν)	τιοι (ν)
Acc	τινα	τινα	τι	τινας	τινας	τινα

§177.5. *Relative pronouns*. These forms have the same ending as the definite article (minus the τ) except in the masculine singular (review §60). Note that all forms are accented and each takes a rough breathing.

CASE	SINGULAR			PLURAL		
	MASCULINE	FEMININE	NEUTER	MASCULINE	FEMININE	NEUTER
Nom	ὅς	ἥ	ὅ	οἵ	αἵ	ἅ
Gen	οὗ	ἧς	οὗ	ὧν	ὧν	ὧν
Abl	οὗ	ἧς	οὗ	ὧν	ὧν	ὧν
Dat	ᾧ	ᾗ	ᾧ	οἷς	αἷς	οἷς
Loc	ᾧ	ᾗ	ᾧ	οἷς	αἷς	οἷς
Inst	ᾧ	ᾗ	ᾧ	οἷς	αἷς	οἷς
Acc	ὅν	ἥν	ὅ	οὕς	ἅς	ἅ

When relative pronouns refer to people, they are translated in the nominative as *who, that*; in the genitive, *of whom*; in the dative *to* or *for whom*; in the accusative *to whom*. Note that the translation into English is the same whether the form occurs in Greek in the singular or in the plural.

Relative pronouns must agree with their antecedent[3] in number and gender. *The case for the relative pronoun is determined by its use in the clause in which it occurs.*

---

[3]Frequently the antecedent is not expressed, but it is nonetheless understood.

Examples: (1) ὁ δοῦλος <u>ὃς</u> διδάσκει ἡμᾶς ἐστὶν ἀγαθός = *the slave <u>who</u> is teaching us is good.* Also οἱ δοῦλοι <u>οἳ</u> διδάσκουσι ἡμᾶς εἰσὶ ἀγαθοί = *the slaves <u>who</u> are teaching us are good.* (2) ὁ δοῦλος <u>ὃν</u> ἔβλεψας εἰσῆλθεν εἰς τὸ ἱερόν = *the slave <u>whom</u> you saw went into the temple.*

In example (1) the relative pronoun ὅς or οἵ both occur in the masculine gender and nominative case. This is so because the antecedent to which each refers is the term ὁ δοῦλος—a masculine noun. In the first sentence, the ὅς is singular; in the second, it is plural. This is so because ὁ δοῦλος is singular in the first instance and plural in the second.

In the second example, the relative pronoun ὅν occurs in the accusative case because, while it has the same masculine singular antecedent, its function in its own clause is to serve as the direct object of the verb ἔβλεψας. It therefore occurs in the accusative masculine singular form.

§177.6. *Indefinite relative pronouns.* This pronoun gets its name from the fact that it is formed by combining the relative ὅς with the definite pronoun τίς. It appears only in the nominative, singular and plural, all genders.

	SINGULAR			**PLURAL**		
CASE	MASCULINE	FEMININE	NEUTER	MASCULINE	FEMININE	NEUTER
Nom	ὅστις	ἥτις	ὅτι	οἵτινες	αἵτινες	ἅτινα

The usual translation is *who, whoever* or *who is of such nature.* The indefinite relative pronoun carries the idea of the *qualitative character* of the antecedent. Example: προσέχετε ἀπὸ τῶν ψευδοπροφητῶν, οἵτινες ἔρχονται πρὸς ὑμᾶς ἐν ἐνδύμασιν προβάτων = *beware of false prophets, who come to you in sheep's clothing* (Matthew 7:15).

§177.7. *Negative pronouns.* The negative pronoun is formed by adding the numeral "one" εἷς, μία, ἕν to the negative particle οὐδέ[4]. The usual translation is *no one.* Note that the negative pronoun is found only in the singular. Example: <u>οὐδ-εὶς</u> ἔρχεται πρὸς τὸν πατέρα εἰ μὴ δι' ἐμοῦ = <u>*no one*</u> *comes to the father if not through me* (John 14:6).

	SINGULAR		
CASE	MASCULINE	FEMININE	NEUTER
Nom	οὐδείς	οὐδεμία	οὐδέν
Gen	οὐδενός	οὐδεμιᾶς	οὐδενός
Abl	οὐδενός	οὐδεμιᾶς	οὐδενός
Dat	οὐδενί	οὐδεμιᾷ	οὐδενί
Loc	οὐδενί	οὐδεμιᾷ	οὐδενί

---

[4]The prefix changes to μη in all moods other than the indicative.

| Inst | οὐδενί | ουδεμιᾷ | οὐδενί |
| Acc | οὐδένα | οὐδεμίαν | οὐδέν |

§177.8. *Reciprocal pronouns* [review §45.3]. The reciprocal pronoun occurs only in the oblique cases of the masculine in the New Testament. It refers to an exchange between members of a plural subject. The reciprocal pronoun is formed by doubling the stem of ἄλλος with *other* (§75). Its three forms (ἀλλήλων, ἀλλήλοις, ἀλλήλους) occur in one of seven cases about 100 times in the New Testament. Example: ἀγαπῶμεν ἀλλήλους = *let us love one another*.

§177.9. *Correlative demonstrative pronouns* [review §70.2]. The correlative demonstrative pronoun is usually translated *such*. It is declined like οὖτος with the τοι prefix.

	SINGULAR			**PLURAL**		
CASE	MASCULINE	FEMININE	NEUTER	MASCULINE	FEMININE	NEUTER
Nom	τοιοῦτος	τοιαύτη	τοιοῦτο	τοιοῦτοι	τοιαῦται	τοιαῦτα
Gen	τοιούτου	τοιαύτης	τοιούτου	τοιούτων	τοιαύτων	τοιούτων
Abl	τοιούτου	τοιαύτης	τοιούτου	τοιούτων	τοιαύτων	τοιούτων
Dat	τοιούτῳ	τοιαύτη	τοιούτῳ	τοιούτοις	τοιαύταις	τοιούτοις
Loc	τοιούτῳ	τοιαύτη	τοιούτῳ	τοιούτοις	τοιαύταις	τοιούτοις
Inst	τοιούτῳ	τοιαύτη	τοιούτῳ	τοιούτοις	τοιαύταις	τοιούτοις
Acc	τοιοῦτον	τοιαύτην	τοιοῦτο	τοιούτους	τοιαύτας	τοιαῦτα

§178. *Practical Application*[5].

§178.1. *1 John 1:5-10.*

Καὶ ἔστιν αὕτη ἡ ἀγγελία ἣν ἀκηκόαμεν ἀπ᾽ αὐτοῦ καὶ ἀναγγέλλομεν ὑμῖν, ὅτι ὁ Θεὸς φῶς ἐστιν καὶ σκοτία ἐν αὐτῷ οὐκ ἔστιν οὐδεμία. 6 Ἐὰν εἴπωμεν ὅτι κοινωνίαν ἔχομεν μετ᾽ αὐτοῦ καὶ ἐν τῷ σκότει περιπατῶμεν, ψευδόμεθα καὶ οὐ ποιοῦμεν τὴν ἀλήθειαν· 7 ἐὰν δὲ ἐν τῷ φωτὶ περιπατῶμεν ὡς αὐτός ἐστιν ἐν τῷ φωτί, κοινωνίαν ἔχομεν μετ᾽ ἀλλήλων καὶ τὸ αἷμα Ἰησοῦ τοῦ υἱοῦ αὐτοῦ καθαρίζει ἡμᾶς ἀπὸ πάσης ἁμαρτίας. 8 ἐὰν εἴπωμεν ὅτι ἁμαρτίαν οὐκ ἔχομεν, ἑαυτοὺς πλανῶμεν καὶ ἡ ἀλήθεια οὐκ ἔστιν ἐν ἡμῖν. 9 ἐὰν ὁμολογῶμεν τὰς ἁμαρτίας ἡμῶν, πιστός ἐστιν καὶ δίκαιος ἵνα ἀφῇ ἡμῖν τὰς ἁμαρτίας καὶ καθαρίσῃ ἡμᾶς ἀπὸ πάσης ἀδικίας. 10 ἐὰν εἴπωμεν ὅτι οὐχ ἡμαρτήκαμεν, ψεύστην ποιοῦμεν αὐτὸν καὶ ὁ λόγος αὐτοῦ οὐκ ἔστιν ἐν ἡμῖν.

---

[5]Beginning with this lesson, the Greek to English sentences will be discontinued. Instead, you will be given a passage from 1 John to translate. Following the passage there will be some *translation aids* to assist you with vocabulary and grammar which has not previously been covered in the text.

§178.1. *Translation aids*.

1 John 1:5. ἀκηκόαμεν = 2nd perfect active indicative 1st person plural (see §151). οὐκ . . . οὐδεμία constitutes an apparent double negative in English and is better translated *there is <u>no</u> darkness <u>at all</u>*. For the location of οὐδεμία see §177.7.

1 John 1:6. μετ' = μετά where the ε elides when the following word begins with a vowel (§12). ἐάν εἴπωμεν . . . περιπατῶμεν. Both verbs are aorist active subjunctive 1st plural because the sentence is of the 3rd class (§163.3) requiring ἐάν + the subjunctive in the protasis and any mood in the apodosis.

1 John 1:8. πλανῶμεν aorist active subjunctive 1st personal plural from πλανάω, *I deceive*.

1 John 1:9. ἀφῇ . . . καθαρίσῃ = aorist active subjunctive 3rd person singular (final subjunctive, §162.2.4).

1 John 1:10. ποιοῦμεν takes two objects (both in the accusative case): ψεύστην and αὐτόν = *we make him a liar*.

Lesson 31

μι Verbs

§179. *Vocabulary.*

ἀφίημι, ἀφήσω, ἀφῆκα, *I forgive, I shall forgive, I forgave*

δίδωμι, δώσω, ἔδωκα, *I give, I shall give, I gave*

ἵστημι, στήσω, ἔστησα, *I set, I shall set, I set*

κρίμα, κρίματος τό, *judgment*

παραδίδωμι, παραδώσω, παρέδωκα, *I hand over, I shall hand over,*
    I handed over

πυρά, ἡ, *fire*

σκοτεινός, σκοτεινή, σκοτεινόν, *dark*

συνίημι, συνήσω, συνῆκα, *I perceive, I shall perceive, I perceived*

τίθημι, θήσω, ἔθηκα, *I place, I shall place, I placed*

§180. *Introduction to μι Verbs.* The Greek verb system may be divided into two subsystems: the ω conjugation (§17)[1] and the μι conjugation. These terms refer to the ending of the first person singular ending in the present active indicative form of the verb. Verbs thus ending in an ω are called *thematic* verbs because they have a variable (or *thematic*) vowel that connects the ending to the stem of the verb. Generally, the thematic vowel is ο/ε in the indicative and ω/ν in the subjunctive.

The μι conjugation is a much smaller class of verbs. These verbs *do not* have the thematic vowel and are thus called *athematic* verbs. The μι verbs differ from the ω verbs only in the present, imperfect, second aorist active and middle, and a few second perfects. In other tenses the μι verbs are conjugated just as the ω verbs. Fortunately, there are only a few μι verbs in the New Testament.[2] The most common is εἰμί (§76). The characteristic mark of the μι verbs is the reduplication of the stem in the *present* tense using an ι instead of the ε normally found in the perfect tense.

---

[1]The -ω conjugation is further sub-divided into the various classes of the so-called contract verbs (see §21, 118, 138).

[2]Of course these occur in various compounded forms, i.e., δίδωμι also occurs as παραδίδωμι.

§181. *Principal Parts of* μι *Verbs*. The principal parts of the μι verbs are as follows:

§181.1. δίδωμι.

δίδωμι, δώσω, ἔδωκα, δέδωκα, δέδομαι, ἐδόθην. The stem is δο. This stem is reduplicated in the present and imperfect tenses and appears as διδο or διδω. The future forms are entirely regular (the stem vowel lengthens before the tense sign σ is added. The first aorist form is ἔδωκα. Again, these forms are perfectly regular except that the aorist tense sign is a κ instead of the more usual σ. In the perfect active the δο lengthens to δω before the tense suffix κ (this lengthening does not occur in the perfect middle/passive since these forms have no tense sign).

§181.2. ἵστημι.

ἵστημι, στήσω, ἔστησα, ἔστηκα, ἔσταμαι, ἐστάθην. The stem is στα. This stem is reduplicated in the present tenses by the addition of an ι together with a rough breathing. The reduplicated σ is lost and the form occurs as ἵστημι—the stem lengthening to compensate for the lost stem vowel. The aorist has a regular first aorist active and passive. These are built on the unduplicated stem στα with the augment ἐ. The stem vowel lengthens to give ἐστη. There are no middle forms in the New Testament. The perefect reduplicates by affixing σε onto the stem στα. The initial σ dropped and the breathing is rough with a stem vowel that has been lengthened. Notice that the tense sign for the perfect occurs *only* in the active forms.

§181.3. τίθημι.

τίθημι, θήσω, ἔθηκα, τέθεικα, τέθειμαι, ἐτέθην. The stem is θε. This stem is reduplicated in the present and imperfect with a τ (see §153.1, #1). Only the present active singular uses the long (η) stem vowel; elsewhere it is ε (ει occurs in the imperfect 2nd and 3rd singular). The aorist active and passive forms are regular first aorist forms except that the stem vowel is lengthened from ε to η. Note that, like δίδωμι, τίθημι requires the aorist tense sign κ instead of the more common σ. The κ occurs only in the aorist active. The aorist middle is formed like a second aorist on the augmented stem θε. The perfect reduplicates like the present except with an ε rather than the ι seen in the present and imperfect tenses. The tense sign κ appears *only* in the perfect active.

§182. *Present System of* μι *Verbs*.

§182.1. *Present active indicative*.

	SINGULAR	PLURAL
1st per	δίδωμι, *I am giving*	δίδομεν, *we are giving*
2nd per	δίδως, *you are giving*	δίδοτε, *you are giving*
3rd per	δίδωσι, *he, she, it is giving*	διδόασι, *they are giving*

SINGULAR	PLURAL
1st per ἵστημι, *I am setting*	ἵσταμεν, *we are setting*
2nd per ἵστης, *you are setting*	ἵστατε, *you are setting*
3rd per ἵστησι, *he, she, it is setting*	ἵστασι, *they are setting*

SINGULAR	PLURAL
1st per τίθημι, *I am placing*	τίθεμεν, *we are placing*
2nd per τίθης, *you are placing*	τίθετε, *you are placing*
3rd per τίθησι, *he, she, it is placing*	τιθέασι, *they are placing*

§182.2. *Present middle/passive indicative.*

SINGULAR	PLURAL
1st per δίδομαι, *I am being given*	διδόμεθα, *we are being given*
2nd per δίδοσαι, *you are being given*	δίδοσθε, *you being are given*
3rd per δίδοται, *he, she, it is being given*	δίδονται, *they are being given*

SINGULAR	PLURAL
1st per ἵσταμαι, *I am being set*	ἱστάμεθα, *we are being set*
2nd per ἵστασαι, *you are being set*	ἵστασθε, *you are being set*
3rd per ἵσταται, *he, she, it is being set*	ἵστανται, *they are being set*

SINGULAR	PLURAL
1st per τίθεμαι, *I am being placed*	τιθέμεθα, *we are being placed*
2nd per τίθεσαι, *you are being placed*	τίθεσθε, *you are being placed*
3rd per τίθεται, *he, she, it is being placed*	τίθενται, *they are being placed*

§183. *Imperfect System of μι Verbs.*

§183.1. *Imperfect active indicative.*

SINGULAR	PLURAL
1st per ἐδίδουν, *I was giving*	ἐδίδομεν, *we were giving*
2nd per ἐδίδους, *you were giving*	ἐδίδοτε, *you were giving*
3rd per ἐδίδου, *he, she, it was giving*	ἐδίδοσαν, *they were giving*

SINGULAR	PLURAL
1st per ἵσταμαι, *I was setting*	ἱστάμεθα, *we were setting*
2nd per ἵστης, *you are setting*	ἵστασθε, *you were setting*

3rd per ἵσταται, *he, she, it was setting*   ἵστανται, *they were setting*

	SINGULAR	PLURAL
1st per	ἐτίθην, *I was placing*	ἐτίθεμεν, *we were placing*
2nd per	ἐτίθεις, *you were placing*	ἐτίθετε, *you were placing*
3rd per	ἐτίθει, *he, she, it was placing*	ἐτίθεσαν, *they were placing*

§183.2. *Imperfect middle/passive indicative.*

	SINGULAR	PLURAL
1st per	ἐδιδόμην, *I was being given*	ἐδιδόμεθα, *we were being given*
2nd per	ἐδίδοσο, *you were being given*	ἐδίδοσθε, *you were being given*
3rd per	ἐδίδοτο, *he, she, it was being given*	ἐδίδοντο, *they were being given*

	SINGULAR	PLURAL
1st per	ἱστάμην, *I was being set*	ἱστάμεθα, *we were being set*
2nd per	ἵστασο, *you were being set*	ἵστασθε, *you were being set*
3rd per	ἵστατο, *he, she, it was being set*	ἵσταντο, *they were being set*

	SINGULAR	PLURAL
1st per	ἐτιθέμην, *I was being placed*	ἐτιθέμεθα, *we were being placed*
2nd per	ἐτίθεσο, *you were being placed*	ἐτίθεσθε, *you were being placed*
3rd per	ἐτίθετο, *he, she, it was being placed*	ἐτιθέντο, *they were being placed*

§184. *Aorist System of μι Verbs.* The aorist active and passive forms follow a regular 1st aorist pattern; the aorist middle follows a second aorist form.

§184.1. *Aorist active indicative.*

	SINGULAR	PLURAL
1st per	ἔδωκα, *I gave*	ἐδώκαμεν, *we gave*
2nd per	ἔδωκας, *you gave*	ἐδώκατε, *you gave*
3rd per	ἔδωκε, *he, she, it gave*	ἔδωκαν, *they gave*

	SINGULAR	PLURAL
1st per	ἔστησα, *I set*	ἐστήσαμεν, *we set*
2nd per	ἔστησας, *you set*	ἐστήσατε, *you set*
3rd per	ἔστησε, *he, she, it set*	ἔστησαν, *they set*

SINGULAR	PLURAL
1st per ἔθηκα, *I placed*	ἐθήκαμεν, *we placed*
2nd per ἔθηκας, *you placed*	ἐθήκατε, *you placed*
3rd per ἔθηκε, *he, she, it placed*	ἔθηκαν, *they placed*

§184.2. *Aorist middle indicative.*

SINGULAR	PLURAL
1st per ἐδόμην, *I gave myself*	ἐδόμεθα, *we gave ourselves*
2nd per ἔδου, *you gave yourself*	ἔδοσθε, *you gave yourselves*
3rd per ἔδοτο, *he gave himself*	ἔδοντο, *they gave themselves*

There are no aorist middle forms of δίδωμι in the New Testament.

SINGULAR	PLURAL
1st per ἐθέμην, *I placed myself*	ἐθέμεθα, *we placed ourselves*
2nd per ἔθου, *you placed yourself*	ἔθεσθε, *you placed yourselves*
3rd per ἔθετο, *he placed himself*	ἔθεντο, *they placed themselves*

§184.3. *Aorist passive indicative.*

SINGULAR	PLURAL
1st per ἐδόθην, *I was given*	ἐδόθημεν, *we were given*
2nd per ἐδόθης, *you were given*	ἐδόθητε, *you were given*
3rd per ἐδόθη, *he, she, it was given*	ἐδόθησαν, *they were given*

SINGULAR	PLURAL
1st per ἐστάθην, *I was set*	ἐστάθημεν, *we were set*
2nd per ἐστάθης, *you were set*	ἐστάθητε, *you were set*
3rd per ἐστάθη, *he, she, it was set*	ἐστάθησαν, *they were set*

SINGULAR	PLURAL
1st per ἐτέθην, *I was placed*	ἐτέθημεν, *we were placed*
2nd per ἐτέθης, *you were placed*	ἐτέθητε, *you were placed*
3rd per ἐτέθη, *he, she, it was placed*	ἐτέθησαν, *they were placed*

§185. *Subjunctive System of* μι *Verbs.*

§185.1. *Present active subjunctive.*

SINGULAR	PLURAL

1st per δίδω̃	διδω̃μεν
2nd per διδω̃ς	διδω̃τε
3rd per διδω̃	διδω̃σι

	SINGULAR	PLURAL
1st per	ἱστω̃	ἱστω̃μεν
2nd per	ἱστη̃ς	ἱστη̃τε
3rd per	ἱστη̃	ἱστω̃σι

	SINGULAR	PLURAL
1st per	τιθω̃	τιθω̃μεν
2nd per	τιθη̃ς	τιθη̃τε
3rd per	τιθη̃	τιθω̃σι

§185.2. *Aorist active subjunctive*.

	SINGULAR	PLURAL
1st per	δω̃	δω̃μεν
2nd per	δω̃ς	δω̃τε
3rd per	δω̃	δω̃σι

	SINGULAR	PLURAL
1st per	στω̃	στω̃μεν
2nd per	στη̃ς	στη̃τε
3rd per	στη̃	στω̃σι

	SINGULAR	PLURAL
1st per	θω̃	θω̃μεν
2nd per	θη̃ς	θη̃τε
3rd per	θη̃	θω̃σι

§186. *Imperative System of* μι *Verbs*.

§186.1. *Present active imperative*.

	SINGULAR	PLURAL
2nd per	δίδου, *you give*	δίδοτε, *you give*
3rd per	διδότω, *let him give*	διδότωσαν, *let them give*

SINGULAR	PLURAL
2nd per ἴστη, *you set*	ἴστατε, *you set*
3rd per ἰστάτω, *let him set*	ἰστάτωσαν, *let them set*

SINGULAR	PLURAL
2nd per τίθει, *you place*	τίθετε, *you place*
3rd per τιθέτω, *let him place*	τιθέτωσαν, *let them place*

§186.2. *Aorist active imperative.*

SINGULAR	PLURAL
2nd per δός, *you give*	δότε, *you give*
3rd per δότω, *let him give*	δότωσαν, *let them give*

SINGULAR	PLURAL
2nd per στῆθι, *you set*	στῆτε, *you set*
3rd per στῆτω, *let him set*	στῆτωσαν *let them set*

SINGULAR	PLURAL
2nd per θές, *you place*	θέτε, *you place*
3rd per θέτω, *let him place*	θέτωσαν, *let them place*

§187. *Infinitive System of* μι *Verbs.*

§187.1. *Present infinitives*

VERB	ACTIVE	MIDDLE/PASSIVE
δίδωμι	διδόναι	δίδοσθαι
ἴστημι	ἰστάναι	ἴστασθαι
τίθημι	τιθέναι	τίθεσθαι

§187.2. *Aorist infinitives.*

VERB	ACTIVE	MIDDLE	PASSIVE
δίδωμι	δοῦναι	δόσθαι	δοθῆναι
ἴστημι	στῆναι	———	σταθῆναι
τίτημι	θεῖναι	θέσθαι	τεθῆναι

§188. *Participle System of* μι *Verbs.* The participles of μι verbs are declined regularly in all genders and voices; therefore, only a single example for each tense will be given.

§188.1. *Present active participle.* The stems for the present participles are: δο (δίδωμι), ιστ (ἴστημι), τιθ (τίθημι).

SINGULAR

CASE	MASCULINE	FEMININE	NEUTER
Nom	διδούς	διδοῦσα	διδόν
Gen	διδόντος	διδούσης	διδόντος
Abl	διδόντος	διδούσης	διδόντος
Dat	διδόντι	διδούσῃ	διδόντι
Loc	διδόντι	διδούσῃ	διδόντι
Inst	διδόντι	διδούσῃ	διδόντι
Acc	διδόντα	διδοῦσαν	διδόν

PLURAL

CASE	MASCULINE	FEMININE	NEUTER
Nom	διδόντες	διδοῦσαι	διδόντα
Gen	διδόντων	διδουσῶν	διδόντων
Abl	διδόντων	διδουσῶν	διδόντων
Dat	διδοῦσι (ν)	διδούσαις	διδοῦσι (ν)
Loc	διδοῦσι (ν)	διδούσαις	διδοῦσι (ν)
Inst	διδοῦσι (ν)	διδούσαις	διδοῦσι (ν)
Acc	διδόντας	διδούσας	διδόντα

§188.2 *Present middle/passive participle.*

SINGULAR

CASE	MASCULINE	FEMININE	NEUTER
Nom	ἱστάμενος	ἱσταμένη	ἱστάμενον
Gen	ἱσταμένου	ἱσταμένης	ἱσταμένου
Abl	ἱσταμένου	ἱσταμένης	ἱσταμένου
Dat	ἱσταμένῳ	ἱσταμένῃ	ἱσταμένῳ
Loc	ἱσταμένῳ	ἱσταμένῃ	ἱσταμένῳ
Inst	ἱσταμένῳ	ἱσταμένῃ	ἱσταμένῳ
Acc	ἱστάμενον	ἱσταμένην	ἱστάμενον

PLURAL

CASE	MASCULINE	FEMININE	NEUTER
Nom	ἱστάμενοι	ἱστάμεναι	ἱστάμενα
Gen	ἱσταμένων	ἱσταμένων	ἱσταμένων
Abl	ἱσταμένων	ἱσταμένων	ἱσταμένων
Dat	ἱσταμένοις	ἱσταμέναις	ἱσταμένοις
Loc	ἱσταμένοις	ἱσταμέναις	ἱσταμένοις
Inst	ἱσταμένοις	ἱσταμέναις	ἱσταμένοις
Acc	ἱσταμένους	ἱσταμένας	ἱστάμενα

§188.3 *Aorist active participle.* The stems for the aorist participles are: δ (δίδωμι), στ (ἵστημι), θ (τιθημι).

SINGULAR

CASE	MASCULINE	FEMININE	NEUTER
Nom	δούς	δοῦσα	δόν
Gen	δόντος	δούσης	δόντος
Abl	δόντος	δούσης	δόντος
Dat	δόντι	δούσῃ	δόντι
Loc	δόντι	δούσῃ	δόντι
Inst	δόντι	δούσῃ	δόντι
Acc	δόντα	δοῦσαν	δόν

PLURAL

CASE	MASCULINE	FEMININE	NEUTER
Nom	δόντες	δοῦσαι	δόντα
Gen	δόντων	δουσῶν	δόντων
Abl	δόντων	δουσῶν	δόντων
Dat	δοῦσι (ν)	δούσαις	δοῦσι (ν)
Loc	δοῦσι (ν)	δούσαις	δοῦσι (ν)
Inst	δοῦσι (ν)	δούσαις	δοῦσι (ν)
Acc	δόντας	δούσας	δόντα

§188.4 *Aorist middle participle*.

SINGULAR

CASE	MASCULINE	FEMININE	NEUTER
Nom	θέμενος	θεμένη	θέμενον
Gen	θεμένου	θεμένης	θεμένου
Abl	θεμένου	θεμένης	θεμένου
Dat	θεμένῳ	θεμένη	θεμένῳ
Loc	θεμένῳ	θεμένη	θεμένῳ
Inst	θεμένῳ	θεμένη	θεμένῳ
Acc	θέμενον	θεμένην	θέμενον

PLURAL

CASE	MASCULINE	FEMININE	NEUTER
Nom	θέμενοι	θέμεναι	θέμενα
Gen	θεμένων	θεμένων	θεμένων
Abl	θεμένων	θεμένων	θεμένων
Dat	θεμένοις	θεμέναις	θεμένοις
Loc	θεμένοις	θεμέναις	θεμένοις
Inst	θεμένοις	θεμέναις	θεμένοις

Acc   θεμένους   θεμένας   θέμενα

§188.5 *Aorist passive participle*.

SINGULAR

CASE	MASCULINE	FEMININE	NEUTER
Nom	σταθείς	σταθεῖσα	σταθέν
Gen	σταθέντος	σταθείσης	σταθέντος
Abl	σταθεντος	σταθείσης	σταθέντος
Dat	σταθέντι	σταθείσῃ	σταθέντι
Loc	σταθέντι	σταθείσῃ	σταθέντι
Inst	σταθέντι	σταθείσῃ	σταθέντι
Acc	σταθέντα	σταθεῖσαν	σταθέν

PLURAL

CASE	MASCULINE	FEMININE	NEUTER
Nom	σταθέντες	σταθεῖσαι	σταθέντα
Gen	σταθέντων	σταθεισῶν	σταθέντων
Abl	σταθέντων	σταθεισῶν	σταθέντων
Dat	σταθεῖσι	σταθείσαις	σταθεῖσι
Loc	σταθεῖσι	σταθείσαις	σταθεῖσι
Inst	σταθεῖσι	σταθείσαις	σταθεῖσι
Acc	σταθέντας	σταθείσας	σταθέντα

§189. *Practical Application*:

§189.1. *1 John 2:1-6.*

1 Τεκνία μου, ταῦτα γράφω ὑμῖν ἵνα μὴ ἁμάρτητε. καὶ ἐάν τις ἁμάρτῃ, Παράκλητον ἔχομεν πρὸς τὸν Πατέρα, Ἰησοῦν Χριστὸν δίκαιον· 2 καὶ αὐτὸς ἱλασμός ἐστιν περὶ τῶν ἁμαρτιῶν ἡμῶν, οὐ περὶ τῶν ἡμετέρων δὲ μόνον ἀλλὰ καὶ περὶ ὅλου τοῦ κόσμου. 3 καὶ ἐν τούτῳ γινώσκομεν ὅτι ἐγνώκαμεν αὐτόν, ἐὰν τὰς ἐντολὰς αὐτοῦ τηρῶμεν. 4 ὁ λέγων ὅτι Ἔγνωκα αὐτόν, καὶ τὰς ἐντολὰς αὐτοῦ μὴ τηρῶν, ψεύστης ἐστίν, καὶ ἐν τούτῳ ἡ ἀλήθεια οὐκ ἔστιν· 5 ὃς δ᾽ ἂν τηρῇ αὐτοῦ τὸν λόγον ἀληθῶς ἐν τούτῳ ἡ ἀγάπη τοῦ Θεοῦ τετελείωται· ἐν τούτῳ γινώσκομεν ὅτι ἐν αὐτῷ ἐσμεν· 6 ὁ λέγων ἐν αὐτῷ μένειν ὀφείλει καθὼς ἐκεῖνος περιεπάτησεν καὶ αὐτὸς οὕτως περιπατεῖν.

§189.2. *Translation aids*.

1 John 2:1. τεκνία = vocative case. μὴ occurs instead of οὐ because it negates the *subjunctive* ἁμάρτητε. παράκλητον = *an advocate [from* παρα = *beside* and καλέω = *I call]*. This term is often transliterated into English as *paraclete*.

Ἰησοῦν χριστὸν δίκαιον = accusative case because the antecedent is παράκλητον which functions as the direct object of ἔχομεν.

1 John 2:2. αὐτὸς = intensive use of the 3rd person personal pronoun *in the nominative case* [see §73.3]. ὅλου = *whole, all.*

1 John 2:3. ἐν τούτῳ = by this, ἐν + instrumental case (see §48.1.4).

1 John 2:5. τετελείωται = perfect passive of τελειόω = *has been perfected.*

1 John 2:6 μένειν = present active infinitive, but translated as though present active
indicative third singular. ὀφείλει . . . καὶ αὐτὸς περιπατεῖν = *ought also
himself to walk about.* The word order is confusing because between the finite
verb and the infinite comes the phrase ἐκεῖνος περιεπάτησεν = *just as that
one walked about.* The whole sentences reads: *The one saying "I remain in him"
ought (himself) to walk about just as that one walked about.*

Lesson 32
Adjectives
Adverbs

§190. *Vocabulary.*
αἰτία, ἡ, *reason*
ἄρτι, *now*
βραχύς, βραχεῖα, βραχύ, *short*
δεύτερος, δευτέρα, δεύτερον, *second*
εὐθύς, *immediately*
ἤδη, *now, already*
ἰσχυρός, ἰσχυρά, ἰσχυρόν, *strong*
ἰστχυρότερος, ἰσχυρότερα, ἰσχυρότερος, *stronger*
μᾶλλον, *more, rather*
μέγας, μεγάλη, μέγα, *great*
πόθεν, *whence*
πολύς, πολλή, πολύ, *much, many*
φανερῶς, *clearly*
ψευδής, ψευδής, ψευδές, *false*
ὥρα, ἡ, *hour*

§191. *Declension of Adjectives* [review §64]. All of the adjectives previously studied were declined regularly, i.e., with first or second declension endings. There are many other adjectives in the New Testament, however, that follow the third declension endings in some or all of their forms through the three genders. There are three groups of such adjectives:

§191.1. *ες stem adjectives*. There are about 60 adjectives in this category and they all use the third declension endings (§143). The masculine and feminine forms are identical.

| | SINGULAR | | | PLURAL | | |
CASE	MASCULINE	FEMININE	NEUTER	MASCULINE	FEMININE	NEUTER
Nom	ψευδής	ψευδής	ψευδές	ψευδεῖς	ψευδεῖς	ψευδῆ
Gen	ψευδοῦς	ψευδοῦς	ψευδοῦς	ψευδῶν	ψευδῶν	ψευδῶν
Abl	ψευδοῦς	ψευδοῦς	ψευδοῦς	ψευδῶν	ψευδῶν	ψευδῶν
Dat	ψευδεῖ	ψευδεῖ	ψευδεῖ	ψευδέσι	ψευδέσι	ψευδέσι
Loc	ψευδεῖ	ψευδεῖ	ψευδεῖ	ψευδέσι	ψευδέσι	ψευδέσι
Inst	ψευδεῖ	ψευδεῖ	ψευδεῖ	ψευδέσι	ψευδέσι	ψευδέσι
Acc	ψευδῆ	ψευδῆ	ψευδές	ψευδεῖς	ψευδεῖς	ψευδῆ

§191.2. *υ stem adjectives.* Some adjectives in the New Testament have a stem ending in an υ. These behave as first declension nouns in the masculine and neuter but like a regular first declension noun in the feminine.

| | SINGULAR | | | PLURAL | | |
CASE	MASCULINE	FEMININE	NEUTER	MASCULINE	FEMININE	NEUTER
Nom	βραχύς	βραχεῖα	βραχύ	βραχεῖς	βραχεῖαι	βραχέα
Gen	βραχέως	βραχείας	βραχέως	βραχέων	βραχειῶν	βραχέων
Abl	βραχέως	βραχείας	βραχέως	βραχέων	βραχειῶν	βραχέων
Dat	βραχεῖ	βραχείᾳ	βραχεῖ	βραχέσι	βραχείαις	βραχέσι
Loc	βραχεῖ	βραχείᾳ	βραχεῖ	βραχέσι	βραχείαις	βραχέσι
Inst	βραχεῖ	βραχείᾳ	βραχεῖ	βραχέσι	βραχείαις	βραχέσι
Acc	βραχύν	βραχεῖαν	βραχύ	βραχεῖς	βραχείας	βραχέα

§191.3. *αντ stem adjectives.* Only two adjectives of this type are found in the New Testament. The more common of these is πᾶς, πᾶσα, πᾶν. Again, these forms follow the third declension in the masculine and neuter; the first declension in the feminine (for the special uses of πᾶς, πᾶσα, πᾶν see §193).

| | SINGULAR | | | PLURAL | | |
CASE	MASCULINE	FEMININE	NEUTER	MASCULINE	FEMININE	NEUTER
Nom	πᾶς	πᾶσα	πᾶν	πάντες	πᾶσαι	πάντα
Gen	παντός	πάσης	παντός	πάντων	πασῶν	πάντων
Abl	παντός	πάσης	παντός	πάντων	πασῶν	πάντων
Dat	παντί	πάσῃ	παντί	πᾶσι	πάσαις	πᾶσι
Loc	παντί	πάσῃ	παντί	πᾶσι	πάσαις	πᾶσι
Inst	παντί	πάσῃ	παντί	πᾶσι	πάσαις	πᾶσι
Acc	πάντα	πᾶσαν	πᾶν	πάντας	πάσας	πάντα

§192. *Irregular adjectives.* Two adjectives do not follow any of these declension patterns in the nominative and accusative cases of the masculine and neuter singular. These four form in each of the following two paradigms must be memorized; otherwise these adjectives follow regular first and second declension forms.

| | SINGULAR | | | PLURAL | | |
CASE	MASCULINE	FEMININE	NEUTER	MASCULINE	FEMININE	NEUTER
Nom	πολύς	πολλή	πολύ	πολλοί	πολλαί	πολλά
Gen	πολλοῦ	πολλῆς	πολλοῦ	πολλῶν	πολλῶν	πολλῶν
Abl	πολλοῦ	πολλῆς	πολλοῦ	πολλῶν	πολλῶν	πολλῶν
Dat	πολλῷ	πολλῇ	πολλῷ	πολλοῖς	πολλαῖς	πολλοῖς
Loc	πολλῷ	πολλῇ	πολλῷ	πολλοῖς	πολλαῖς	πολλοῖς
Inst	πολλῷ	πολλῇ	πολλῷ	πολλοῖς	πολλαῖς	πολλοῖς
Acc	πολύν	πολλήν	πολύ	πολλούς	πολλάς	πολλά

| | SINGULAR | | | PLURAL | | |
CASE	MASCULINE	FEMININE	NEUTER	MASCULINE	FEMININE	NEUTER
Nom	μέγας	μεγάλη	μέγα	μεγάλοι	μεγάλαι	μεγάλα
Gen	μεγάλου	μεγάλης	μεγάλου	μεγάλων	μεγάλων	μεγάλων
Abl	μεγάλου	μεγάλης	μεγάλου	μεγάλων	μεγάλων	μεγάλων
Dat	μεγάλῳ	μεγάλη	μεγάλῳ	μεγάλοις	μεγάλαις	μεγάλοις
Loc	μεγάλῳ	μεγάλη	μεγάλῳ	μεγάλοις	μεγάλαις	μεγάλοις
Inst	μεγάλῳ	μεγάλη	μεγάλῳ	μεγάλοις	μεγάλαις	μεγάλοις
Acc	μέγαν	μεγάλην	μέγα	μεγάλους	μεγάλας	μεγάλα

§193. *Special Uses of πᾶς, πᾶσα, πᾶν.*

§193.1. *Predicate position.* When πᾶς occurs in the predicate position it is translated *all*. Example: πάντες οἱ μαθηταὶ βλέπουσι τὸν Ἰησοῦν = *all the disciples are seeing Jesus.*

§193.2. *Attributive position.* When πᾶς occurs in the attributive position it is translated *whole*. Example: ὁ πᾶς ὄχλος ἔβλεψε τὸν Ἰησοῦν = *the whole crowd saw Jesus.*

§193.3. *Predicate position with a participle.* When πᾶς occurs in the predicate position *with a participle* it is translated *everyone* in the singular and *all these* in the plural. Examples: πᾶς ὁ πιστεύων σωθήσεται = *everyone who believes will be saved* or πάντες οἱ πιστεύοντες σωθήσονται = *all those who believe will be saved.*

§193.4. *Anarthrous use.* When πᾶς occurs in the singular and anathrously, i.e., without the definite article, it is translated *every*. Example: οἱ ἀπόστολοι ἔλυσαν πάντα δοῦλον = *the apostles loosed every slave.*

§194. *Comparison of Adjectives.* Just as in English, Greek adjectives have three degrees of comparison (though the third is rarely used in the Greek New Testament): positive (*sweet*); comparative (*sweeter*); superlative (*sweetest*).

§194.1. *Regular adjectives.* Adjectives that are regular in comparison form their comparative and superlative degrees by adding τερος[1] (comparative) or τατος (superlative) to the regular adjective:

> ὁ ἰσχυρός = *the strong man*
> ὁ ἰσχυρότερος = *the strong man*
> ἡ ἰσχυροτέρα = *the stronger woman*
> τὸ ἰσχυρότερον = *the stronger thing*
> ὁ ἰσχυρότατος = *the strongest man*
> ἡ ἰσχυροτάτη = *the strongest woman*
> τὸ ἰσχυρότατον = *the strongest thing*

§194.2. *Irregular adjectives.* Adjectives that are irregular in comparison form their comparative and superlative degrees by a more radical change (as in English *good, better, best*). Example: μικρός = *little;* ἐλάσσων = *less;* ἐλάχιστος = *least.*

§195. *Practical Application.*

§195.1. *1 John 2:7-11.*

7 Ἀγαπητοί, οὐκ ἐντολὴν καινὴν γράφω ὑμῖν, ἀλλ' ἐντολὴν παλαιὰν ἣν εἴχετε ἀπ'. ἀρχῆς· ἡ ἐντολὴ ἡ παλαιά ἐστιν ὁ λόγος ὃν ἠκούσατε. 8 πάλιν ἐντολὴν καινὴν γράφω ὑμῖν, ὅ ἐστιν ἀληθὲς ἐν αὐτῷ καὶ ἐν ὑμῖν, ὅτι ἡ σκοτία παράγεται καὶ τὸ φῶς τὸ ἀληθινὸν ἤδη φαίνει. 9 ὁ λέγων ἐν τῷ φωτὶ εἶναι καὶ τὸν ἀδελφὸν αὐτοῦ μισῶν ἐν τῇ σκοτίᾳ ἐστὶν ἕως ἄρτι. 10 ὁ ἀγαπῶν τὸν ἀδελφὸν αὐτοῦ ἐν τῷ φωτὶ μένει, καὶ σκάνδαλον ἐν αὐτῷ οὐκ ἔστιν· 11 ὁ δὲ μισῶν τὸν ἀδελφὸν αὐτοῦ ἐν τῇ σκοτίᾳ ἐστὶν καὶ ἐν τῇ σκοτίᾳ περιπατεῖ, καὶ οὐκ οἶδεν ποῦ ὑπάγει, ὅτι ἡ σκοτία ἐτύφλωσεν τοὺς ὀφθαλμοὺς αὐτοῦ.

§195.2. *Translation aids.*

1 John 2:7. Ἀγαπητοὶ = vocative, plural. εἴχετε = imperfect active indicative 2nd person plural from ἔχω. παλαιὰν = feminine accusative singular adjective meaning *old.* ὃν = accusative, object of ἠκούσατε.

1 John 2:8. παράγεται = present active indicative third singular from παράγω = *I lead beside.*

---

[1]Some adjectives add ιων, ιων, ιον. These endings follow the third declension. Example: πολύς, πολλή, πολύ = πλείων, πλείων, πλεῖον

1 John 2:9. εἶναι = present infinitive of εἰμί, translated as present indicative (cf. 2:6, μένειν above).

1 John 2:11. οὐκ οἶδεν = perfect tense but usually translated as though it were present tense = *he does not know*.

Lesson 33
Definite Article

§196. *Vocabulary*.
ἀγρός, ὁ, *field*
ἀδελφή, ἡ, *sister*
ἀνήρ, ἀνδρός, ὁ, *man, husband*
ἀντίχριστος, ὁ, *antichrist*
ἄξιος, ἀξία, ἄξιον, *worthy*
διαθήκη, διαθήκης, ἡ, *covenant*
δώδεκα, *twelve*
μισέω, μισήσω, ἐμίσησα, *I hate, I shall hate, I hated*
νεανίσκος, ὁ, *young man*
νικάω, νικήσω, ἐνίκησα, *I overcome, I shall overcome, I overcame*
ψεῦδος, ψεύδους, τό, *lie*

§197. *Introduction to the Use of the Article* [review §60]. The definite article may have originally functioned as a demonstrative pronoun. It retains something of that force in many instances in the New Testament. Thus when the definite article accompanies a noun *specific identity* is intended. When the article is omitted the reference is to the *general quality* of the noun. Example: ὁ θεός = *God* (the Jewish-Christian God); θεός = *a god* (in the sense of "any god").

§198. *Uses of the Article*.

§198.1. *General uses*.

§198.1.1. To point out specific nouns or objects. Examples: ὁ ἀπόστολος, ἡ ἐντολή.

§198.1.2. In cases where English generally omits the definite article:

§198.1.2.1. With proper names. Examples: ὁ θεός, ὁ ᾿Ιησοῦς.

§198.1.2.2. With abstract nouns. Examples: ἡ χάρις, ἡ ἀλήθεια .

§198.1.2.3. With classes or groups. Example: τὰ πετεινά = *birds*.

§198.1.3. *With infinitives* [review §173.1.2]. In this construction the article employed always occurs in the neuter.

§198.1.4. As a noun. Example: αἱ ἐν τῷ ἱερῷ = *the women who are in the temple*.

§198.2. *Special uses*.

§198.2.1. As a demonstrative pronoun. Example: αἱ ἀκούουσιν αὐτόν = *these women are hearing him*.

§198.2.2. As a relative pronoun. Example: τοῦτό ἐστιν τὸ αἷμά μου τὸ περὶ πολλῶν δίδωμι = *this is my blood which I am giving for many*.

§198.2.3. As a possessive pronoun. Example: ἔπεμψα μετ᾽ αὐτοῦ τὸν ἀδελφόν = *I sent with him his brother*.

§198.2.4. With nouns linked by εἰμί. When dual substantives are preceded by the articile and are joined together by a form of εἰμί the substantives are interchangeable in terms of which is the subject and which the predicate. Example: ἡ δύναμις τῆς ἁμαρτίας ἐστὶν ὁ νόμος = *the power of the sin is the law* or *the law is the power of sin*. If only *one* of the two substantives occurs with the definite article then *that* one functions as the subject of the sentence. Example: ὁ θεὸς ἀγάπη ἐστίν = *God is love*.

§198.2.5. Uses with καί. When two substantives are joined together with the conjunction καί they refer to the different persons or things *if* both are preceded by the definite article. Example: ὁ ἀπόστολος καὶ ὁ ἀδελφός = *the apostle and the brother* (where different persons are intended). But if only one substantive is preceded by the article then the same person or object is intended. Example: ὁ ἀπόστολος καὶ ἀδελφός = *the apostle and brother* (where they are one in the same person).

§199. *Practical Application*.

§199.1.1. *John 2:12-17*.

12 Γράφω ὑμῖν, τεκνία, ὅτι ἀφέωνται ὑμῖν αἱ ἁμαρτίαι διὰ τὸ ὄνομα αὐτοῦ. 13 γράφω ὑμῖν, πατέρες, ὅτι ἐγνώκατε τὸν ἀπ᾽ ἀρχῆς. γράφω ὑμῖν, νεανίσκοι, ὅτι νενικήκατε τὸν πονηρόν. 14 ἔγραψα ὑμῖν, παιδία, ὅτι ἐγνώκατε τὸν Πατέρα. ἔγραψα ὑμῖν, πατέρες, ὅτι ἐγνώκατε τὸν ἀπ᾽ ἀρχῆς. ἔγραψα ὑμῖν, νεανίσκοι, ὅτι ἰσχυροί ἐστε καὶ ὁ λόγος τοῦ Θεοῦ ἐν ὑμῖν μένει καὶ νενικήκατε τὸν πονηρόν. 15 Μὴ ἀγαπᾶτε τὸν κόσμον μηδὲ τὰ ἐν

τῷ κόσμῳ. ἐάν τις ἀγαπᾷ τὸν κόσμον, οὐκ ἔστιν ἡ ἀγάπη τοῦ Πατρὸς ἐν αὐτῷ· 16 ὅτι πᾶν τὸ ἐν τῷ κόσμῳ, ἡ ἐπιθυμία τῆς σαρκὸς καὶ ἡ ἐπιθυμία τῶν ὀφθαλμῶν καὶ ἡ ἀλαζονεία τοῦ βίου, οὐκ ἔστιν ἐκ τοῦ Πατρός, ἀλλ᾽ ἐκ τοῦ κόσμου ἐστίν. 17 καὶ ὁ κόσμος παράγεται καὶ ἡ ἐπιθυμία αὐτοῦ, ὁ δὲ ποιῶν τὸ θέλημα τοῦ Θεοῦ μένει εἰς τὸν αἰῶνα.

§199.1. *Translation aids.*
1 John 2:12. ἀφέωνται = perfect, passive, indicative, 3rd, plural from ἀφίημι.
1 John 2:13. νενικήκατε = perfect, active, indicative, 2nd, plural from νικάω.

Appendix 1
Supplemental Readings

§200. *1 John 2:18-25.*

18 Παιδία, ἐσχάτη ὥρα ἐστίν, καὶ καθὼς ἠκούσατε ὅτι ἀντίχριστος ἔρχεται, καὶ νῦν ἀντίχριστοι πολλοὶ γεγόνασιν· ὅθεν γινώσκομεν ὅτι ἐσχάτη ὥρα ἐστίν. 19 ἐξ ἡμῶν ἐξῆλθαν, ἀλλ᾽ οὐκ ἦσαν ἐξ ἡμῶν· εἰ γὰρ ἐξ ἡμῶν ἦσαν, μενενήκεισαν ἂν μεθ᾽ ἡμῶν· ᾽αλλ᾽ ἵνα φανερωθῶσιν ὅτι οὐκ εἰσὶν πάντες ἐξ ἡμῶν. 20 καὶ ὑμεῖς χρῖσμα ἔχετε ἀπὸ τοῦ Ἁγίου, καὶ οἴδατε πάντες. 21 οὐκ ἔγραψα ὑμῖν ὅτι οὐκ οἴδατε τὴν ἀλήθειαν, ἀλλ᾽ ὅτι οἴδατε αὐτήν, καὶ ὅτι πᾶν ψεῦδος ἐκ τῆς ἀληθείας οὐκ ἔστιν. 22 Τίς ἐστιν ὁ ψεύστης εἰ μὴ ὁ ἀρνούμενος ὅτι Ἰησοῦς οὐκ ἔστιν ὁ Χριστός; οὗτός ἐστιν ὁ ἀντίχριστος, ὁ ἀρνούμενος τὸν Πατέρα καὶ τὸν Υἱόν. 23 πᾶς ὁ ἀρνούμενος τὸν Υἱὸν οὐδὲ τὸν Πατέρα ἔχει· ὁ ὁμολογῶν τὸν Υἱὸν καὶ τὸν Πατέρα ἔχει. 24 ὑμεῖς ὃ ἠκούσατε ἀπ᾽ ἀρχῆς, ἐν ὑμῖν μενέτω. ἐὰν ἐν ὑμῖν μείνῃ ὃ ἀπ᾽ ἀρχῆς ἠκούσατε, καὶ ὑμεῖς ἐν τῷ Υἱῷ καὶ ἐν τῷ Παρτὶ μενεῖτε. 25 καὶ αὕτη ἐστὶν ἡ ἐπαγγελία ἣν αὐτὸς ἐπηγγείλατο ἡμῖν, τὴν ζωὴν τὴν αἰώνιον.

§201. *1 John 2:26-3:3*

26 Ταῦτα ἔγραψα ὑμῖν περὶ τῶν πλανώντων ὑμᾶς. 27 καὶ ὑμεῖς τὸ χρῖσμα ὃ ἐλάβετε ἀπ᾽ αὐτοῦ μένει ἐν ὑμῖν, καὶ οὐ χρείαν ἔχετε ἵνα τις διδάσκῃ ὑμᾶς· ἀλλ᾽ ὡς τὸ αὐτοῦ χρῖσμα διδάσκει ὑμᾶς περὶ πάντων, καὶ ἀληθές ἐστιν καὶ οὐκ ἔστιν ψεῦδος, καὶ καθὼς ἐδίδαξεν ὑμᾶς, μένετε ἐν αὐτῷ.

28 Καὶ νῦν, τεκνία, μένετε ἐν αὐτῷ, ἵνα ἐὰν φανερωθῇ σχῶμεν παρρη-σίαν καὶ μὴ αἰσχυνθῶμεν ἀπ᾽ αὐτοῦ ἐν τῇ παρουσίᾳ αὐτοῦ. 29 ἐὰν εἰδῆτε ὅτι δίκαιός ἐστιν, γινώσκετε ὅτι καὶ πᾶς ὁ ποιῶν τὴν δικαιοσύνην ἐξ αὐτοῦ γεγέννηται. 3:1 ἴδετε ποταπὴν ἀγάπην δέδωκεν ἡμῖν ὁ πατὴρ ἵνα τέκνα θεοῦ κληθῶμεν, καὶ ἐσμέν. διὰ τοῦτο ὁ κόσμος οὐ γινώσκει ἡμᾶς, ὅτι

οὐκ ἔγνω αὐτόν. 2 Ἀγαπητοί, νῦν τέκνα θεοῦ ἐσμεν, καὶ οὔπω ἐφανερώθη τί ἐσόμεθα. οἴδαμεν ὅτι ἐὰν φανερωθῇ ὅμοιοι αὐτῷ ἐσόμεθα, ὅτι ὀψόμεθα αὐτὸν καθώς ἐστιν. 3 καὶ πᾶς ὁ ἔχων τὴν ἐλπίδα ταύτην ἐπ᾽ αὐτῷ ἁγνίζει ἑαυτὸν καθὼς ἐκεῖνος ἁγνός ἐστιν.

§202. *1 John 3:4-10.*

4 πᾶς ὁ ποιῶν τὴν ἁμαρτίαν καὶ τὴν ἀνομίαν ποιεῖ, καὶ ἡ ἁμαρτία ἐστὶν ἡ ἀνομία. 5 καὶ οἴδατε ὅτι ἐκεῖνος ἐφανερώθη ἵνα τὰς ἁμαρτίας ἄρῃ, καὶ ἁμαρτία ἐν αὐτῷ οὐκ ἔστιν. 6 πᾶς ὁ ἐν αὐτῷ μένων οὐκ ἁμαρτάνει· πᾶς ὁ ἁμαρτάνων οὐχ ἑώρακεν αὐτὸν οὐδὲ ἔγνωκεν αὐτόν. 7 Τεκνία, μηδεὶς πλανάτω ὑμᾶς· ὁ ποιῶν τὴν δικαιοσύνην δίκαιός ἐστιν, καθὼς ἐκεῖνος δίκαιός ἐστιν· 8 ὁ ποιῶν τὴν ἁμαρτίαν ἐκ τοῦ διαβόλου ἐστίν, ὅτι ἀπ᾽ ἀρχῆς ὁ διάβολος ἁμαρτάνει. εἰς τοῦτο ἐφανερώθη ὁ υἱὸς τοῦ θεοῦ, ἵνα λύσῃ τὰ ἔργα τοῦ διαβόλου. 9 Πᾶς ὁ γεγεννημένος ἐκ τοῦ θεοῦ ἁμαρτίαν οὐ ποιεῖ, ὅτι σπέρμα αὐτοῦ ἐν αὐτῷ μένει· καὶ οὐ δύναται ἁμαρτάνειν, ὅτι ἐκ τοῦ θεοῦ γεγέννηται. 10 ἐν τούτῳ φανερά ἐστιν τὰ τέκνα τοῦ θεοῦ καὶ τὰ τέκνα τοῦ διαβόλου· πᾶς ὁ μὴ ποιῶν δικαιοσύνην οὐκ ἔστιν ἐκ τοῦ Θεοῦ, καὶ ὁ μὴ ἀγαπῶν τὸν ἀδελφὸν αὐτοῦ.

Appendix 2
Accents

§203. *General Principles of Accenting*. Virtually every word in the Greek New Testament has an accent mark.[1] These accent marks are not placed randomly, but according to precise rules. Some general considerations follow. You must study these carefully.

§203.1. *Accent marks* [§11]. The accent marks in Greek:

acute = ´
circumflex = ˜
grave = `

§203.2. *Syllables*. A Greek word has as many syllables as it has vowels and/or diphthongs. Example:

ἄνθρωπος
εὐαγγελίζομαι

§203.3. *Tonal value of syllables*. Syllables may be long or short in tonal value. Syllables are long if the vowel is η, ω, or a diphthong.[2] Syllables are short if the vowel is ε or ο. Syllables with α, ι, or υ may be either long or short.

§203.4. *Syllable placement*. An accent may occur on any of the final three syllables of a word. The names for the final three syllables are:

ἄνθρω<u>πος</u> = ultima
ἄν<u>θρω</u>πος = penult
<u>ἄν</u>θρωπος = antipenult

§203.5. *Rules of accent*.

§203.5.1. *Acute accent*. The acute accent may sustain as many as three syl-

---

[1]Except enclitics and proclitics (see §71.1, §27.2, 71.2).
[2]Except ει and οι when final.

lables, i.e., it may stand on the antepenult, the penult, or the ultima.

§203.5.1.1. The acute accent may stand on either long or short syllables. Examples: ἤδη, λόγος.

§203.5.1.2. The acute accent may stand on any of the final three syllables. Example: ἄνθρωπος, λόγος, ἱερόν.

§203.5.1.3. The acute accent may not stand on the antepenult when the ultima sustains a long tonal value. Example: with a short ultima = ἄνθρωπος the acute stands on the antepenult; however, when the ultima becomes *long* the accent may not stand on a long penult when the ultima sustains a short tonal value. Example: with a short ultima the accent becomes circumflex = δοῦλος but with a long ultima the acute is retained[3] = δούλου.

§203.5.1.4. An acute accent on the ultima of a *nominative singular noun* becomes a circumflex when the ultima becomes long except in the accusative plural. Example: καρπός, καρποῦ.

§203.5.2. *Circumflex accent.* The circumflex accent may sustain as many as two syllables, i.e., it may stand on the penult or the ultima.

§203.5.2.1. The circumflex accent may stand on long syllables only. Examples: οἶκος, γλῶσσα.

§203.5.2.2. The circumflex accent may stand on either the penult or the ultima. Examples: οἶκος, καρπῶν.

§203.5.2.3. The circumflex accent may not stand on the penult when the ultima sustains a long tonal value. Example: with a short ultima = δοῦλος the circumflex stands on the penult; however, when the ultima is *long* the accent becomes acute = δούλου.

§203.5.2.4. The circumflex accent must stand on an accented penult when the ultima sustains a short tonal value. Example: with a short ultima = οἶκος the circumflex *must* stand *if an accent falls on the penult*.

§203.5.3. *Grave accent.* The grave accent is found on an accented ultima when the accent is *acute* and when *there follows another word without any intervening punctuation (note that the circumflex accent never changes to grave). Example:* ἐκεῖνος ἐστιν ὁ καρπός but ἐκεῖνος ἐστιν ὁ καρπὸς ἐμοῦ.

§203.6. *Accents on enclitics* [see §71.1]. An enclitic normally has no accent of

---

[3]The accent of the second inflected form in both the singular and plural is irregular and stands on the *antepenult* even when the ultima is long.

its own; it is pronounced with the word that precedes it. Example: ὁ λόγος μου. This phrase could actually be conceived of as one four syllable word = ὁλόγοσμου. The long ultima ου does not preclude the accent on the antipenult because when an enclitic has a long syllable it is considered short for the purpose of accenting.

§203.6.1. When an enclitic begins a sentence it retains its accent since no word precedes it. Example: εἰμὶ ἡ ὁδός.

§203.6.2. An enclitic (or a proclitic, § 27.2) accented before another enclitic. Example: ὁ ἀδελφός μού ἐστιν ἀγαθός.

§203.6.3. The acute accent does *not* change to a grave before an enclitic. ὁ ἀδελθός ἐστιν ἀγαθός.

§203.6.4. If a word preceeding an enclitic has an accent on the antipenult or a circumflex accent on the penult, there will be added an additional acute accent on the ultima. ὁ ἀπόστολός ἐστιν ἀγαθός or ὁ οἶκός ἐστιν ἀγαθός.

§203.6.5. If a word preceeding an enclitic (of one syllable) has an acute accent on the penult or a circumflex on the ultima, the enclitic will not be accented. Example: ὁ λόγος μου. But in the same situation when the enclitic has *two* syllables, the enclitic retains its accent. Example: ὁ λόγος ἐστὶν ἀληθινός.

§204. *Accenting Verbs and Nouns.*

§204.1. *Verbs.* The accent on verbs will be placed as far forward in the word as the general rules of accenting will permit, i.e., if the ultima is *long* place the accent on the penult (ἐλυόμην); if the ultima is *short* place the accent on the antipenult (λυόμενα).

For contract verbs follow these special rules:

(1) Write the <u>un</u>contracted form and accent it according to the rules for verbs discussed above.

(2) Note whether the accent falls on one of the contracting vowels (in the uncontracted form). If it does, it is important to note *which* of the two vowels is accented.

(3) Should the accent fall on the first member (from the left) of the two vowels to be contracted, the resulting *contracted form* will be accented with the circumflex. Example: τιμάω = τιμῶ

(4) Should the accent appear on the second member (from the left) of the two vowels to be contracted, the resulting *contracted form* will be accented with the acute. Example: τιμαόμεθα = τιμώμεθα.

§204.2. *Nouns.* You must learn where the accent falls on the nominative singular form of each noun because the accent will stay on that syllable unless the general rules of accenting dictate that it shift. Study these examples to see how the accent remains where it starts unless the general rules come into play (the number in [   ] after certain forms indicates the sub-paragraph in §203.5 where the rule may be found to account for the shift).

ACUTE ACCENT ON ANTIPENULT	ACUTE ACCENT ON PENULT	ACUTE ACCENT ON ULTIMA	CIRCUMFLEX ACCENT ON PENULT
SINGULAR			
ἄνθρωπος	τόπος	ἀδελφός	οἶκος
ἀνθρώπου [1.3]	τόπου	ἀδελφοῦ [1.5]	οἴκου [2.3]
ἀνθρώπου [1.3]	τόπου	ἀδελφοῦ [1.5]	οἴκου [2.3]
ἀνθρώπῳ [1.3]	τόπῳ	ἀδελφῷ [1.5]	οἴκῳ [2.3]
ἀνθρώπῳ [1.3]	τόπῳ	ἀδελφῷ [1.5]	οἴκῳ [2.3]
ἀνθρώπῳ [1.3]	τόπῳ	ἀδελφῷ [1.5]	οἴκῳ [2.3]
ἄνθρωπον	τόπον	ἀδελφόν	οἶκον
PLURAL			
ἄνθρωποι[4]	τόποι	ἀδελφοί	οἶκοι[4]
ἀνθρώπων [1.3]	τόπων	ἀδελφῶν	οἴκων
ἀνθρώπων [1.3]	τόπων	ἀδελφῶν	οἴκων
ἀνθρώποις	τόποις	ἀδελφοῖς	οἴκοις
ἀνθρώποις	τόποις	ἀδελφοῖς	οἴκοις
ἀνθρώποις	τόποις	ἀδελφοῖς	οἴκοις
ἀνθρώπους [1.3]	τόπους	ἀδελφούς [1.3]	οἴκους

---

[4] οι is short when final, as is αι.

Appendix 3
Principal Parts of Some Irregular Verbs

(§205)

PRESENT	FUTURE	AORIST	PERFECT	PERFECT MIDDLE/ PASSIVE	AORIST PASSIVE
ἄγω	ἄξω	ἤγαγον	—	—	ἤχθην
αἴρω	ἀρῶ	ἦρα	ἦρκα	ἦρμαι	ἤρθην
ἀκούω	ἀκούσω	ἤκουσα	ἀκήκοα	—	ἠκούσθην
ἁμαρτάνω	ἁμαρτήσω	ἡμάρτησα	ἡμάρτηκα	—	—
ἀποθνῄσκω	ἀποθανοῦμαι	ἀπέθανον	—	—	—
ἀποκτείνω	ἀποκτενῶ	ἀπέκτεινα	—	—	ἀπεκτάνθην
ἄρχω	ἄρξω	ἦρξα	—	—	—
ἀφίημι	ἀφήσω	ἀφῆκα	ἀφεῖκα	ἀφεῖμαι	—
βαίνω	βήσομαι	ἔβην	βέβηκα	—	ἐβήθην
βάλλω	βαλῶ	ἔβαλον	βέβληκα	βέβλημαι	ἐβλήθην
γίνομαι	γενήσομαι	ἐγενόμην	γέγονα	γεγένημαι	ἐγενήθην
γινώσκω	γνώσομαι	ἔγνων	ἔγνωκα	ἔγνωσμαι	ἐγνώσθην
γράφω	γράψω	ἔγραψα	γέγραφα	γέγραμμαι	ἐγράφην

δέχομαι	δέξομαι	ἐδεξάμην	——	δέδεγμαι	ἐδέχθην
διδάσκω	διδάξω	ἐδίδαξα	——	——	ἐδιδάχθην
δίδωμι	δώσω	ἔδωκα	δέδωκα	δέδομαι	ἐδόθην
ἐγγίζω	ἐγγίσω	ἤγγισα	ἤγγικα	——	——
εἰμί	ἔσομαι				
ἐλπίζω	ἐλπιῶ	ἤλπισα	ἤλπικα	——	——
ἔρχομαι	ἐλεύσομαι	ἦλθον	ἐλήλυθα	——	——
ἐσθίω	φάγομαι	ἔφαγον	——	——	——
θέλω	θελήσω	ἠθέλησα			
ἵστημι	στήσω	ἔστησα	ἕστηκα	——	ἐστάθην
καλέω	καλέσω	ἐκάλεσα	κέκληκα	κέκλημαι	ἐκλήθην
κρίνω	κρινῶ	ἔκρινα	κέκρικα	κέκριμαι	ἐκρίθην
λαμβάνω	λήμψομαι	ἔλαβον	εἴληφα	εἴλημμαι	ἐλήμφθην
λείπω	λείψω	ἔλιπον	——	λέλειμμαι	ἐλείφθην
μένω	μενῶ	ἔμεινα	μεμένηκα	——	——
πάσχω	——	ἔπαθον	πέπονθα		
πείθω	πείσω	ἔπεισα	πέποιθα	πέπεισμαι	ἐπείσθην
σῴζω	σώσω	ἔσωσα	σέσωκα	σέσωσμαι	ἐσώθην
τίθημι	θήσω	ἔθηκα	τέθεικα	τέθειμαι	ἐτέθην
φαίνω	φανοῦμαι				ἐφάνην
φέρω	οἴσω	ἤνεγκα	ἐνήνοχα	——	ἠνέχθην

Appendix 4
Paradigms

§206. *Nouns*.

§206.1. *First declension*.

§206.1.1. *Feminine* [§57].

CASE	SINGULAR ε, ι, ϱ	SINGULAR σ, λλ, ψ, ξ, ς	SINGULAR ANY OTHER LETTER	PLURAL ALL
Nom	ἐκκλησία	γλῶσσα	διδαχή	_____-αι
Gen	ἐκκλησίας	γλώσσης	διδαχῆς	_____-ων
Abl	ἐκκλησίας	γλώσσης	διδαχῆς	_____-ων
Dat	ἐκκλησίᾳ	γλώσσῃ	διδαχῇ	_____-αις
Loc	ἐκκλησίᾳ	γλώσσῃ	διδαχῇ	_____-αις
Inst	ἐκκλησίᾳ	γλώσσῃ	διδαχῇ	_____-αις
Acc	ἐκκλησίαν	γλῶσσαν	διδαχήν	_____-ας

§206.1.2. *Masculine* [§58].

CASE	SINGULAR ε, ι, π	SINGULAR ANY OTHER LETTER	PLURAL ALL
Nom	μεσσίας	μαθητής	_____-αι
Gen	μεσσίου	μαθητοῦ	_____-ων
Abl	μεσσίου	μαθητοῦ	_____-ων
Dat	μεσσίᾳ	μαθητῇ	_____-αις
Loc	μεσσίᾳ	μαθητῇ	_____-αις
Inst	μεσσίᾳ	μαθητῇ	_____-αις
Acc	μεσσίαν	μαθητήν	_____-ας

§206.2. *Second declension*.

§206.2.1. *Masculine and feminine* [§28.1].

	SINGULAR		**PLURAL**
CASE	MASCULINE	FEMININE	ALL
Nom	λόγος	ὁδός	_____-οι
Gen	λόγου	ὁδοῦ	_____-ων
Abl	λόγου	ὁδοῦ	_____-ων
Dat	λόγῳ	ὁδῷ	_____-οις
Loc	λόγῳ	ὁδῷ	_____-οις
Inst	λόγῳ	ὁδῷ	_____-οις
Acc	λόγον	ὁδόν	_____-ους

§206.2.2. *Neuter* [§28.2].

	SINGULAR	**PLURAL**
CASE		
Nom	δῶρον	_____-α
Gen	δώρου	_____-ων
Abl	δώρου	_____-ων
Dat	δώρῳ	_____-οις
Loc	δώρῳ	_____-οις
Inst	δώρῳ	_____-οις
Acc	δῶρον	_____-α

§206.3. *Third declension.*

§206.3.1. *Liquid* [§144].

	SINGULAR		**PLURAL**
CASE	λ, μ, ω, ρ	ερ	ALL
Nom	αἰών	πατήρ	_____-ες
Gen	αἰῶνος	πατρός	_____-ων
Abl	αἰῶνος	πατρός	_____-ων
Dat	αἰῶνι	πατρί	_____-ασι (ν)
Loc	αἰῶνι	πατρί	_____-ασι (ν)
Inst	αἰῶνι	πατρί	_____-ασι (ν)
Acc	αἰῶνα	πατέρα	_____-ας

§206.3.2. *Mute* [§145].

	SINGULAR		**PLURAL**
CASE	MONOSYLLABIC	ANY OTHER LETTER	ALL
Nom	νύξ	ἐλπίς	_____-ες
Gen	νυκτός	ἐλπίδος	_____-ων
Abl	νυκτός	ἐλπίδος	_____-ων
Dat	νυκτί	ἐλπίδι	_____-σι (ν)
Loc	νυκτί	ἐλπίδι	_____-σι (ν)
Inst	νυκτί	ἐλπίδι	_____-σι (ν)

| Acc | νύκτα | ἐλπίδα | _____-ας |

§206.3.3. *Neuter* [§148].

CASE	SINGULAR		PLURAL ALL
	ματ	ες	
Nom	ὄνομα	γένος	_____-α
Gen	ὀνόματος	γένους	_____-ων
Abl	ὀνόματος	γένους	_____-ων
Dat	ὀνόματι	γένει	_____-σι (ν)
Loc	ὀνόματι	γένει	_____-σι (ν)
Inst	ὀνόματι	γένει	_____-σι (ν)
Acc	ὄνομα	γένος	_____-α

§206.3.4 *Vowel stem* [§149].

CASE	SINGULAR			PLURAL ALL
	ι STEM	υ STEM	ευ STEM	
Nom	πόλις	στάχυς	βασιλεύς	_____-ες
Gen	πόλεως	στάχυος	βασιλέως	_____-ων
Abl	πόλεως	στάχυος	βασιλέως	_____-ων
Dat	πόλει	στάχυι	βασιλεῖ	_____-σι (ν)
Loc	πόλει	στάχυι	βασιλεῖ	_____-σι (ν)
Inst	πόλει	στάχυι	βασιλεῖ	_____-σι (ν)
Acc	πόλιν	στάχυν	βασιλέα	_____-ας

§207. *Pronouns.*

§207.1. *Personal pronouns* [§70.1].

FIRST PERSON

CASE	SINGULAR	PLURAL
Nom	ἐγώ, *I*	ἡμεῖς, *we*
Gen	ἐμοῦ (or μου), *of me*	ἡμῶν, *of us*
Abl	ἐμοῦ (or μου), *from me*	ἡμῶν, *from us*
Dat	ἐμοί (or μοι), *to* or *for me*	ἡμῖν, *to* or *for us*
Loc	ἐμοί (or μοι), *in me*	ἡμῖν, *in us*
Inst	ἐμοί (or μοι), *by me*	ἡμῖν, *by us*
Acc	ἐμέ (or με), *me*	ἡμᾶς, *us*

SECOND PERSON

CASE	SINGULAR	PLURAL
Nom	σύ, *you*	ὑμεῖς, *you*
Gen	σοῦ, *of you*	ὑμῶν, *of you*
Abl	σοῦ, *from you*	ὑμῶν, *from you*

Dat	σοί, *to* or *for you*	ὑμῖν, *to* or *for you*
Loc	σοί, *in you*	ὑμῖν, *in you*
Inst	σοί, *by you*	ὑμῖν, *by you*
Acc	σέ, *you*	ὑμᾶς, *you*

THIRD PERSON - SINGULAR

CASE	MASCULINE	FEMININE	NEUTER
Nom	αὐτός, *he*	αὐτή, *she*	αὐτό, *it*
Gen	αὐτοῦ, *of him*	αὐτῆς, *of her*	αὐτοῦ, *of it*
Abl	αὐτοῦ, *from him*	αὐτῆς, *from her*	αὐτοῦ, *from it*
Dat	αὐτῷ, *to* or *for him*	αὐτῇ, *to* or *for her*	αὐτῷ, *to* or *for it*
Loc	αὐτῷ, *in him*	αὐτῇ, *in her*	αὐτῷ, *in it*
Inst	αὐτῷ, *by him*	αὐτῇ, *by her*	αὐτῷ, *by it*
Acc	αὐτόν, *him*	αὐτήν, *her*	αὐτό, *it*

THIRD PERSON - PLURAL

CASE	MASCULINE	FEMININE	NEUTER
Nom	αὐτοί, *they*	αὐταί, *they*	αὐτά, *they*
Gen	αὐτῶν, *of them*	αὐτῶν, *of them*	αὐτῶν, *of them*
Abl	αὐτῶν, *from them*	αὐτῶν, *from them*	αὐτῶν, *from them*
Dat	αὐτοῖς, *to* or *for them*	αὐταῖς, *to* or *for them*	αὐτοῖς, *to* or *for them*
Loc	αὐτοῖς, *in them*	αὐταῖς, *in them*	αὐτοῖς, *in them*
Inst	αὐτοῖς, *by them*	αὐταῖς, *by them*	αὐτοῖς, *by them*
Acc	αὐτούς, *them*	αὐτάς, *them*	αὐτά, *them*

§207.2. *Demonstrative pronouns* [§70.2].

SINGULAR

CASE	THIS - NEAR MASCULINE	FEMININE	NEUTER	THAT - REMOTE MASCULINE	FEMININE	NEUTER
Nom	οὗτος	αὕτη	τοῦτο	ἐκεῖνος	ἐκείνη	ἐκεῖνο
Gen	τούτου	ταύτης	τούτου	ἐκείνου	ἐκείνης	ἐκείνου
Abl	τούτου	ταύτης	τούτου	ἐκείνου	ἐκείνης	ἐκείνου
Dat	τούτῳ	ταύτῃ	τούτῳ	ἐκείνῳ	ἐκείνῃ	ἐκείνῳ
Loc	τούτῳ	ταύτῃ	τούτῳ	ἐκείνῳ	ἐκείνῃ	ἐκείνῳ
Inst	τούτῳ	ταύτῃ	τούτῳ	ἐκείνῳ	ἐκείνῃ	ἐκείνῳ
Acc	τοῦτον	ταύτην	τοῦτο	ἐκεῖνον	ἐκείνην	ἐκεῖνο

PLURAL

CASE	THESE - NEAR MASCULINE	FEMININE	NEUTER	THOSE - REMOTE MASCULINE	FEMININE	NEUTER
Nom	οὗτοι	αὗται	ταῦτα	ἐκεῖνοι	ἐκεῖναι	ἐκεῖνα

Gen	τούτων	ταύτων	τούτων	ἐκείνων	ἐκείνων	ἐκείνων
Abl	τούτων	ταύτων	τούτων	ἐκείνων	ἐκείνων	ἐκείνων
Dat	τούτοις	ταύταις	τούτοις	ἐκείνοις	ἐκείναις	ἐκείνοις
Loc	τούτοις	ταύταις	τούτοις	ἐκείνοις	ἐκείναις	ἐκείνοις
Inst	τούτοις	ταύταις	τούτοις	ἐκείνοις	ἐκείναις	ἐκείνοις
Acc	τούτους	ταύτας	ταῦτα	ἐκείνους	ἐκείνας	ἐκεῖνα

§207.3. *Possessive pronouns* [§177.1].

FIRST PERSON SINGULAR

| | SINGULAR | | | PLURAL | | |
CASE	MASCULINE	FEMININE	NEUTER	MASCULINE	FEMININE	NEUTER
Nom	ἐμός	ἐμή	ἐμόν	ἐμοί	ἐμαί	ἐμά
Gen	ἐμοῦ	ἐμῆς	ἐμοῦ	ἐμῶν	ἐμῶν	ἐμῶν
Abl	ἐμοῦ	ἐμῆς	ἐμοῦ	ἐμῶν	ἐμῶν	ἐμῶν
Dat	ἐμῷ	ἐμῇ	ἐμῷ	ἐμοῖς	ἐμαῖς	ἐμοῖς
Loc	ἐμῷ	ἐμῇ	ἐμῳ	ἐμοῖς	ἐμαῖς	ἐμοῖς
Inst	ἐμῷ	ἐμῇ	ἐμῷ	ἐμοῖς	ἐμαῖς	ἐμοῖς
Acc	ἐμόν	ἐμήν	ἐμόν	ἐμούς	ἐμάς	ἐμά

SECOND PERSON SINGULAR

| | SINGULAR | | | PLURAL | | |
CASE	MASCULINE	FEMININE	NEUTER	MASCULINE	FEMININE	NEUTER
Nom	σός	σή	σόν	σοί	σαί	σά
Gen	σοῦ	σῆς	σοῦ	σῶν	σῶν	σῶν
Abl	σοῦ	σῆς	σοῦ	σῶν	σῶν	σῶν
Dat	σῷ	σῇ	σῷ	σοῖς	σαῖς	σοῖς
Loc	σῷ	σῇ	σῷ	σοῖς	σαῖς	σοῖς
Inst	σῷ	σῇ	σῷ	σοῖς	σαῖς	σοῖς
Acc	σόν	σήν	σόν	σούς	σάς	σά

FIRST PERSON PLURAL

| | SINGULAR | | | PLURAL | | |
CASE	MASCULINE	FEMININE	NEUTER	MASCULINE	FEMININE	NEUTER
Nom	ἡμέτερος	ἡμετέρα	ἡμέτερον	ἡμέτεροι	ἡμέτεραι	ἡμέτερα
Gen	ἡμετέρου	ἡμετέρας	ἡμετέρου	ἡμετέρων	ἡμετέρων	ἡμετέρων
Abl	ἡμετέρου	ἡμετέρας	ἡμετέρου	ἡμετέρων	ἡμετέρων	ἡμετέρων
Dat	ἡμετέρῳ	ἡμετέρα	ἡμετέρῳ	ἡμετέροις	ἡμετέραις	ἡμετέροις
Loc	ἡμετέρῳ	ἡμετέρα	ἡμετέρῳ	ἡμετέροις	ἡμετέραις	ἡμετέροις
Inst	ἡμετέρῳ	ἡμετέρα	ἡμετέρῳ	ἡμετέροις	ἡμετέραις	ἡμετέροις
Acc	ἡμέτερον	ἡμετέραν	ἡμέτερον	ἡμετέρους	ἡμετέρας	ἡμέτερα

SECOND PERSON PLURAL

| | SINGULAR | | | PLURAL | | |
CASE	MASCULINE	FEMININE	NEUTER	MASCULINE	FEMININE	NEUTER

Nom	ὑμέτερος	ὑμετέρα	ὑμέτερον	ὑμέτεροι	ὑμέτεραι	ὑμέτερα
Gen	ὑμετέρου	ὑμετέρας	ὑμετέρου	ὑμετέρων	ὑμετέρων	ὑμετέρων
Abl	ὑμετέρου	ὑμετέρας	ὑμετέρου	ὑμετέρων	ὑμετέρων	ὑμετέρων
Dat	ὑμετέρῳ	ὑμετέρα	ὑμετέρῳ	ὑμετέροις	ὑμετέραις	ὑμετέροις
Loc	ὑμετέρῳ	ὑμετέρα	ὑμετέρῳ	ὑμετέροις	ὑμετέραις	ὑμετέροις
Inst	ὑμετέρῳ	ὑμετέρα	ὑμετέρῳ	ὑμετέροις	ὑμετέραις	ὑμετέροις
Acc	ὑμέτερον	ὑμετέραν	ὑμέτερον	ὑμετέρους	ὑμετέρας	ὑμέτερα

§207.4. *Reflexive pronouns* [§177.2].

FIRST PERSON

	SINGULAR - MYSELF			PLURAL - OURSELVES		
CASE	MASCULINE	FEMININE	NEUTER	MASCULINE	FEMININE	NEUTER
Gen	ἐμαυτοῦ	ἐμαυτῆς	-	ἑαυτῶν	ἑαυτῶν	-
Abl	ἐμαυτοῦ	ἐμαυτῆς	-	ἑαυτῶν	ἑαυτῶν	-
Dat	ἐμαυτῷ	ἐμαυτῇ	-	ἑαυτοῖς	ἑαυταῖς	-
Loc	ἐμαυτῷ	ἐμαυτῇ	-	ἑαυτοῖς	ἑαυταῖς	-
Inst	ἐμαυτῷ	ἐμαυτῇ	-	ἑαυτοῖς	ἑαυταῖς	-
Acc	ἐμαυτόν	ἐμαυτήν	-	ἑαυτούς	ἑαυτάς	-

SECOND PERSON

	SINGULAR - YOURSELF			PLURAL - YOURSELVES		
CASE	MASCULINE	FEMININE	NEUTER	MASCULINE	FEMININE	NEUTER
Gen	σεαυτοῦ	σεαυτῆς	-	ἑαυτῶν	ἑαυτῶν	-
Abl	σεαυτοῦ	σεαυτῆς	-	ἑαυτῶν	ἑαυτῶν	-
Dat	σεαυτῷ	σεαυτῇ	-	ἑαυτοῖς	ἑαυταῖς	-
Loc	σεαυτῷ	σεαυτῇ	-	ἑαυτοῖς	ἑαυταῖς	-
Inst	σεαυτῷ	σεαυτῇ	-	ἑαυτοῖς	ἑαυταῖς	-
Acc	σεαυτόν	σεαυτήν	-	ἑαυτούς	ἑαυτάς	-

THIRD PERSON

	SINGULAR - HIMSELF			PLURAL - THEMSELVES		
CASE	MASCULINE	FEMININE	NEUTER	MASCULINE	FEMININE	NEUTER
Gen	ἑαυτοῦ	ἑαυτῆς	ἑαυτοῦ	ἑαυτῶν	ἑαυτῶν	ἑαυτῶν
Abl	ἑαυτοῦ	ἑαυτῆς	ἑαυτοῦ	ἑαυτῶν	ἑαυτῶν	ἑαυτῶν
Dat	ἑαυτῷ	ἑαυτῇ	ἑαυτῷ	ἑαυτοῖς	ἑαυταῖς	ἑαυτοῖς
Loc	ἑαυτῷ	ἑαυτῇ	ἑαυτῷ	ἑαυτοῖς	ἑαυταῖς	ἑαυτοῖς
Inst	ἑαυτῷ	ἑαυτῇ	ἑαυτῷ	ἑαυτοῖς	ἑαυταῖς	ἑαυτοῖς
Acc	ἑαυτόν	ἑαυτήν	ἑαυτό	ἑαυτούς	ἑαυτάς	ἑαυτά

§207.5. *Interrogative pronouns* [§177.3].

	SINGULAR			PLURAL		
CASE	MASCULINE	FEMININE	NEUTER	MASCULINE	FEMININE	NEUTER
Nom	τίς	τίς	τί	τίνες	τίνες	τίνα
Gen	τίνος	τίνος	τίνος	τίνων	τίνων	τίνων

Abl	τίνος	τίνος	τίνος	τίνων	τίνων	τίνων
Dat	τίνι	τίνι	τίνι	τίσι (ν)	τίσι (ν)	τίσι (ν)
Loc	τίνι	τίνι	τίνι	τίσι (ν)	τίσι (ν)	τίσι (ν)
Inst	τίνι	τίνι	τίνι	τίσι (ν)	τίσι (ν)	τίσι (ν)
Acc	τίνα	τίνα	τί	τίνας	τίνας	τίνα

§207.6. *Indefinite pronouns* [§177.4].

	SINGULAR			PLURAL		
CASE	MASCULINE	FEMININE	NEUTER	MASCULINE	FEMININE	NEUTER
Nom	τις	τις	τι	τινες	τινες	τινα
Gen	τινος	τινος	τινος	τινων	τινων	τινων
Abl	τινος	τινος	τινος	τινων	τινων	τινων
Dat	τινι	τινι	τινι	τισι (ν)	τισι (ν)	τισι (ν)
Loc	τινι	τινι	τινι	τισι (ν)	τισι (ν)	τισι (ν)
Inst	τινι	τινι	τινι	τισι (ν)	τισι (ν)	τισι (ν)
Acc	τινα	τινα	τι	τινας	τινας	τινα

§207.7. *Relative pronouns* [§177.5].

	SINGULAR			PLURAL		
CASE	MASCULINE	FEMININE	NEUTER	MASCULINE	FEMININE	NEUTER
Nom	ὅς	ἥ	ὅ	οἵ	αἵ	ἅ
Gen	οὖ	ἧς	οὖ	ὧν	ὧν	ὧν
Abl	οὖ	ἧς	οὖ	ὧν	ὧν	ὧν
Dat	ᾧ	ᾗ	ᾧ	οἷς	αἷς	οἷς
Loc	ᾧ	ᾗ	ᾧ	οἷς	αἷς	οἷς
Inst	ᾧ	ᾗ	ᾧ	οἷς	αἷς	οἷς
Acc	ὅν	ἥν	ὅν	οὕς	ἅς	ἅ

§207.8. *Indefinite relative pronouns* [§177.6].

	SINGULAR			PLURAL		
CASE	MASCULINE	FEMININE	NEUTER	MASCULINE	FEMININE	NEUTER
Nom	ὅστις	ἥτις	ὅτι	οἵτινες	αἵτινες	ἅτινα

§207.9. *Negative pronouns* [§177.7].

	SINGULAR		
CASE	MASCULINE	FEMININE	NEUTER
Nom	οὐδείς	οὐδεμία	οὐδέν
Gen	οὐδενός	οὐδεμιᾶς	οὐδενός
Abl	οὐδενός	οὐδεμιᾶς	οὐδενός
Dat	οὐδενί	οὐδεμιᾷ	οὐδενί
Loc	οὐδενί	οὐδεμιᾷ	οὐδενί
Inst	οὐδενί	ουδεμιᾷ	οὐδενί

Acc   οὐδένα   οὐδεμίαν   οὐδέν

§207.10. *Reciprocal pronouns* [§177.8].
      ἀλλήλων   ἀλλήλοις   ἀλλήλους

§207.11. *Correlative pronouns* [§177.9].

	SINGULAR			**PLURAL**		
CASE	MASCULINE	FEMININE	NEUTER	MASCULINE	FEMININE	NEUTER
Nom	τοιοῦτος	τοιαύτη	τοιοῦτο	τοιοῦτοι	τοιαῦται	τοιαῦτα
Gen	τοιούτου	τοιαύτης	τοιούτου	τοιούτων	τοιαύτων	τοιούτων
Abl	τοιούτου	τοιαύτης	τοιούτου	τοιούτων	τοιαύτων	τοιούτων
Dat	τοιούτῳ	τοιαύτῃ	τοιούτῳ	τοιούτοις	τοιαύταις	τοιούτοις
Loc	τοιούτῳ	τοιαύτῃ	τοιούτῳ	τοιούτοις	τοιαύταις	τοιούτοις
Inst	τοιούτῳ	τοιαύτῃ	τοιούτῳ	τοιούτοις	τοιαύταις	τοιούτοις
Acc	τοιοῦτον	τοιαύτην	τοιοῦτο	τοιούτους	τοιαύτας	τοιαῦτα

§208. *Adjectives.*

§208.1. *ες stem adjectives* [§191.1].

	SINGULAR			**PLURAL**		
CASE	MASCULINE	FEMININE	NEUTER	MASCULINE	FEMININE	NEUTER
Nom	ψευδής	ψευδής	ψευδές	ψευδεῖς	ψευδεῖς	ψευδῆ
Gen	ψευδοῦς	ψευδοῦς	ψευδοῦς	ψευδῶν	ψευδῶν	ψευδῶν
Abl	ψευδοῦς	ψευδοῦς	ψευδοῦς	ψευδῶν	ψευδῶν	ψευδῶν
Dat	ψευδεῖ	ψευδεῖ	ψευδεῖ	ψευδέσι	ψευδέσι	ψευδέσι
Loc	ψευδεῖ	ψευδεῖ	ψευδεῖ	ψευδέσι	ψευδέσι	ψευδέσι
Inst	ψευδεῖ	ψευδεῖ	ψευδεῖ	ψευδέσι	ψευδέσι	ψευδέσι
Acc	ψευδῆ	ψευδῆ	ψευδές	ψευδεῖς	ψευδεῖς	ψευδῆ

§208.2. *υ stem adjectives* [§191.2].

	SINGULAR			**PLURAL**		
CASE	MASCULINE	FEMININE	NEUTER	MASCULINE	FEMININE	NEUTER
Nom	βραχύς	βραχεῖα	βραχύ	βραχεῖς	βραχεῖαι	βραχέα
Gen	βραχέως	βραχείας	βραχέως	βραχέων	βραχειῶν	βραχέων
Abl	βραχέως	βραχείας	βραχέως	βραχέων	βραχειῶν	βραχέων
Dat	βραχεῖ	βραχείᾳ	βραχεῖ	βραχέσι	βραχείαις	βραχέσι
Loc	βραχεῖ	βραχείᾳ	βραχεῖ	βραχέσι	βραχείαις	βραχέσι
Inst	βραχεῖ	βραχείᾳ	βραχεῖ	βραχέσι	βραχείαις	βραχέσι
Acc	βραχύν	βραχεῖαν	βραχύ	βραχεῖς	βραχείας	βραχέα

§208.3. *αντ stem adjectives* [§191.3].

CASE	SINGULAR			PLURAL		
	MASCULINE	FEMININE	NEUTER	MASCULINE	FEMININE	NEUTER
Nom	πᾶς	πᾶσα	πᾶν	πάντες	πᾶσαι	πάντα
Gen	παντός	πάσης	παντός	πάντων	πασῶν	πάντων
Abl	παντός	πάσης	παντός	πάντων	πασῶν	πάντων
Dat	παντί	πάσῃ	παντί	πᾶσι	πάσαις	πᾶσι
Loc	παντί	πάσῃ	παντί	πᾶσι	πάσαις	πᾶσι
Inst	παντί	πάσῃ	παντί	πᾶσι	πάσαις	πᾶσι
Acc	πάντα	πᾶσαν	πᾶν	πάντας	πάσας	πάντα

§208.4. *Irregular adjectives* [§192].

CASE	SINGULAR			PLURAL		
	MASCULINE	FEMININE	NEUTER	MASCULINE	FEMININE	NEUTER
Nom	πολύς	πολλή	πολύ	πολλοί	πολλαί	πολλά
Gen	πολλοῦ	πολλῆς	πολλοῦ	πολλῶν	πολλῶν	πολλῶν
Abl	πολλοῦ	πολλῆς	πολλοῦ	πολλῶν	πολλῶν	πολλῶν
Dat	πολλῷ	πολλῇ	πολλῷ	πολλοῖς	πολλαῖς	πολλοῖς
Loc	πολλῷ	πολλῇ	πολλῷ	πολλοῖς	πολλαῖς	πολλοῖς
Inst	πολλῷ	πολλῇ	πολλῷ	πολλοῖς	πολλαῖς	πολλοῖς
Acc	πολύν	πολλήν	πολύ	πολλούς	πολλάς	πολλά

§209. *Verbs.*

§209.1. *Present tense.*

§209.1.1. *Indicative.*

§209.1.1.1. *Active* [§16].

	SINGULAR	PLURAL
1st per	λύω, *I am loosing*	λύομεν, *we are loosing*
2nd per	λύεις, *you are loosing*	λύετε, *you are loosing*
3rd per	λύει, *he, she, it is loosing*	λύουσι(ν), *they are loosing*

§209.1.1.2. *Middle/passive*[2] [§38].

	SINGULAR	PLURAL
1st per	λύομαι, *I am loosing myself*	λυόμεθα, *we are loosing ourselves*
2nd per	λύῃ, *you are loosing yourself*	λύεσθε, *you are loosing yourselves*
3rd per	λύεται, *he is loosing himself*	λύονται, *they are loosing themselves*

---

[2]In those case where the middle and passive forms are *identical* the forms will only be listed once and the translation will be given for the *middle* voice only.

§209.1.2. *Subjunctive.*

§209.1.2.1. *Active* [§161.1].

	SINGULAR	PLURAL
1st per	λύω	λύωμεν
2nd per	λύῃς	λύητε
3rd per	λύῃ	λύωσι (ν)

§209.1.2.2. *Middle/passive* [§161.2].

	SINGULAR	PLURAL
1st per	λύωμαι	λυώμεθα
2nd per	λύῃ	λύησθε
3rd per	λύηται	λύωνται

§209.1.3. *Imperative.*

§209.1.3.1. *Active* [§169.1].

	SINGULAR	PLURAL
2nd per	λῦε, *you loose*	λύετε, *you loose*
3rd per	λυέτω, *let him, her, it loose*	λυέτωσαν, *let them loose*

§209.1.3.2. *Middle/passive* [§169.2].

	SINGULAR	PLURAL
2nd per	λύου, *you loose for yourself*	λύεσθε, *you loose for yourselves*
3rd per	λυέσθω, *let him loose for himself*	λυέσθωσαν, *let them loose for themselves*

§209.1.4. *Participle.*

§209.1.4.1. *Active* [124.1].

SINGULAR

CASE	MASCULINE	FEMININE	NEUTER
Nom	λύων	λύουσα	λῦον
Gen	λύοντος	λυούσης	λύοντος
Abl	λύοντος	λυούσης	λύοντος
Dat	λύοντι	λυούσῃ	λύοντι
Loc	λύοντι	λυούσῃ	λύοντι
Inst	λύοντι	λυούσῃ	λύοντι
Acc	λύοντα	λύουσαν	λῦον

PLURAL

CASE	MASCULINE	FEMININE	NEUTER
Nom	λύοντες	λύουσαι	λύοντα
Gen	λυόντων	λυουσῶν	λυόντων

Abl	λυόντων	λυουσῶν	λυόντων
Dat	λύουσι (ν)	λυούσαις	λύουσι (ν)
Loc	λύουσι (ν)	λυούσαις	λύουσι (ν)
Inst	λύουσι (ν)	λυούσαις	λύουσι (ν)
Acc	λύοντας	λυούσας	λύοντα

§209.1.4.2. *Middle/passive* [§124.2].

SINGULAR

CASE	MASCULINE	FEMININE	NEUTER
Nom	λυόμενος	λυομένη	λυόμενον
Gen	λυομένου	λυομένης	λυομένου
Abl	λυομέμου	λυομένης	λυομένου
Dat	λυομένῳ	λυομένη	λυομένῳ
Loc	λυομένῳ	λυομένη	λυομένῳ
Inst	λυομένῳ	λυομένη	λυομένῳ
Acc	λυόμενον	λυομένην	λυόμενον

PLURAL

CASE	MASCULINE	FEMININE	NEUTER
Nom	λυόμενοι	λυόμεναι	λυόμενα
Gen	λυομένων	λυομένων	λυομένων
Abl	λυομένων	λυομένων	λυομένων
Dat	λυομένοις	λυομέναις	λυομένοις
Loc	λυομένοις	λυομέναις	λυομένοις
Inst	λυομένοις	λυομέναις	λυομένοις
Acc	λυομένους	λυομένας	λυόμενα

§209.1.5. *Infinitive*.

ACTIVE	MIDDLE	PASSIVE
λύειν	λύεσθαι	λύεσθαι
to loose	*to loose oneself*	*to be loosed*

§209.2. *Imperfect tense*.

§209.2.1. *Indicative*.[1]

§209.2.1.1. *Active* [§84.1].

	SINGULAR	PLURAL
1st per	ἔλυον, *I was loosing*	ἐλύομεν, *we were loosing*
2nd per	ἐλύες, *you were loosing*	ἐλύετε, *you were loosing*
3rd per	ἔλυε, *he, she, it was loosing*	ἔλυον, *they were loosing*

---

[1]The imperfect and pluperfect occur only in the indicative mood in the New Testament.

§209.2.1.2. *Middle/passive* [§84.2].

SINGULAR	PLURAL
1st per ἐλυόμην, *I was loosing myself*	ἐλυόμεθα, *we were loosing ourselves*
2nd per ἐλύου, *you were loosing yourself*	ἐλύεσθε, *you were loosing yourselves*
3rd per ἐλύετο, *he was loosing himself*	ἐλύοντο, *they were loosing themselves*

§209.3. *Future tense.*

§209.3.1. *Indicative.*

§209.3.1.1. *Active* [§95].

SINGULAR	PLURAL
1st per ἀκούσω, *I shall hear*	ἀκούσομεν, *we shall hear*
2nd per ἀκούσεις, *you will hear*	ἀκούσετε, *you will hear*
3rd per ἀκούσει, *he, she, it will hear*	ἀκούσουσι, *they will hear*

§209.3.1.2. *Middle* [§95].

SINGULAR	PLURAL
1st per ἀκούσομαι, *I shall hear myself*	ἀκουσόμεθα, *we shall hear ourselves*
2nd per ἀκούσῃ, *you will hear yourself*	ἀκούσεσθε, *you will hear yourselves*
3rd per ἀκούσεται, *he will hear himself*	ἀκούσονται, *they will hear themselves*

§209.3.1.3. *Passive* [§115].

SINGULAR	PLURAL
1st per λυθήσομαι, *I shall be loosed*	λυθησόμεθα, *we shall be loosed*
2nd per λυθήσῃ, *you will be loosed*	λυθήσεσθε, *you will be loosed*
3rd per λυθήσεται, *he, she, it will be loosed*	λυθήσονται, *they will be loosed*

§209.3.2. *Participle.*

§209.3.2.1. *Active* [124.3].

SINGULAR

CASE	MASCULINE	FEMININE	NEUTER
Nom	λύσων	λύσουσα	λῦσον
Gen	λύσοντος	λυσούσης	λύσοντος
Abl	λύσοντος	λυσούσης	λύσοντος
Dat	λύσοντι	λυσούσῃ	λύσοντι
Loc	λύσοντι	λυσούσῃ	λύσοντι

Inst	λύσοντι	λυσούσῃ	λύσοντι
Acc	λύσοντα	λύσουσαν	λῦσον

PLURAL

CASE	MASCULINE	FEMININE	NEUTER
Nom	λύσοντες	λύσουσαι	λύσοντα
Gen	λυσόντων	λυσουσῶν	λυσόντων
Abl	λυσόντων	λυσουσῶν	λυσόντων
Dat	λύσουσι (ν)	λυσούσαις	λύσουσι (ν)
Loc	λύσουσι (ν)	λυσούσαις	λύσουσι (ν)
Inst	λύσουσι (ν)	λυσούσαις	λύσουσι (ν)
Acc	λύσοντας	λυσούσας	λύσοντα

§209.3.2.2. *Middle* [§124.4].

SINGULAR

CASE	MASCULINE	FEMININE	NEUTER
Nom	λυσόμενος	λυσομένη	λυσόμενον
Gen	λυσομένου	λυσομένης	λυσομένου
Abl	λυσομένου	λυσομένης	λυσομένου
Dat	λυσομένῳ	λυσομένη	λυσομένῳ
Loc	λυσομένῳ	λυσομένη	λυσομένῳ
Inst	λυσομένῳ	λυσομένη	λυσομένῳ
Acc	λυσόμενον	λυσομένην	λυσόμενον

PLURAL

CASE	MASCULINE	FEMININE	NEUTER
Nom	λυσόμενοι	λυσόμεναι	λυσόμενα
Gen	λυσομένων	λυσομένων	λυσομένων
Abl	λυσομένων	λυσομένων	λυσομένων
Dat	λυσομένοις	λυσομέναις	λυσομένοις
Loc	λυσομένοις	λυσομέναις	λυσομένοις
Inst	λυσομένοις	λυσομέναις	λυσομένοις
Acc	λυσομένους	λυσομένας	λυσόμενα

§209.3.2.3. *Passive* [§124.5].

SINGULAR

CASE	MASCULINE	FEMININE	NEUTER
Nom	λυθησόμενος	λυθησομένη	λυθησόμενον
Gen	λυθησομένου	λυθησομένης	λυθησομένου
Abl	λυθησομένου	λυθησομένης	λυθησομένου
Dat	λυθησομένῳ	λυθησομένη	λυθησομένῳ

Loc	λυθησομένῳ	λυθησομένη	λυθησομένῳ
Inst	λυθησομένῳ	λυθησομένη	λυθησομένῳ
Acc	λυθησόμενον	λυθησομένην	λυθησόμενον

PLURAL

CASE	MASCULINE	FEMININE	NEUTER
Nom	λυθησόμενοι	λυθησόμεναι	λυθησόμενα
Gen	λυθησομένων	λυθησομένων	λυθησομένων
Abl	λυθησομένων	λυθησομένων	λυθησομένων
Dat	λυθησομένοις	λυθησομέναις	λυθησομένοις
Loc	λυθησομένοις	λυθησομέναις	λυθησομένοις
Inst	λυθησομένοις	λυθησομέναις	λυθησομένοις
Acc	λυθησομένους	λυθησομένας	λυθησόμενα

§209.3.3. *Infinitive.*

ACTIVE	MIDDLE	PASSIVE
λύσειν	λύσεσθαι	λυθήσεσθαι
to loose	*to loose oneself*	*to be loosed*

§209.4. *Aorist tense.*

§209.4.1. *Indicative.*

§209.4.1.1. *Active.*

FIRST AORIST [§103.1]

	SINGULAR	PLURAL
1st per	ἔλυσα, *I loosed*	ἐλύσαμεν, *we loosed*
2nd per	ἔλυσας, *you loosed*	ἐλύσατε, *you loosed*
3rd per	ἔλυσε (ν), *he, she, it loosed*	ἔλυσαν, *they loosed*

SECOND AORIST [§108.1]

	SINGULAR	PLURAL
1st per	ἔλαβον, *I took*	ἐλάβομεν, *we took*
2nd per	ἔλαβες, *you took*	ἐλάβετε, *you took*
3rd per	ἔλαβε (ν), *he, she, it took*	ἔλαβον, *they took*

§209.4.1.2. *Middle.*

FIRST AORIST [§103.2]

	SINGULAR	PLURAL
1st per	ἐλυσάμην, *I loosed myself*	ἐλυσάμεθα, *we loosed ourselves*
2nd per	ἐλύσω, *you loosed yourself*	ἐλύσασθε, *you loosed yourselves*
3rd per	ἐλύσατο, *he loosed himself*	ἐλύσαντο, *they loosed themselves*

SECOND AORIST [§108.2]

SINGULAR	PLURAL

1st per	ἐλαβόμην, *I took myself*	ἐλαβόμεθα, *we took ourselves*
2nd per	ἐλάβου, *you took yourself*	ἐλάβεσθε, *you took yourselves*
3rd per	ἐλάβετο, *he took himself*	ἐλάβοντο, *they took themselves*

§209.4.1.3. *Passive.*
FIRST AORIST [§112.1.3]

	SINGULAR	PLURAL
1st per	ἐλύθην, *I was loosed*	ἐλύθημεν, *we were loosed*
2nd per	ἐλύθης, *you were loosed*	ἐλύθητε, *you were loosed*
3rd per	ἐλύθη, *he, she, it was loosed*	ἐλύθησαν, *they were loosed*

SECOND AORIST [§112.2]

	SINGULAR	PLURAL
1st per	ἐγράφην, *I was written*	ἐγράφημεν, *we were written*
2nd per	ἐγράφης, *you were written*	ἐγράφητε, *you were written*
3rd per	ἐγράφη, *he, she, it was written*	ἐγράφησαν, *they were written*

§209.4.2. *Subjunctive.*

§209.4.2.1. *Active.*
FIRST AORIST [§161.3]

	SINGULAR	PLURAL
1st per	λύσω	λύσωμεν
2nd per	λύσῃς	λύσητε
3rd per	λύσῃ	λύσωσι (ν)

SECOND AORIST [§161.5]

	SINGULAR	PLURAL
1st per	λάβω	λάβωμεν
2nd per	λάβῃς	λάβητε
3rd per	λάβῃ	λάβωσι (ν)

§209.4.2.2. *Middle.*
FIRST AORIST [§161.4]

	SINGULAR	PLURAL
1st per	λύσωμαι	λυσώμεθα
2nd per	λύσῃ	λύσησθε
3rd per	λύσηται	λύσωνται

SECOND AORIST [§161.6]

	SINGULAR	PLURAL
1st per	λάβωμαι	λαβώμεθα
2nd per	λάβῃ	λάβησθε

| 3rd per | λάβηται | λάβωνται |

§209.4.2.3. *Passive.*

FIRST AORIST [§161.7]

	SINGULAR	PLURAL
1st per	λυθῶ	λυθῶμεν
2nd per	λυθῇς	λυθῆτε
3rd per	λυθῇ	λυθῶσι (ν)

SECOND AORIST [§161.8]

	SINGULAR	PLURAL
1st per	λίπωμαι	λιπώμεθα
2nd per	λίπῃ	λίπησθε
3rd per	λίπηται	λίπωνται

§209.4.3. *Imperative.*

§209.4.3.1. *Active.*

FIRST AORIST [§169.3]

	SINGULAR	PLURAL
2nd per	λῦσον, *you loose*	λύσατε, *you loose*
3rd per	λυσάτω, *let him, her, it loose*	λυσάτωσαν, *let them loose*

SECOND AORIST [§169.6]

	SINGULAR	PLURAL
2nd per	λάβε, *you take*	λάβετε, *you take*
3rd per	λαβέτω, *let him, her, it take*	λαβέτωσαν, *let them take*

§209.4.3.2. *Middle.*

FIRST AORIST [§169.4]

	SINGULAR	PLURAL
2nd per	λῦσαι, *you loose yourself*	λύσασθε, *you loose yourselves*
3rd per	λυσάσθω, *let him loose himself*	λυσάσθωσαν, *let them loose themselves*

SECOND AORIST [§169.7]

	SINGULAR	PLURAL
2nd per	λαβοῦ, *you take for yourself*	λάβεσθε, *you take for yourselves*
3rd per	λαβέσθω, *let him take for himself*	λαβέσθωσαν, *let them take for themselves*

§209.4.3.3. *Passive.*

FIRST AORIST [§169.5]

	SINGULAR	PLURAL
2nd per	λύθητι, *you be loosed*	λύθητε, *you be loosed*

3rd per   λυθήτω, *let him, her, it be loosed*   λυθήτωσαν, *let them be loosed*

SECOND AORIST [§169.8]

	SINGULAR	PLURAL
2nd per	λάβηθι, *you be taken*	λάβητε, *you be taken*
3rd per	λαβήτω, *let him, her, it be taken*	λαβήτωσαν, *let them be taken*

§209.4.4. *Participle.*

§209.4.4.1. *Active.*

FIRST AORIST [§129.1]

SINGULAR

CASE	MASCULINE	FEMININE	NEUTER
Nom	λύσας	λύσασα	λῦσαν
Gen	λύσαντος	λυσάσης	λύσαντος
Abl	λύσαντος	λυσάσης	λύσαντος
Dat	λύσαντι	λυσάσῃ	λύσαντι
Loc	λύσαντι	λυσάσῃ	λύσαντι
Inst	λύσαντι	λυσάσῃ	λύσαντι
Acc	λύσαντα	λύσασαν	λῦσαν

PLURAL

CASE	MASCULINE	FEMININE	NEUTER
Nom	λύσαντες	λύσασαι	λύσαντα
Gen	λυσάντων	λυσασῶν	λυσάντων
Abl	λυσάντων	λυσασῶν	λυσάντων
Dat	λύσασι (ν)	λυσάσαις	λύσασι (ν)
Loc	λύσασι (ν)	λυσάσαις	λύσασι (ν)
Inst	λύσασι (ν)	λυσάσαις	λύσασι (ν)
Acc	λύσαντας	λυσάσας	λύσαντα

SECOND AORIST [§129.3]

SINGULAR

CASE	MASCULINE	FEMININE	NEUTER
Nom	λιπών	λιποῦσα	λιπόν
Gen	λιπόντος	λιπούσης	λιπόντος
Abl	λιποντος	λιπούσης	λιπόντος
Dat	λιπόντι	λιπούσῃ	λιπόντι
Loc	λιπόντι	λιπούσῃ	λιπόντι
Inst	λιπόντι	λιπούσῃ	λιπόντι
Acc	λιπόντα	λιποῦσαν	λιπόν

PLURAL

CASE	MASCULINE	FEMININE	NEUTER

Nom	λιπόντες	λιποῦσαι	λιπόντα
Gen	λιπόντων	λιπουσῶν	λιπόντων
Abl	λιπόντων	λιπουσῶν	λιπόντων
Dat	λιποῦσι (ν)	λιπούσαις	λιποῦσι (ν)
Loc	λιποῦσι (ν)	λιπούσαις	λιποῦσι (ν)
Inst	λιποῦσι (ν)	λιπούσαις	λιποῦσι (ν)
Acc	λιπόντας	λιπούσας	λιπόντα

§209.4.4.2. *Middle*.

FIRST AORIST [§129.2]

SINGULAR

CASE	MASCULINE	FEMININE	NEUTER
Nom	λυσάμενος	λυσαμένη	λυσάμενον
Gen	λυσαμένου	λυσαμένης	λυσαμένου
Abl	λυσαμένου	λυσαμένης	λυσαμένου
Dat	λυσαμένῳ	λυσσμένη	λυσαμένῳ
Loc	λυσαμένῳ	λυσαμένη	λυσαμένῳ
Inst	λυσαμένῳ	λυσαμένη	λυσαμένῳ
Acc	λυσάμενον	λυσαμένην	λυσάμενον

PLURAL

CASE	MASCULINE	FEMININE	NEUTER
Nom	λυσάμενοι	λυσάμεναι	λυσάμενα
Gen	λυσαμένων	λυσαμένων	λυσαμένων
Abl	λυσαμένων	λυσαμένων	λυσαμένων
Dat	λυσαμένοις	λυσαμέναις	λυσαμένοις
Loc	λυσαμένοις	λυσαμέναις	λυσαμένοις
Inst	λυσαμένοις	λυσαμέναις	λυσαμένοις
Acc	λυσαμένους	λυσαμένας	λυσάμενα

SECOND AORIST [§129.4]

SINGULAR

CASE	MASCULINE	FEMININE	NEUTER
Nom	λιπόμενος	λιπομένη	λιπόμενον
Gen	λιπομένου	λιπομένης	λιπομένου
Abl	λιπομένου	λιπομένης	λιπομένου
Dat	λιπομένῳ	λιπομένη	λιπομένῳ
Loc	λιπομένῳ	λιπομένη	λιπομένῳ
Inst	λιπομένῳ	λιπομένη	λιπομένῳ
Acc	λιπόμενον	λιπομένην	λιπόμενον

PLURAL

CASE	MASCULINE	FEMININE	NEUTER
Nom	λιπόμενοι	λιπόμεναι	λιπόμενα
Gen	λιπομένων	λιπομένων	λιπομένων
Abl	λιπομένων	λιπομένων	λιπομένων
Dat	λιπομένοις	λιπομέναις	λιπομένοις
Loc	λιπομένοις	λιπομέναις	λιπομένοις
Inst	λιπομένοις	λιπομέναις	λιπομένοις
Acc	λιπομένους	λιπομένας	λιπόμενα

§209.4.4.3. *Passive.*

FIRST AORIST [134.1]

SINGULAR

CASE	MASCULINE	FEMININE	NEUTER
Nom	λυθείς	λυθεῖσα	λυθέν
Gen	λυθέντος	λυθείσης	λυθέντος
Abl	λυθέντος	λυθείσης	λυθέντος
Dat	λυθέντι	λυθείσῃ	λυθέντι
Loc	λυθέντι	λυθείσῃ	λυθέντι
Inst	λυθέντι	λυθείσῃ	λυθέντι
Acc	λυθέντα	λυθεῖσαν	λυθέν

PLURAL

CASE	MASCULINE	FEMININE	NEUTER
Nom	λυθέντες	λυθεῖσαι	λυθέντα
Gen	λυθέντων	λυθεισῶν	λυθέντων
Abl	λυθέντων	λυθεισῶν	λυθέντων
Dat	λυθεῖσι (ν)	λυθείσαις	λυθεῖσι (ν)
Loc	λυθεῖσι (ν)	λυθείσαις	λυθεῖσι (ν)
Inst	λυθεῖσι (ν)	λυθείσαις	λυθεῖσι (ν)
Acc	λυθέντας	λυθείσας	λυθέντα

SECOND AORIST [§134.2]

SINGULAR

CASE	MASCULINE	FEMININE	NEUTER
Nom	ἀποσταλείς	ἀποσταλεῖσα	ἀποσταλέν
Gen	ἀποσταλέντος	ἀποσταλείσης	ἀποσταλέντος
Abl	ἀποσταλέντος	ἀποσταλείσης	ἀποσταλέντος
Dat	ἀποσταλέντι	ἀποσταλείσῃ	ἀποσταλέντι
Loc	ἀποσταλέντι	ἀποσταλείσῃ	ἀποσταλέντι
Inst	ἀποσταλέντι	ἀποσταλείσῃ	ἀποσταλέντι
Acc	ἀποσταλέντα	ἀποσταλεῖσαν	ἀποσταλέν

PLURAL

CASE	MASCULINE	FEMININE	NEUTER
Nom	ἀποσταλέντες	ἀποσταλεῖσαι	ἀποσταλέντα
Gen	ἀποσταλέντων	ἀποσταλεισῶν	ἀποσταλέντων
Abl	ἀποσταλέντων	ἀποσταλεισῶν	ἀποσταλέντων
Dat	ἀποσταλεῖσι (ν)	ἀποσταλείσαις	ἀποσταλεῖσι (ν)
Loc	ἀποσταλεῖσι (ν)	ἀποσταλείσαις	ἀποσταλεῖσι (ν)
Inst	ἀποσταλεῖσι (ν)	ἀποσταλείσαις	ἀποσταλεῖσι (ν)
Acc	ἀποσταλέντας	ἀποσταλείσας	ἀποσταλέντα

§209.4.5. *Infinitive.*

FIRST AORIST

ACTIVE	MIDDLE	PASSIVE
λῦσαι	λύσασθαι	λυθῆναι

SECOND AORIST

ACTIVE	MIDDLE	PASSIVE
λιπεῖν	λιπέσθαι	λιπῆναι

§209.5. *Perfect tense.*

§209.5.1. *Indicative.*

§209.5.1.1. *Active* [§152.1].

	SINGULAR	PLURAL
1st per	λέλυκα, *I have loosed*	λελύκαμεν, *we have loosed*
2nd per	λέλυκας, *you have loosed*	λελύκατε, *you have loosed*
3rd per	λέλυκε, *he, she, it has loosed*	λελύκασι, *they have loosed*

§209.5.1.2. *Middle/passive* [§152.2]

	SINGULAR	PLURAL
1st per	λέλυμαι, *I have loosed myself*	λελύμεθα, *we have loosed ourselves*
2nd per	λέλυσαι, *you have loosed yourself*	λέλυσθε, *you have loosed yourselves*
3rd per	λέλυται, *he has loosed himself*	λέλυνται, *they have loosed themselves*

§209.5.2. *Participle.*

§209.5.2.1. *Active* [§152.3]

SINGULAR

CASE	MASCULINE	FEMININE	NEUTER
Nom	λελυκώς	λελυκυῖα	λελυκός
Gen	λελυκότος	λελυκυίας	λελυκότος
Abl	λελυκότος	λελυκυίας	λελυκότος
Dat	λελυκότι	λελυκυίᾳ	λελυκότι
Loc	λελυκότι	λελυκυίᾳ	λελυκότι

| Inst | λελυκότι | λελυκυίᾳ | λελυκότι |
| Acc | λελυκότα | λελυκυῖαν | λελυκός |

PLURAL

CASE	MASCULINE	FEMININE	NEUTER
Nom	λελυκότες	λελυκυῖαι	λελυκότα
Gen	λελυκότων	λελυκυιῶν	λελυκότων
Abl	λελυκότων	λελυκυιῶν	λελυκότων
Dat	λελυκόσι (ν)	λελυκυίαις	λελυκόσι (ν)
Loc	λελυκόσι (ν)	λελυκυίαις	λελυκόσι (ν)
Inst	λελυκόσι (ν)	λελυκυίαις	λελυκόσι (ν)
Acc	λελυκότας	λελυκυίας	λελυκότα

§209.5.2.2. *Middle/passive* [§152.4].

SINGULAR

CASE	MASCULINE	FEMININE	NEUTER
Nom	λελυμένος	λελυμένη	λελυμένον
Gen	λελυμένου	λελυμένης	λελυμένου
Abl	λελυμένου	λελυμένης	λελυμένου
Dat	λελυμένῳ	λελυμένη	λελυμένῳ
Loc	λελυμένῳ	λελυμένη	λελυμένῳ
Inst	λελυμένῳ	λελυμένη	λελυμένῳ
Acc	λελυμένον	λελυμένην	λελυμένον

PLURAL

CASE	MASCULINE	FEMININE	NEUTER
Nom	λελυμένοι	λελυμέναι	λελυμένα
Gen	λελυμένων	λελυμένων	λελυμένων
Abl	λελυμένων	λελυμένων	λελυμένων
Dat	λελυμένοις	λελυμέναις	λελυμένοις
Loc	λελυμένοις	λελυμέναις	λελυμένοις
Inst	λελυμένοις	λελυμέναις	λελυμένοις
Acc	λελυμένους	λελυμένας	λελυμένα

§209.5.3. *Infinitive* [§152.5, 174].

ACTIVE	MIDDLE	PASSIVE
λελυκέναι	λελύσθαι	λελύσθαι

§209.6. *Pluperfect Tense*.

§209.6.1. *Indicative*.

§209.6.1.1. *Active* [§155.1].

	SINGULAR	PLURAL
1st per	ἐλελύκειν, *I had loosed*	ἐλελύκειμεν, *we had loosed*
2nd per	ἐλελύκεις, *you had loosed*	ἐλελύκειτε, *you had loosed*
3rd per	ἐλελύκει, *he, she, it had loosed*	ἐλελύκεισαν, *they had loosed*

§209.6.1.2. Middle/passive [§155.2].

	SINGULAR	PLURAL
1st per	ἐλελύμην, *I had loosed myself*	ἐλελύμεθα, *we had loosed ourselves*
2nd per	ἐλέλυσο, *you had loosed yourself*	ἐλέλυσθε, *you had loosed yourselves*
3rd per	ἐλέλυτο, *he had loosed himself*	ἐλέλυντο, *they had loosed themselves*

§209.7. εἰμί.

§209.7.1. Indicative.

§209.7.1.1. Present [§76].

	SINGULAR	PLURAL
1st per	εἰμί, *I am*	ἐσμέν, *we are*
2nd per	εἶ, *you are*	ἐστέ, *you are*
3rd per	ἐστί(ν), *he, she, it is*	εἰσί(ν), *they are*

§209.7.1.2. Imperfect [§84.4].

	SINGULAR	PLURAL
1st per	ἤμην, *I was*	ἦμεν, *we were*
2nd per	ἦς, *you were*	ἦτε, *you were*
3rd per	ἦν, *he, she, it was*	ἦσαν, *they were*

§209.7.1.3. Future [§98].

	SINGULAR	PLURAL
1st per	ἔσομαι, *I shall be*	ἐσόμεθα, *we shall be*
2nd per	ἔση, *you will be*	ἔσεσθε, *you will be*
3rd per	ἔσται, *he, she, it will be*	ἔσονται, *they will be*

§209.7.2. Subjunctive [§161.9].

	SINGLUAR	PLURAL
1st per	ὦ	ὦμεν
2nd per	ἦς	ἦτε
3rd per	ἦ	ὦσι (ν)

§209.7.3. Imperative [§169.9].

	SINGULAR	PLURAL
2nd per	ἴσθι, *you be*	ἔστε, *you be*

3rd per ἔστω, *let him, her, it be* ἔστωσαν, *let them be*

§209.7.4. *Infinitive* [§90.1.3].

εἶναι

§209.7.5. *Participle* [§124.6].

SINGULAR

CASE	MASCULINE	FEMININE	NEUTER
Nom	ὤν	οὖσα	ὄν
Gen	ὄντος	οὔσης	ὄντος
Abl	ὄντος	οὔσης	ὄντος
Dat	ὄντι	οὔσῃ	ὄντι
Loc	ὄντι	οὔσῃ	ὄντι
Inst	ὄντι	οὔσῃ	ὄντι
Acc	ὄντα	οὖσαν	ὄν

PLURAL

CASE	MASCULINE	FEMININE	NEUTER
Nom	ὄντες	οὖσαι	ὄντα
Gen	ὄντων	οὐσῶν	ὄντων
Abl	ὄντων	οὐσῶν	ὄντων
Dat	οὖσι (ν)	οὔσαις	οὖσι (ν)
Loc	οὖσι (ν)	οὔσαις	οὖσι (ν)
Inst	οὖσι (ν)	οὔσαις	οὖσι (ν)
Acc	ὄντας	οὔσας	ὄντα

Appendix 5

Glossaries
Greek-English

§210. This glossary consists of all vocabulary words contained in the lessons. Each word is listed alphabetically, first in Greek (§210), and then in English (§211). A general "translation" is given, but you should consult a lexicon such as Arndt-Gingrich or Kittel for more specific usages of a given term.

The paragraph number following the entry indicates the point at which the term was first mentioned in the text.

There are approximately 300 words in the Greek New Testament that occur 50 times or more. These words are marked in the Greek to English vocabulary with an (*). Note, however, that the asterick *does not precede the word unless that specific term occurs fifty times or more*, i.e., the asterick does not precede a term even if that term appears more than fifty times when these occurences result from its use in compounds.

*ἀγαθός, ἀγαθή, ἀγαθόν, *good,* §62

*ἀγαπάω, ἀγαπήσω, ἠγάπησα, ἠγάπηκα, ἠγάπημαι, ἠγαπήθην, *I love,* §117

*ἀγάπη, ἡ, *love,* §54

*ἀγαπητός, ἀγαπητή, ἀγαπητόν, *beloved,* §62

*ἀγγελία, ἡ, *message,* §131

*ἄγγελος, ὁ, *messenger, angel,* §25

ἁγιάζω, _____, ἡγίησα, _____, ἡγίασμαι, ἡγιάσθην, *I sanctify,* §117

*ἅγιος, ἁγία, ἅγιον, *holy,* §171

ἀγρός, ὁ, *field,* §196

*ἄγω, ἄξω, ἤγαγον, _____, _____, ἤχθην, *I lead,* §42

ἀδελφή, ἡ, *sister,* §196

*ἀδελφός, ὁ, *brother,* §25

ἀδικία, ἡ, *unrighteousness,* §126

*αἷμα, αἵματος, τό, *blood,* §147

*αἴρω, ἀρῶ, ἦρα, ἦρκα, ἦρμαι, ἤρθην, *I take up, I take away,* §42

*αἰτέω, αἰτήσω, ᾔτησα, ᾔτηκα, _____, ᾐτήθην, *I ask,* §166

αἰτία, ἡ, *reason,* §190

*αἰών, αἰῶνος, ὁ, *age,* §142

*ἀκούω, ἀκούσω, ἤκουσα, ἀκήκοα, _____, ἠκούσθην, *I hear,* §15

*ἀλήθεια, ἡ, *truth,* §54

ἀληθινός, ἀληθινή, ἀληθινόν, *true,* §151

ἀληθῶς, *truly,* §166

ἁλιεύς, ἁλιέως, ὁ, *fisherman,* §151

*ἀλλά, *but,* §62

*ἀλλήλων, ἀλλήλοις, ἀλλήλους, *one another,* §176

*ἄλλος, ἄλλη, ἄλλο, *another,* §75

ἁμαρτάνω, ἁμαρτήσω, ἡμάρτησα, ἡμάρτηκα, _____, _____, *I sin,* §89

*ἁμαρτία, ἡ, *sin,* §54

ἁμαρτωλός, ὁ, *sinner,* §89

ἀνά, *up, up to, again,* §48

*ἀναβαίνω, (see principal parts under βαίνω), *I go up,* §89

ἀναγγέλλω, ἀναγγελῶ, ἀνήγγελα, _____, _____, ἀνηγγέλην, *I announce,* §166

ἀναγινώσκω, (see principal parts under γινώσκω), *I read,* §83

ἀνάστασις, ἀναστάσεως, ἡ, *resurrection,* §147

*ἀνήρ, ἀνδρός, ὁ, *man,* §196

*ἄνθρωπος, ὁ, *man,* §25

ἀντί, *over against,* §48

ἀντίχριστος, ὁ, *antichrist,* §196

ἄξιος, ἀξία, ἄξιον, *worth,* §196

*ἀπό, *from, away from,* §48

*ἀποθνήσκω, ἀποθανοῦμαι, ἀπέθανον, _____, _____, _____, *I die,* §126

*ἀποκρίνομαι, ἀποκρινοῦμαι, ἀπεκρινάμην, _____, _____, ἀπεκρίθην, I answer, §75

*ἀποκτείνω, ἀποκτενῶ, ἀπέκτεινα, _____, _____, ἀπεκτάνθην, I kill, §122

*ἀποστέλλω, ἀποστελῶ, ἀπέστειλα, ἀπέσταλκα, ἀπέσταλμαι, ἀπεστάλην, I send, §83

*ἀπόστολος, ὁ, apostle, §25

ἄρτι, now, §190

*ἄρτος, ὁ, bread, §25

*ἀρχή, ἡ, beginning, §131

*ἀρχιερεύς, ἀρχιερέως, ὁ, high priest, §151

*ἄρχω, ἄρξω, ἦρξα, _____, _____, _____, I rule, §83 (middle voice ἄρχομαι, I begin, §75)

ἄρχων, ἄρχοντος, ὁ, ruler, §142

*αὐτός, αὐτή, αὐτό, he, she, it, §69

*ἀφίημι, ἀφήσω, ἀφῆκα, ἀφεῖκα, ἀφεῖμαι, _____, I forgive, §179.

βάθος, βάθους, τό, depth, §151

βαίνω, βήσομαι, ἔβην, βέβηκα, _____, ἐβήθην, I go, §89

*βάλλω, βαλῶ, ἔβαλον, βέβληκα, βέβλημαι, ἐβλήθην, I throw, §36

*βαπτίζω, βαπτίσω, ἐβάπτισα, _____, βεβάπτισμαι, ἐβαπτίσθην, I baptize, §36

*βασιλεία, ἡ, kingdom, §54

*βασιλεύς, βασιλέως, ὁ, king, §147

βασιλικός, βασιλική, βασιλικόν, royal, §62

βιβλίον, τό, book, §89

βίος, ὁ, life, §137

*βλέπω, βλέψω, ἔβλεψα, _____, _____, _____, I see, §15

γάμος, ὁ, marriage, §25

*γάρ, for, §89

γένος, γένους, τό, race, §147

*γεννάω, γεννήσω, ἐγέννησα, γεγέννηκα, γεγέννημαι, ἐγεννήθην, I give birth to, §117

*γῆ, γῆς, ἡ, earth, §166

*γίνομαι, γενήσομαι, ἐγενόμην, γέγονα, γεγένημαι, ἐγενήθην, *I become*, §75

*γινώσκω, γνώσομαι, ἔγνων, ἔγνωκα, ἔγνωσμαι, ἐγνώσθην, *I know*, §15

*γλῶσσα, ἡ, *tongue*, §54

γνῶσις, γνώσεως, ἡ, *knowledge*, §147

*γραμματεύς, γραμματέως, ὁ, *scribe*, §147

*γραφή, ἡ, *writing*, §62

*γράφω, γράψω, ἔγραψα, γέγραφα, γέγραμμαι, ἐγράφην, *I write*, §15

*δαιμόνιον, τό, *demon*, §101

*δέ, *but*, §62

δεύτερος, δευτέρα, δεύτερον, *second*, §190

*δέχομαι, δέξομαι, ἐδεξάμην, _____, δέδεγμαι, ἐδέχθην, *I receive*, §131

δηλόω, δηλώσω, ἐδήλωσα, _____, _____, ἐδηλώθην, *I show*, §137

διά, *through, by*, §48

διαθήκη, διαθήκης, ἡ, *covenant*, §196

διακονία, ἡ, *ministry*, §131

*διδάσκαλος, ὁ, *teacher*, §89

*διδάσκω, διδάξω, ἐδίδαξα, _____. _____, ἐδιδάχθην, *I teach*, §15

διδαχή, ἡ, *teaching*, §54

*δίδωμι, δώσω, ἔδωκα, δέδωκα, δέδομαι, ἐδόθην, *I give*, §179

διέρχομαι (see principal parts under ἔρχομαι), *I come through*, §75

*δίκαιος, δικαία, δίκαιον, *righteous, just*, §62

*δικαιοσύνη, ἡ, *righteousness*, §159

δικαιόω, δικαιώσω, ἐδικαίωσα, _____, δεδικαίωμαι, ἐδικαιώθην, *I justify*, §166

διώκω, διώξω, ἐδίωξα, _____, δεδίωγμαι, ἐδιώχθην, *I persecute*, §117

*δόξα, ἡ, *glory*, §62

*δοξάζω, δοξάσω, ἐδόξασα, _____, δεδόξασμαι, ἐδοξάσθην, *I glorify*, §42

*δοῦλος, ὁ, *slave*, §25

*δύναμις, δυνάμεως, ἡ, *power*, §147

*δώδεκα, *twelve*, §196

δῶρον, τό, *gift*, §25

*ἐάν, *if*, §159

ἐγγίζω, ἐγγίσω, ἤγγισα, ἤγγικα, _____. _____, *I come near*, §166

*ἐγείρω, ἐγερῶ, ἤγειρα, _____, ἐγήγερμαι, ἠγέρθην, *I raise up*, §36

*ἐγώ, *I*, §69

*ἔθνος, ἔθνους, τὸ, *nation*, §147

*εἰ, *if*, §159

*εἰμί, ἔσομαι, *I am*, §75

*εἰρήνη, ἡ, *peace*, §62

*εἰς, *into*, §48

*εἰσέρχομαι (see principal parts under ἔρχομαι), *I come into*, §75

*ἐκ, *out of*, §48

*ἐκεῖνος, ἐκείνη, ἐκεῖνο, *that*, §69

*ἐκκλησία, ἡ, *church*, §54

ἔλεος, ἐλέους, τό, *mercy*, §147

ἐλπίζω, ἐλπιῶ, ἤλπισα, ἤλπικα, _____, _____, *I hope*, §126

*ἐλπίς, ἐλπίδος, ἡ, *hope*, §142

ἐμαυτοῦ, ἐμαυτῆς, *(of) myself*, §176

*ἐμός, ἐμή, ἐμόν, *my*, §176

*ἐν, *in* §36

*ἐντολή, ἡ, *commandment*, §54

*ἐξέρχομαι, (see principal parts under ἔρχομαι, *I come out*, §75

*ἐξουσία, ἡ, *authority*, §117

*ἐπαγγελία, ἡ, *promise*, §89

*ἐπερωτάω, ἐπερωτήσω, _____, _____, _____, _____, *I ask a question of*, §117

*ἐπί, *upon, on*, §48

ἐπιθυμία, ἡ, *lust*, §137

*ἔργον, τό, *work*, §111

ἔρημος, ἡ, *desert*, §83

*ἔρχομαι, ἐλεύσομαι, ἦλθον, ἐλήλυθα, _____, _____, *I come, I go*, §75

*ἐρωτάω, ἐρωτήσω, ἠρώτησα, _____, _____, ἠρωτήθην, *I ask*, §117

*ἐσθίω, φάγομαι, ἔφαγον, _____, _____, _____, *I eat*, §42

*ἔσχατος, ἐσχάτη, ἔσχατον, *last*, §62

*ἕτερος, ἑτέρα, ἕτερον, *another*, §62

*ἔτι, *still, yet*, §126

ἑτοιμάζω, ἑτοιμάσω, ἡτοίμασα, ἡτοίμακα, ἡτοίμασμαι, ἡτοιμάσθην, *I prepare*, §126

*εὐαγγελίζομαι, _____, εὐηγγέλισα, _____, εὐηγγέλισμαι, εὐηγγελίσθην, *I preach the gospel*, §171

*εὐαγγέλιον, τό, *gospel*, §89

*εὐθύς, *immediately*, §188

εὐλογέω, εὐλογήσω, εὐλόγησα, εὐλόγηκα, εὐλόγημαι, εὐλογήθην, *I bless*, §20

*εὑρίσκω, εὑρήσω, εὗρον, εὕρηκα, _____, εὑρέθην, *I find*, §106

ἐχθρός, ὁ, *enemy*, §171

*ἔχω, ἕξω, ἔσχον, ἔσχηκα, _____, _____, *I have*, §15

*ζάω, ζήσω, ἔζησα, _____, _____, _____, *I live*, §117

*ζητέω, ζητήσω, ἐζήτησα, _____, _____, _____, *I seek*, §20

*ζωή, ἡ, *life*, §83

*ἤδη, *now, already*, §190

ἥλιος, ὁ, *sun*, §166

*ἡμεῖς, *we*, §69

*ἡμέρα, ἡ, *day*, §54

θάλασσα, ἡ, *sea*, §117

*θάνατος, ὁ, *death*, §25

θαυμάζω, θαυμάσομαι, ἐθαύμασα, _____, _____, ἐθαυμάσθην, *I marvel*, §117

*θέλημα, θελήματος, τό, *will*, §147

*θέλω, θελήσω, ἠθέλησα, _____, _____, _____, *I wish*, §171

*θεός, ὁ, *God*, §25

θεραπεύω, θεραπεύσω, ἐθεράπευσα, _____, τεθεράπευμαι, ἐθεραπεύθην, *I heal*, §122

θεωρέω, θεωρήσω, ἐθεώρησα, _____, _____, _____, *I behold*, §20

θυγάτηρ, θυγατρός, ἡ, *daughter*, §159

ἱερεύς, ἱερέως, ὁ, *priest*, §147

*ἱερόν, τό, *temple*, §25

Ἰησοῦς, ὁ, *Jesus*, §122

ἱλασμός, ὁ, *propitiation*, §137

*ἵνα, *in order that*, §159

*ἵστημι, στήσω, ἔστησα, ἔστηκα, _____, ἐστάθην, *I set*, §179

ἰσχυρός, ἰσχυρά, ἰσχυρόν, *strong*, §190

ἰσχυρότερος, ἰσχυρότερα, ἰσχυρότερος, *stronger*, §190

ἰχθύς, ἰχθύος, ὁ, *fish*, §101

καθαρίζω, καθαριῶ, ἐκαθάρισα, _____, _____, ἐκαθαρίσθην, *I cleanse*,
    §101

*καί, *and*, §25

καινός, καινή, καινόν, *new*, §62

*κακός, κακή, κακόν, *bad, evil*, §62

*καλέω, καλέσω, ἐκάλεσα, κέκληκα, κέκλημαι, ἐκλήθην, *I call*, §20

*καλός, καλή, καλόν, *good*, §62

καλῶς, *well*, §171

*καρδία, ἡ, *heart*, §83

*καρπός, ὁ, *fruit*, §42

*κατά, *down, down from*, §48

*καταβαίνω (see principal parts under βαίνω), *I go down*, §89

κατέρχομαι (see principal parts under ἔρχομαι) *I come down*, §75

*κεφαλή, ἡ, *head*, §131

*κηρύσσω, κηρύξω, ἐκήρυξα, _____, _____, ἐκηρύχθην, *I preach, I pro-
    claim*, §36

κοινωνία, ἡ, *fellowship*, §131

*κόσμος, ὁ, *world*, §36

κρίμα, κρίματος, ὁ, *judgment*, §179

*κρίνω, κρινῶ, ἔκρινα, κέκρικα, κέκριμαι, ἐκρίθην, *I judge*, §42

κρίσις, κρίσεως, ἡ, *judgment*, §147

*κύριος, ὁ, *lord, the Lord*, §75

*λαλέω, λαλήσω, ἐλάλησα, λελάληκα, λελάλημαι, ἐλαλήθην, *I speak*, §20

*λαμβάνω, λήμψομαι, ἔλαβον, εἴληφα, εἴλημμαι, ἐλήμφθην, *I take, I receive*,
    §15

*λαός, ὁ, *people*, §83

*λέγω, ἐρῶ, εἶπον, εἴρηκα, εἴρημαι, ἐρρέθην, *I say*, §15

λείπω, λείψω, ἔλιπον, _____, λέλειμμαι, ἐλείφθην, *I leave*, §106

*λίθος, ὁ, *stone*, §42

*λόγος, ὁ, *word*, §25

λύω, λύσω, ἔλυσα, λέλυκα, λέλυμαι, ἐλύθην, *I loose, I destroy*, §15

*μαθητής, ὁ, *disciple*, §54

*μᾶλλον, *more, rather*, §190

μαρτυρία, ἡ, *witness*, §159

*μέγας, μεγάλη, μέγα, *great*, §190

*μέν . . . δέ, *on the one hand . . . on the other hand*, §122

*μένω, μενῶ, ἔμεινα, μεμένηκα, _____, _____, *I abide*, §36

μεσσίας, ὁ, *Messiah*, §54

*μετά, *with*, §48

*μήτηρ, μητρός, ἡ, *mother*, §142

μικρός, μικρά, μικρόν, *small*, §75

μισέω, μισήσω, ἐμίσησα, μεμίσηκα, _____, _____, *I hate*, §196

*μόνος, μόνη, μόνον, *only*, §75

μου, *my*, §69

νεανίσκος, ὁ, *young man*, §196

*νεκρός, νεκρά, νεκρόν, *dead*, §75

νικάω, νικήσω, ἐνίκησα, νενίκηκα, _____, _____, *I overcome*, §196

*νόμος, ὁ, *law*, §25

*νῦν, *now*, §83

*νύξ, νυκτός, ἡ, *night*, §142

*ὁδός, ἡ, *way*, §83

*οἶκος, ὁ, *house*, §42

ὁμολογέω, ὁμολογήσω, ὡμολόγησα, _____, _____, _____, *I confess*, §20

*ὄνομα, ὀνόματος, τό, *name*, §147

*ὅς, ἥ, ὅ, *who, which*, §176

*ὅστις, ἥτις, ὅτι, *whoever*, §176

*ὅτι, *because, that*, §89

*οὐ (οὐκ before a vowel; οὐχ before a vowel with a rough breathing), *not*, §75

*οὐδέ, *and not, nor, not even*, §122

*οὐδείς, οὐδεμία, οὐδέν, *no one*, §176

οὐκέτι, *no longer*, §101

*οὐρανός, ὁ, *heaven*, §42

*οὗτος, αὕτη, τοῦτο, *this*, §68

*ὀφθαλμός, ὁ, *eye*, §131

*ὄχλος, ὁ, *crowd*, §42

παιδίον, τό, *child*, §166

πάντοτε, *always*, §171

*παρά, *beside, beyond, above*, §48

*παραβολή, ἡ, *parable*, §62

*παραδίδωμι (see principal parts under δίδωμι), *I hand over*, §179

*παρακαλέω (see principal parts under καλέω), *I comfort, I exhort*, §20

παράκλητος, ὁ, *advocate*, §126

παρρησία, ἡ, *boldness*, §126

*πᾶς, πᾶσα, πᾶν, *all, whole*, §142

πάσχω, _____, ἔπαθον, πέπονθα, _____, _____, *I suffer*, §106

*πατήρ, πατρός, ὁ, *father*, §142

*πείθω, πείσω, ἔπεισα, πέποιθα, πέπεισμαι, ἐπείσθην, *I persuade*, §101

πειράζω, πειράσω, ἐπείρασα, _____, πεπείρασμαι, ἐπειράσθην, *I tempt*, §171

*πέμπω, πέμψω, ἔπεμψα, _____, _____, ἐπέμφθην, *I send*, §15

*περί, *about, concerning*, §48

*περιπατέω, περιπατήσω, περιεπάτησα, περιπεπάτηκα, _____, _____, *I walk about*, §20

Πέτρος, ὁ, *Peter*, §126

*πίνω, πίομαι, ἔπιον, πέπωκα, _____, ἐπόθην, *I drink*, §111

*πιστεύω, πιστεύσω, ἐπίστευσα, πεπίστευκα, πεπίστευμαι, ἐπιστεύθην, *I believe*, §75

*πίστις, πίστεως, ἡ, *faith*, §159

*πιστός, πιστή, πιστόν, *faithful*, §75

*πληρόω, πληρώσω, ἐπλήρωσα, πεπλήρωκα, πεπλήρωμαι, ἐπληρώθην, *I fulfill*, §137

*πλοῖον, τό, *boat*, §101

*πνεῦμα, πνεύματος, τό, *spirit*, §159

πόθεν, *whence*, §190

*ποιέω, ποιήσω, ἐποίησα, πεποίηκα, πεποίημαι, _____, *I do, I make*, §20

*πόλις, πόλεως, ἡ, *city*, §147

*πολύς, πολλή, πολύ, *much, many*, §188

*πονηρός, πονηρά, πονηρόν, *evil*, §75

*πορεύομαι, πορεύσομαι, ἐπορευσάμην, _____, πεπόρευμαι, ἐπορεύθην, *I go*, §83

ποῦ, *where*, §166

πρίν, *before*, §171

πρό, *in front of, before*, §48

*πρός, *at*, §48

*προφήτης, ὁ, *prophet*, §54

*πρῶτος, πρώτη, πρῶτον, *first*, §75

πυρά, ἡ, *fire*, §179

*ῥῆμα, ῥήματος, τό, *word*, §159

*σάββατον, τό, *Sabbath*, §166

*σάρξ, σαρκός, ἡ, *flesh*, §142

*σημεῖον, τό, *miracle*, §122

σκάνδαλον, τό, *stumbling block*, §122

σκοτεινός, σκοτεινή, σκοτεινόν, *dark*, §179

σκοτία, ἡ, *darkness*, §111

σκότος, σκότους, τό, *darkness*, §159

*σοφία, ἡ, *wisdom*, §126

σταυρόω, σταυρώσω, ἐσταύρωσα _____, ἐσταύρωμαι, ἐσταυρώθην, *I crucify*, §137

στάχυς, στάχυος, ὁ, *ear of corn*, §147

*στόμα, στόματος, τό, *mouth*, §159

*σύ, *you*, §69

*σύν, *with*, §48

συνάγω (see principal parts under ἄγω), *I gather together,* §83

συναγωγή, *synagogue,* §151

συνέρχομαι (see principal parts under ἔρχομαι), *I come with,* §75

συνίημι (see principal parts under ἀφίημι), *I perceive,* §179

*σῴζω, σώσω, ἔσωσα, σέσωκα, σέσωσμαι, ἐσώθην, *I save,* §36

*σῶμα, σώματος, τό, *body,* §147

σωτηρία, ἡ, *salvation,* §131

*τέκνον, τό, *child,* §36

τέλος, τέλους, τό, *end,* §147

*τίθημι, θήσω, ἔθηκα, τέθεικα, τέθειμαι, ἐτέθην, *I place,* §179

τιμάω, τιμήσω, ἐτίμησα, _____, τετίμημαι, _____, *I honor,* §117

*τις, τι, *somebody, something,* §176

*τίς, τί, *who, which,* §176

*τοιοῦτος, τοιαύτη, τοιοῦτο, *such,* §176

*τόπος, ὁ, *place,* §36

*τότε, *then,* §83

*υἱός, ὁ, *son,* §42

*ὑμεῖς, *you (pl),* §68

*ὑπέρ, *in behalf of, instead of,* §48

*ὑπό, *from,* §36

ὑποστρέφω, ὑποστρέψω, ὑπέστρεψα, _____, _____, _____, *I return,*
   §101

φαίνω, φανοῦμαι, _____, _____, _____, ἐφάνην, *I shine,* §122

φανερόω, φανερώσω, ἐφανέρωσα, _____, πεφανέρωμαι, ἐφανερώθην, *I make manifest,* §166

φανερῶς, *clearly,* §190

*φέρω, οἴσω, ἤνεγκα, ἐνήνοχα, _____, ἠνέχθην, *I bear, I bring,* §36

*φωνή, ἡ, *voice,* §83

*χαίρω, χαρήσομαι, _____, _____, _____, ἐχάρην, *I rejoice,* §122

*χαρά, ἡ, *joy,* §89

*χάρις, χάριτος, ἡ, *grace,* §142

*χείρ, χειρός, ἡ, *hand,* §151

χρεία, ἡ, *need*, §171

χριστός, ὁ, *Christ*, §83

*χρόνος, ὁ, *time*, §171

ψεύδομαι, _____, ἐψευσάμην, _____, _____, _____, *I lie*, §122

ψεῦδος, ψεύδους, τό, *lie*, §196

ψεύστης, ὁ, *liar*, §122

*ὥρα, ἡ, *hour*, §190

English-Greek

§211. In cases where there are multiple English translations possible for a given Greek term, only the most common is indexed.

(I) abide, μένω, §36

about, concerning, περί, §48

advocate, παράκλητος, §126

age, αἰών, §142

all, whole, πᾶς, πᾶσα, πᾶν, §142

already, ἤδη, §190

always, πάντοτε, §171

(I) am, εἰμί, §75

and, καί, §25

angel, ἄγγελος, §25

(I) announce, ἀναγγέλλω, §166

another (of the same kind), ἄλλος, ἄλλη, ἄλλο, §75; another (of a different kind), ἕτερος, ἑτέρα, ἕτερον, §62

(I) answer, ἀποκρίνομαι, §75

antichrist, ἀντίχριστος, §196

apostle, ἀπόστολος, §25

(I) ask, αἰτέω, §166

(I) ask ἐρωτάω, §117

(I) ask a question of, ἐπερωτάω, §117

at, πρός, §48

authority, ἐξουσία, §117

away from, ἀπό, §48

bad, κακός, κακή, κακόν, §62

(I) baptize, βαπτίζω, §36

(I) bear, I bring, φέρω, §36

because, that, ὅτι, §89

(I) become, γίνομαι, §75

before, πρίν, §171

(I) begin, ἄρχομαι, §75

beginning, ἀρχή, §131

(I) behold, θεωρέω, §20

(I) believe, πιστεύω, §75

beloved, ἀγαπητός, ἀγαπητή, ἀγαπητόν, §62

beside, beyond, along, παρά, §48

(I) bless, εὐλογέω, §20

blood, αἷμα, §147

boat, πλοῖον, §101

body, σῶμα, §147

boldness, παρρησία, §126

book, βιβλίον, §89

bread, ἄρτος, §25

brother, ἀδελφός, §25

but, ἀλλά, §62˙ δέ, §62

by, ὑπό, §36

(I) call, καλέω, §20

child, παιδίον, §166; τέκνον, §36

Christ, χριστός, §83

church, ἐκκλησία, §54

city, πόλις, §147

(I) cleanse, καθαρίζω, §101

clearly, φανερῶς, §188

(I) come, I go, ἔρχομαι, §75

(I) come down, κατέρχομαι, §75

(I) come into, εἰσέρχομαι, §75

(I) come near, ἐγγίζω, §166

(I) come out, ἐξέρχομαι, §75

(I) come through, διέρχομαι, §75

(I) come with, συνέρχομαι, §75

(I) comfort, I exhort, παρακαλέω, §20

commandment, ἐντολή, §54

(I) confess, ὁμολογέω, §20

covenant, διαθήκη, §196

crowd, ὄχλος, §42

(I) crucify, σταυρόω, §137

dark, σκοτεινός, σκοτεινή, σκοτεινόν, §179

darkness, σκοτία, §111

darkness, σκότος, §159

daughter, θυγάτηρ, §159

day, ἡμέρα, §54

dead, νεκρός, §75

death, θάνατος, §25

demon, δαιμόνιον, §101

depth, βάθος, §151

desert, ἔρημος, §83

(I) destroy, λύω, §15

(I) die, ἀποθνήσκω, §126

disciple, μαθητής, §54

(I) do, I make, ποιέω, §20

down, down from, κατά, §48

(I) drink, πίνω, §111

ear of corn, στάχυς, §147

earth, γῆ, §166

(I) eat, ἐσθίω, §42

end, τέλος, §147

enemy, ἐχθρός, §171

evil, πονηρός, §75

eye, ὀφθαλμός, §131

faith, πίστις, §159

faithful, πιστός, πιστή, πιστόν, §75

father, πατήρ, §142

fellowship, κοινωνία, §131

field, ἀγρός, §196

(I) find, εὑρίσκω, §106

fire, πυρά, §179

first, πρῶτος, πρώτη, πρῶτον, §75

fish, ἰχθύς, §159

fisherman, ἁλιεύς, §151

flesh, σάρξ, §142

for, γάρ, §89

(I) forgive, ἀφίημι, §179

from, away from, ἀπό, §48

fruit, καρπός, §42

(I) fulfill, πληρόω, §137

(I) gather together, συνάγω, §83

gift, δῶρον, §25

(I) give, δίδωμι, §179

(I) give birth to, γεννάω, §117

(I) glorify, δοξάζω, §42

glory, δόξα, §62

(I) go, βαίνω, §89

(I) go, πορεύομαι, §83

(I) go down, καταβαίνω, §89

(I) go up, ἀναβαίνω, §89

god, God, θεός, §28

good, καλός, καλή, καλόν, §62; ἀγαθός, ἀγαθή, ἀγαθόν, §62

gospel, εὐαγγέλιον, §89

grace, χάρις, §142

great, μέγας, μεγάλη, μέγα, §190

hand, χείρ, §151

(I) hand over, παραδίδωμι, §179

(I) hate, μισέω, §196

(I) have, ἔχω, §15

he, she, it, αὐτός, αὐτή, αὐτό, §68

head, κεφαλή, §131

(I) heal, θεραπεύω, §122

(I) hear, ἀκούω, §15

heart, καρδία, §83

heaven, οὐρανός, §42

high priest, ἀρχιερεύς, §151

hold fast, κρατέω, §196

holy, ἅγιος, ἁγία, ἅγιον, §171

(I) honor, τιμάω, §117

hope, ἐλπίς, §142

(I) hope, ἐλπίζω, §126

hour, ὥρα, §190

house, οἶκος, §42

husband, ἀνήρ, §196

I, ἐγώ, §68

if (with the indicative), εἰ, §159; ἐάν, §159 (with all other moods)

immediately, εὐθύς, §188

in, ἐν, §36

in behalf of, instead of, ὑπέρ, §48
in front of, before, πρό, §48
in order that, ἵνα, §159
(I) intend (to), μέλλω, §196
into, εἰς, §48

Jesus, Ἰησοῦς, §122
joy, χαρά, §89
(I) judge, κρίνω, §42
judgment, κρίσις, §147
judgment, decision, κρίμα, §179
just, δίκαιος, δικαία, δίκαιον, §62
(I) justify, δικαιόω, §166

(I) kill, ἀποκτείνω, §122
king, βασιλεύς, §147
kingdom, βασιλεία, §54
(I) know, γινώσκω, §15
knowledge, γνῶσις, §147

last, ἔσχατος, ἐσχάτη, ἔσχατον, §62
law, νόμος, §25
(I) lead, ἄγω, §42
(I) leave, λείπω, §106
liar, ψεύστης, §122
lie, ψεῦδος, §196
(I) lie, ψεύδομαι, §122
life, βίος, §137
life, ζωή, §83
(I) live, ζάω, §117
(I) loose, I destroy, λύω, §15
lord, the Lord, κύριος, §75
love, ἀγάπη, §54
(I) love, ἀγαπάω, §117
lust, ἐπιθυμία, §137

(I) make, I do, ποιέω, §20

(I) make manifest, φανερόω, §166

man, ἄνθρωπος, §25; ἀνήρ, §196

marriage, γάμος, §25

(I) marvel, θαυμάζω, §117

mercy, ἔλεος, §147

message, ἀγγελία, §131

messenger, angel, ἄγγελος, §25

Messiah, μεσσίας, §54

ministry, διακονία, §131

miracle, σημεῖον, §122

mother, μήτηρ, §142

mouth, στόμα, §142

more, rather, μᾶλλον, §190

much, many, πολύς, πολλή, πολύ, §190

my, ἐμός, §176; μου, §68

(of) myself, ἐμαυτοῦ, §176

name, ὄνομα, §147

nation, ἔθνος, §147

need, χρεία, §171

new, καινός, καινή, καινόν, §62

night, νύξ, §142

no longer, οὐκέτι, §101

no one, οὐδείς, §176

not, οὐ (οὐκ, οὐχ), §75

nor, not ever, οὐδέ, §122

now, ἄρτι, §190

now, νῦν, §83

on the one hand . . . on the other hand, μέν . . . δέ, §122

one another, ἀλλήλων, §176

only, μόνος, μόνη, μόνον, §75

out of, ἐκ, §48

over against, ἀντί, §48

(I) overcome, νικάω, §196

parable, παραβολή, §62

peace, εἰρήνη, §62

people, λαός, §83

(I) perceive, συνίημι, §179

(I) persecute, διώκω, §117

(I) persuade, πείθω, §101

Peter, Πέτρος, §126

place, τόπος, §36

place, τίθημι, §179

power, δύναμις, §147

(I) preach, I proclaim, κηρύσσω, §36

(I) preach the gospel, εὐαγγελίζομαι, §171

(I) prepare, ἑτοιμάζω, §126

priest, ἱερεύς, §147

promise, ἐπαγγελία, §89

prophet, προφήτης, §54

propitiation, ἱλασμός, §137

race, γένος, §147

(I) raise up, ἐγείρω, §36

(I) read, ἀναγινώσκω, §83

reason, αἰτία, §190

(I) receive, δέχομαι, §131; λαμβάνω, §15

(I) rejoice, χαίρω, §122

resurrection, ἀνάστασις, §147

(I) return, ὑποστρέφω, §101

righteous, δίκαιος, δικαία, δίκαιον, §62

righteousness, δικαιοσύνη, §159

royal, βασιλικός, §62

(I) rule, ἄρχω, §83

ruler, ἄρχων, §142

synagogue, συναγωγή, §151

(I) take, I receive, λαμβάνω, §15

(I) take up, I take away, αἴρω, §42

(I) teach, διδάσκω, §15

teacher, διδάσκαλος, §89

teaching, διδαχή, §54

temple, ἱερόν, §25

(I) tempt, πειράζω, §171

that, ἐκεῖνος, ἐκείνη, ἐκεῖνο, §69

then, τότε, §83

this, οὗτος, αὕτη, τοῦτο, §68

through, by, διά, §48

(I) throw, βάλλω, §36

time, χρόνος, §171

tongue, γλῶσσα, §54

true, ἀληθινός, ἀληθινή, ἀληθινόν, §151

truly, ἀληθῶς, §166

truth, ἀλήθεια, §54

twelve, δώδεκα, §196

unrighteousness, ἀδικία, §126

up, up to, again, ἀνά, §48

upon, on, ἐπί, §48

voice, φωνή, §83

(I) walk about, περιπατέω, §20

way, ὁδός, §83

we, ἡμεῖς, §68

well, καλῶς, §171

whence, πόθεν, §190

where, ποῦ, §166

who, which, τίς, §176; ὅς, §176

whoever, ὅστις, §176

whole, all, πᾶς, §142

will, θέλημα, §147
wisdom, σοφία, §126
(I) wish, θέλω, §171
with, σύν, §48; μετά, §48
witness, μαρτυρία, §159
word, λόγος, §25; ῥῆμα, §159
work, ἔργον, §111
world, κόσμος, §36
worthy, ἄξιος, §196
(I) write, γράφω, §15
writing, γραφή, §62

you (pl), ὑμεῖς, §68
you (sing), σύ, §68
young man, νεανίσκος, §196

Appendix 6
Bibliography

(§212)

Abbott-Smith, G. *A Manual Greek Lexicon of the New Testament*. 3rd ed. T. & T. Clark, 1937.

Alsop, John R. *An Index to the Bauer-Arndt-Gingrich Greek Lexicon*. Zondervan, 1972.

Bauer, Walter. *A Greek-English Lexicon of the New Testament and Other Early Christian Literature*. Trans. William F. Arndt and F. Wilbur Gingrich. Rev. ed. University of Chicago Press, 1979.

Blass, Friedrich and A. Debrunner. *A Greek Grammar of the New Testament*. University of Chicago, 1964.

Chamberlain, William Douglas. *An Exegetical Grammar of the Greek New Testament*. Macmillan, 1941.

Dana, H. E. and J. R. Mantey. *A Manual Grammar of the Greek New Testament*. Macmillan, 1927.

Davis, W. Hersey. *Beginner's Grammar of the Greek New Testament*. Harper & Row, 1923.

Drumwright, Huber L., Jr. *An Introduction to New Testament Greek*. Broadman, 1910.

Kaufman, Paul L. *An Introductory Grammar of New Testament Greek*. Western Baptist Press, 1978.

Koster, A. J. *The Greek Accents*. E. J. Brill, 1962.

Kubo, Sakae. *A Beginner's New Testament Greek Grammar*. University Press of America, 1979.

_____. *A Reader's Greek-English Lexicon of the New Testament*. Andrews University Press, 1975.

Mare, W. Harold. *Mastering New Testament Greek*. Baker Book House, 1975.

Metzger, Bruce M. *The Text of the New Testament*. Clarendon Press, 1964.

Morgenthaler, Robert. *Statistik des Neutestamentlichen Wortschatzes*. Gotthelf-Verlag, 1958.

Moulton, James H. *A Grammar of New Testament Greek, Vols. I and II*. T. & T. Clark, 1908.

Moulton, James H. and George Milligan. *The Vocabulary of the Greek New Testament*. Hodder and Stoughton, 1949.

Nida, Eugene A. *Morphology: The Descriptive Analysis of Words*. University of Michigan Press, 1946.

Powers, Ward. *Learn to Read the Greek New Testament*. Eerdmans, 1979.

Robertson, A. T. *A Grammar of the Greek New Testament in the Light of Historical Research*. Broadman, 1914.

Robertson, A. T. and W. Hersey Davis. *A New Short Grammar of the Greek New Testament*. Harper & Brothers, 1908.

Smyth, Herbert W. *Greek Grammar*. Harvard University Press, 1956.

Stegenga, J. *The Greek-English Analytical Concordance of the Greek-English New Testament*. Zondervan, 1963.

Summers, Ray. *Essentials of New Testament Greek*. Broadman, 1950.

Turner, Nigel. *A Grammar of New Testament Greek. Vol. III: Syntax*. T. & T. Clark, 1963.

Appendix 7

Indexes

§214. *Scripture.*

Matthew 5:17, §162.2.2; 7:15, §177.6; 8:9, §91; 11:15, §168.3; 26:44, §73.1; 26:74, §79

Luke 1:31, §99; 9:22, §173.2.1; 12:24, §91

John 1:1-8, §14; 1:23, §9; 6:44, §173.2.2; 6:68, §99; 14:6, §177.7; 14:26, §99

Romans 8:16, §73.2

1 John 1:5, §178.1; 1:5-10, §178.1; 1:6, §178.1; 1:8, §178.1; 1:9, §178.1; 1:10, §178.1; 2:1, §189.2; 2:1-6, §189.1; 2:2, §189.2; 2:3, §189.2; 2:5, §189.2; 2:6, §189.2; 2:7, §195.2; 2:7-11, §195.1; 2:8, §195.2; 2:9, §195.2; 2:11, §195.2; 2:12, §199.2; 2:12-17, §199.1; 2:13, §199.2; 2:15, §163.3; 2:18-25, §200; 2:26-3:3, §201; 3:4-10, §202; 4:7, §162.2.1

Revelation, 1:8, §1